11/28/23

$1

THE MYTH OF PSYCHOLOGY

THE MYTH of PSYCHOLOGY

Fred Newman

Foreword by Lenora B. Fulani

 New York

Castillo International, Inc.
500 Greenwich Street, Suite 201
New York, New York 10013

Library of Congress Catalog Number: 91-076608

Newman, Fred
The Myth of Psychology

Includes bibliographical references.

ISBN 0-9628621-2-6

TYPOGRAPHY BY ILENE ADVERTISING, NEW YORK
BOOK DESIGN BY DAVID NACKMAN

95   94   93   92   91   5   4   3   2   1

Manufactured in the United States of America

In our view, the limited and uneven advances of this psychology derive from the essentially solipsist *character of this basic assumption, methods of inquiry, and sources of experiential datum.* Solipsism *is the perspective that only the "self" exists or can be proven to exist. The dominant psychology is founded and imbued with the outlook that (a) the Euro-American world view is the only or best world view; (b) positivism or neo-positivism is the only or best approach to the conduct of scientific inquiry; and (c) the experiences of white, middle-class males are the only or most valid experiences in the world. The first of these I call* assumptive solipsism; *the second,* methodological solipsism *and the third,* experiential solipsism. *These three types of solipsism interpenetrate and influence one another. Together they form the foundations of Eurocentric psychology.*

—**Hussein Abdilahi Bulhan**
Frantz Fanon and the Psychology of Oppression

CONTENTS

FOREWORD

LENORA B. FULANI, Ph.D.

I.

The first person to teach me anything seriously useful about politics and/or psychology was the man I am about to introduce to you: Dr. Fred Newman.

I first heard him lecture on psychology, actually on social therapy, in the late '70s. Although I did not understand everything that he was saying, I was very intrigued by the progressiveness of the politics guiding his talk. I went into group therapy with Dr. Newman in the early '80s while I was in individual therapy with a Black lesbian gestalt therapist. I remained in that arrangement for a year; when Susan (as I'll call her here) announced her intention to begin a gestalt group, I announced to my social therapy group my intention to leave social therapy. My position — as someone who was in the forefront of challenging traditional psychology's blatant racism — was that all one had to do to turn this around was to replace white psychologists who work with Black folks with Black psychologists. And off I went to do group therapy with my Black gestalt therapist, never anticipating how critical that year would be to my development as a social therapist.

The gestalt group was a disaster — although I learned something about the power of methodology while I was in it. There we were, with all the proper ingredients for doing something different: we were Black, white, Jewish; gay and straight; working class and middle class; and all women. We were sensitive, caring and compassionate. But the *practice* of our therapy was Eurocentric, straight and male to the core. We never touched on the real differences that existed among people — even the ones in that room — because if we had the group would have dissolved. In fact, whenever racism or any other contentious issue was raised it got redefined in some psychoanalytical language and the situation was cooled out. Which was just as well, because the limits of the methodology (regardless of the good intentions of our Black therapist) made it impossible for her work to result in the empowerment of her patients.

It was in Fred Newman's social therapy group that I was able to learn some profound lessons about racism. I could take a look at what I was conveying to my then eight-year-old daughter — which was that if she was smart and charming enough, her personality would conquer racism. It was in the context of Dr. Newman's group that I learned all kinds of things about myself as a woman, my sexuality, my belief that I had a lot more control over men and their abusiveness than it was possible for me to have. It was from him that I learned about the insidiousness of the "isms" and that I could, without even knowing it, be anti-Semitic towards him (a Jew whom I had come to love and trust) by using a common refrain among Black folks: "All white people are the same to me" (obviously Adolph Hitler could tell the difference). He also taught me how these "isms" rarely appear alone; if you begin to work on racism or sexism or anti-Semitism in a group, before long another raises its ugly head. So we began the very difficult job of learning to deal with these issues — and what must be built just to make this possible.

I remember sitting in a group in my early years of training with Dr. Newman, watching him create the context in which a white, upper middle class businessman who had finally exposed why he never spoke — the utter disdain which he felt for the rest of us who were women, Black, gay or working class — was challenged to struggle with working on the problem of his disdain (not us) as a precondition for remaining in social therapy. As an African American woman who had spent many years in white liberal environments where racial and class issues were always hedged on (if they were discussed at all), I realized that social therapy — and its founder, Dr. Newman — were about something very different.

The work reflected in this book represents the most advanced, and successful, attempt I know of to develop a radically humanistic theory and practice of psychology, Black or white.

II.

In addition to being a therapist I am also the chairperson of America's fourth largest political party — the New Alliance Party. While NAP is not a Black party (it is Black-led and multi-racial), it is indeed the party of the Black community. Similarly, social therapy is not a Black therapy but it is in my opinion by far the most effective, coherent and useful approach to the treatment of the emotional struggles of the African American community that exists anywhere. No other approach even comes close.

The brilliance of Fred Newman's work as the manager of my various electoral campaigns — including my '88 and '92 Presidential runs — to shape and inform the nascent independent political movement in this country is something I have delighted in sharing with friends and supporters around the country. It is very exciting to have this opportunity to share with you some of the discoveries he has made in the area of human development.

The first person to teach me anything about Karl Marx and the meaning of his work was Fred Newman. Early in our relationship, while I was aggressively searching for a way to contribute to the fight for the empowerment of Black people, I asked Dr. Newman why he was a Marxist. His response had a profound impact on me. He said that after reading the first page of the *Communist Manifesto* (in which Marx wrote that what it meant to be a communist was that you did not support any system based on the exploitation of one human being by another), he knew that's what he was.

Marxists in this country (and in the rest of the world) have, for the most part, avoided the application of Marxist science to the domain of interpersonal issues. However, it was clear to Dr. Newman that the economic and social status quo in America is not only maintained by the institutions that are clearly identifiable as political (political parties, the judicial system, the military, etc.), but by such "private" institutions as marriage, child rearing, sexuality and emotionality. In recent years it's become clear that the failure of traditional (orthodox) Marxism to engage these issues is not only a source of tremendous emotional pain for our people; it has also been a source of the profound failure of revolutionary movements and organizations the world over.

One of the most destructive forces in the African American community is the impact of what passes for the treatment of emotional illness perpetrated by the so-called helping professions/mental health industry. Once caught up in that system, most people lose their capacity to grow and develop; many end up being destroyed by it. But the solution to the destructiveness of traditional psychology does not lie in attempts by Black psychologists to "color" the pseudo-science of psychology Black! No! The demand is that psychology as an institution be challenged at its very *roots*. And Dr. Newman's work — its theory, its practice, its method — does just that.

III.

My training as a social therapist began during my work as a patient in Dr. Newman's group. I then spent a year at the East Side Center for Social Therapy under the supervision of Debra Pearl, doing therapy with middle class white patients. That year of training was invaluable. It taught me a lot about the how-to's of social therapy and the usefulness of this approach for all kinds of people. By the time I reached our clinic in Harlem, I felt ready for the task of empowering my people.

One of my initial reactions to arriving in Harlem and meeting the Harlem community was a combination of frustration and dismay when I saw that the patients (Black and Latino working class people) shared the same negative perspectives of themselves as did the broader society. They used labels and explanations and understandings that were extremely limiting to their growth and development. Black psychology has sometimes managed to replace the Eurocentric labels with new sets of understandings and labels which — though nicer and more humane — are not much more conducive to development and usually precipitate a tug of war between patient and therapist over whose label is "right."

Dr. Newman had developed a non-labeling approach which left the therapists and patients with the awkward and unguided job of getting to *know* each other — not as labels or "diagnostic categories" but as real people in the world.

The power of social therapy does not lie in "making nice" or covering up the real differences that exist among people in our society; rather, it is a tool for building environments (in the therapy office and in the rest of the world) where something new, something decent, can be created by people *using* their differences. What is crucial in creating such new environments is that people must relate to themselves and to others not as victims but as builders capable of changing the conditions of their lives.

The last thing that the promoters of traditional psychology (let alone the powers-that-be) want is for poor people, people of color, gay people and women to identify themselves as changers of their environment. My challenge as a Black therapist learning to do social therapy was to forsake my fantasy of "saving" the Black working class and take on the activity of getting down with Black working class people to create the tools necessary to change the conditions of their lives.

As a Black psychologist who spent years searching for ways to do a more relevant psychology in the Black community, I had read many critiques of traditional psychology from "a Black point of view." But although I did not realize it at the time, almost all of that work focused on the *content* of traditional psychology. Use language that is more relevant to the Black community. Study cultural aspects of Africa and somehow translate that into explanations of African American neuroses. Replace white psychologists with Black ones to treat Black patients. This is what radical/alternative Black psychologists viewed as the solution to the problems inherent in traditional (white) psychology.

In "Talkin' Transference" Dr. Newman speaks about social therapy as a qualitative extension of the radical therapies of the '60s. He points out that, while in their content many of these therapies — including Black psychology — were nowhere near as pernicious, racist or sexist as their traditional counterparts, they were insufficiently radical in their presuppositions, their method, their actual practice.

Which means that regardless of their intentions, no matter how Afrocentric their cultural accoutrements, Black psychologists have ended up practicing a Eurocentric psychology. I began to discover this in the '70s, when the well-intentioned Black psychologists who had taken the place of whites as analysts and experts on the Black community began to find the very same flaws in poor and working class Black people as whites had been "discovering" about us for years!

When I met Dr. Newman and began studying with him I obviously carried with me all of the Eurocentric and methodological hang-ups that most of us automatically inherit by living in the United States and being trained as psychologists in this country. However, I was also very insistent that my practice of psychology had to be rooted in a politic that was centered on the empowerment of Black people. Long before I began to grasp the issues of methodology raised by Dr. Newman (and I still struggle to understand them more fully), I understood and felt very close to his politics. I knew that what ailed Black folks was not our "low IQ's," our "low self-esteem" or our "lack of ambition." I also understood that challenging Black people to become changers of their lives (emotional and otherwise) had to go beyond teaching them African history. I spent years studying everything I could about Africa. In every undergraduate or graduate paper I wrote (whether it was in English literature, psychology or math) I found a way to discuss Black history; I learned a lot by doing that (including how to fight with my mostly white professors, who deeply resented my attempts to make my work and study relevant to my people). But it was also clear that although I was helping to create a niche for myself as a Black psychologist, what I was doing had no impact upon the conditions of the lives of the Black working class.

IV.

One of the points that Dr. Newman makes throughout his work is that social therapy does not adapt people to their societal roles but instead adapts them to historical ones. I'd like to say why I think this is critical for Black psychologists.

In a section of "Talkin' Transference" Dr. Newman speaks

about American exceptionalism — the attitude that "it can't happen here." He is addressing 'he widespread belief in this country that because of American pluralism, America will always be able (institutionally, politically, ideologically) to fit all things in; that strength, the exceptionalists say, is what makes it possible to avoid fascism — a rapid transformation of American society such as the one which produced Nazism in Germany. I believe that this point of view (which in my opinion is profoundly mistaken) finds expression in the work even of some of the most militant Black political activists and psychologists. How so?

At first glance you would think that Frances Cress Welsing, Na'im Akbar and Amos Wilson are saying that, given the nature of white folks, anything can happen to Black people in this country. But if you look closely at the explanations they offer, you will discover that (1) they are timeless (ahistorical), and (2) they assume that Black people can adjust to their oppression by being "Blacker." Some of the most militant psychologists actually include lists of things that folks can do (usually with their families) within the context of this society to make us Blacker and therefore to adapt better to things as they are. Granting that strategy might work in a stable society (it wouldn't), such an "analysis" leaves out the crucial fact that American society is changing!

One of the basic assumptions that guides all of my work — building a Black-led, multi-racial independent political movement in this country, and practicing therapy in Harlem — is that the African American working class cannot be integrated into American society as it is currently organized. By integration, I do not mean cultural integration or assimilation — the demand (disguised as an "opportunity") that people of color become like white people. I am referring to the kind of integration that made it possible for the majority of American Jews, for example, to enter the middle class (mostly by means of the professions) in the 1940s and

'50s, when the economy was booming. Today, as the economy shrinks, the broad masses of Black people and our sisters and brothers of color are no longer necessary as a source of labor (even unskilled labor) to those who run the United States (and the world).

And because the powers-that-be do not envision a future in which the American economy will be "born again," there is no need — from their point of view — even to keep us alive, let alone to establish the conditions for our children to grow and develop. I think it is this fundamental fact of American economic life at the close of the 20th century which explains the passage (with bipartisan support) of the life-threatening Gramm-Rudman bill, the official acquiescence in the epidemic of police brutality in cities all over the country, the deployment in massive numbers of Black troops to the front lines in the recent Gulf war, the inundation of our communities with murderous drugs — what genocide looks like, close up. If the cops and the crack don't finish the job, despair and self-destruction will.

Social therapy is a pro-Black, pro-working class political (not psychological) response to the murderously anti-working class and racist conditions of our people's lives. It is not political in the narrow sense of being about the election of this or that candidate (although electoral politics is obviously an important part of the struggle at this moment in history). Rather, it is political in the broadest sense — it is about the reorganization of power. We are not helping people to think or feel differently about society-as-it-is (and thereby to adjust to exploitation and oppression), but to do a different activity — to participate in changing a profoundly exploitative and oppressive world.

If Black people cannot be integrated into American society in its current state of advanced decay, then it is clear that our survival and our development depend on our ability to play a leadership role in the radical restructuring of that society. Our ability to play the historical role of revolutionaries — human beings capable of participating in the process of transforming totalities — depends to a large degree on whether we can break with our adjustment (or maladjustment) to our social role of victims. This is precisely what social therapy teaches people to do.

Dr. Newman was originally trained to work in a machine shop as a tool and die maker — someone who makes tools specifically designed for a particular job for which no ready-made tools are appropriate. Social therapy is such a made-to-order tool. As a Black psychologist deeply concerned with the emotional agony Black people have been living through for 400 years, I am extremely grateful to have something so powerful to help my people — "help" not in the social worker/therapist/liberal sense of easing the pain of their day-to-day lives a little bit, but help in the radical/revolutionary sense of curing the pain by giving them the tools they need to engage in the activity of reorganizing the totality (including, but not restricted to, the emotionality) of life.

PREFACE

This book has been written over a period of almost ten years. And the anti-therapy that ultimately came to be (and to be called) social therapy was practiced (under various names) by me and a handful of others for about a decade before that. Now hundreds of professionals are using social therapy to help tens of thousands directly, and perhaps millions indirectly.

Is the transformation of the 1960s radical anti-therapy into social therapy a grand reconciliation or, more graphically, a dirty, rotten sell-out? I, of course, think not. It is, rather, a recognition that (1) while psychology is a myth it nevertheless impacts profoundly, *qua* myth, on all of us, sometimes positively, typically negatively (Santa Claus does a little bit of good and enormous harm); and (2) the only way to engage a myth is to develop an anti-mythic historical (pro-human) *practice* (in Marx's language a practical-critical, i.e. revolutionary *activity*; in Vygotsky's language a dialectical tool *and* result methodology) which does not simply offer a *cognitive* critique (myths eat cognitive critiques for breakfast) but which *organizes* people (the rabble) to destroy the myth and then to use the rubble to build something of use for us — for our species, for our class-*for*-itself.

So this book is *about* building a new psychology. But while it is *now about that*, the work of creating these words, sentences, paragraphs, etc. was not in its historical origins *about* anything; rather, it was the attempt to create tools *and* results (a method that, in Vygotsky's formulation, "... is simultaneously prerequisite and product...") useful in the activity of helping people out of their pain and oppression.

Many academics, as much products as teachers of some form of behaviorism and/or positivism, will no doubt have knee-jerk (economically determined, in the vulgarist sense) reactions to calling psychology a myth. I can hear them now: a chorus of Skinnerean pigeons cackling, "Mr. Newman, what precisely do you mean by psychology? (tee hee, tee hee)." I turn to an academic for an answer. Hussein Abdilahi Bulhan, the author of *Frantz Fanon and the Psychology of Oppression,* offers us a succinct historical "definition" of psychology:

> From the fourteenth century to the present, Europe and its descendants have been embarked on an unprecedented mission of violence and self-aggrandizement throughout the world. Meanwhile, an intellectual debate on the human condition had been raging in academic circles. A discipline called "psychology" emerged by the sixteenth century, when Philipp Melanchthon, a friend of Luther, coined the term, even though the roots of this new discipline reach back to ancient civilizations. In time, the new discipline flourished and proliferated in various aspects of society. It developed its own concepts, won numerous adherents, evolved its own tradition, won a measure of respectability, and defined a jealously guarded turf. As Europe conquered much of the world, the European imposing as the only honorable model of humanity, the discipline of psychology too emerged as a powerful specialty and a scientific arbiter of human experience.

The discipline of psychology did not of course emerge

in a social vacuum unrelated to Europe's history of conquest and violence. From its beginning to the present, the discipline has been enmeshed in that history of conquest and violence. This fact is all too often unappreciated and conveniently avoided. Yet for a discipline known for its commitment to unmask the repressed and for its profusion of studies, such neglect and avoidance of human history and the role of psychologists in that history are curious indeed.

Myths, you see, do not drop from the sky. They are *constructed* accompaniments serving the interests of controlling forces even as they are (if effective) self-destructively adopted by those under control. *The Myth of Psychology*, as both polemic and practice, seeks to "deconstruct" psychology not in order to create still another myth but to participate in the building of another world (obviously not George Bush's New World Order) in which myth will no longer be required.

This book is dedicated to people of color the world over from Zaire (formerly the Congo) to Azania to Haiti to Cuba to El Salvador to the Philippines to Guatemala to Palestine to Nicaragua to the Mohawk Nation to Crown Heights and Harlem and East Los Angeles to Vietnam and on and on, who continue to lead the struggle to destroy the myths that destroy our humanity. *Hasta la victoria siempre! La lutta continua!*

— *F.N.*
New York City
October 1991

ACKNOWLEDGEMENTS

Thanks to the thousands with whom I have had years of *activist dialogue* and who have made this book possible; and in particular to my dear friend and colleague, the most distinguished African American psychologist and political activist Dr. Lenora B. Fulani, for her foreword, which speaks so simply, eloquently and passionately of our history and its significance, and for her extraordinary creativity in building the community that shapes all that we do; to Dr. Lois Holzman, my intellectual *comrade collaborator* and wonderful friend whose influence is in every one of these writings, for her invaluable introduction and for co-writing "Vygotsky's Method"; to Gabrielle Kurlander, who is not only the talented publisher of this book, but the love of my life; to my pal Diane Stiles, Castillo's production chief, whose hard work, leadership and grace have transformed these words into a book; to David Nackman, a designer of great talent (and an extraordinary actor/comedian!) whose vision has given this book shape; to the gifted Ilene Hinden and her crew at Ilene Advertising for the book's typography; to Dr. Dan Friedman, my very good friend, collaborator and editor, for putting it all together and filling in all the g-a-p-s; to Dr. Phyllis Goldberg and Warren Liebesman, two dear old friends and copyeditors, for putting the final polish on the often crude words; to proofreaders Margo Grant, Kate Henselmans, Anne Bettman, Janet

Weigel, and Jeff Roby for making sure all the language was in the right order; to Routledge for permission to publish Chapter III of the forthcoming *Lev Vygotsky: Revolutionary Scientist*, appearing here as "Vygotsky's Method"; and, of course, to all the workers of the Castillo collective and the East Side Center for Social Therapy collective who have literally made *this book* and every day make so much other progressive culture, psychology and intellectual activity.

INTRODUCTION

LOIS HOLZMAN, Ph.D.

As you read this book, it will become clear that the subject of Fred Newman's writings is us — human beings as changers. According to Newman, what makes us unique is not that we think, or have thumbs, or stand upright, but that we are changers-of-totalities — we reshape the very environments that shape us. Newman calls this ability "revolutionary activity." The work gathered in this volume is an examination of traditional psychology's role in repressing revolutionary activity — and his discoveries about how to reinitiate it.

Newman's work is a challenge to the assumption of traditional psychology that people are objects to be changed, rather than changers. It is therefore a challenge to the myth that psychology *helps* people. To Newman, helping people can only mean helping them to change their environment, to reorganize the totality of their lives, to be changers. Help, Newman says, is not to be found in psychology (which attempts to adapt people to take their places within the world as it is) but in people changing the world to meet human needs — and in the process, changing themselves. Newman always relates to his patients as revolutionaries, as people who are changers.

"The Patient as Revolutionary," first delivered to the Congress of the Interamerican Society of Psychology at the Karl Marx

Theatre in Havana, Cuba in June, 1986 — the first time that the Society had met in Cuba since the revolution — was a challenge to the American delegation, as well as to the Cuban and Latin American psychologists in attendance.

Newman and I, along with several of our colleagues, traveled from New York City to participate in the conference — which was attended by 2,000 psychologists and psychiatrists, primarily from Latin America.

The president of the Interamerican Society of Psychology, Dr. Harry Triandas — an American — opened the congress by warning the attendees: "The society was founded on the premise that it is possible to have a science that is beyond politics," and that they should steer clear of politics. There was room for all in the Society, Triandas continued, since "all theories are valid under some conditions." All theories except, apparently, Marxism, since it maintains that science and politics are intimately related.

The subject of the talks Newman and our colleagues gave at the conference was the relationship between science and politics. In an earlier work by Newman and me, *The Practice of Method*, we first made the distinction between revolutionary activity and making the revolution:

> One is capable of historical transformation as an individual only insofar as one is *involved in* (more accurately, *is*) the activity of changing society in a self-conscious manner. This should not be taken to mean that one must be a revolutionary in order to change; being a revolutionary is working to change society in a very particular way. But while being involved in the activity of self-consciously changing society is not identifiable with being a revolutionary, it is identifiable with having revolutionary consciousness, or with revolutionary, practical-critical activity in the sense Marx explicates in the *Theses on Feuerbach*.

In Cuba, a country that had made a revolution, Newman, in his talk, challenged the Cubans and everyone else in attendance to engage in revolutionary activity. The Cubans and other Latin American psychologists were excited by what Newman had to say about social therapy and what he had been building in the U.S.. Despite the very real achievements of the revolution, social relations were not very advanced, e.g., the racism, sexism, and homophobia we experienced in Cuba were palpable. While the revolution had fed the hungry, cured the sick and taught the ignorant to read, it had not yet begun to create the new human being. The old communism has died in no small measure because it failed to create a psychology in the service of a revolutionary politic, to revolutionize the human being.

"Talkin' Transference," by putting two pressing historical/psychological questions together, comes up with a major discovery about the link between ideology and psychology. The first question is: "How could Germany — the most politically progressive and culturally and scientifically creative nation in Europe — be transformed into the barbarism of Nazism so quickly? How could the Holocaust have happened?" The second question is: "What must the human mind be like to adapt to a society so thoroughly alienated and commodified as ours?" The linkage of those questions is the major development articulated in this essay. And that link is transference.

In 1982, when the Institute for Social Therapy and Research — where the practice and theory of social therapy were first developed — had been in existence for only four years, we woke up one Wednesday to "Psychopolitics," an attack on our work by a journalist named Joe Conason on the front page of the once-liberal weekly New York newspaper, the *Village Voice*.

Like Harry Triandas at the Congress of the Interamerican

Society of Psychology in Cuba, who maintained that you could do science without politics, Conason's position was that not only *could* you do therapy without politics but that you *should;* then he attacked social therapy for not meeting his criterion.

In response, Newman delivered a talk, "Talkin' Transference," which while carefully examining the assumptions of Conason's position teaches about the psychology of politics and the politics of psychology as well as about a critically important aspect of how social therapy works, namely its non-transferential nature.

In response to Conason's charge that social therapy uses traditional psychology's transference mechanism to "brainwash" people into being radicals, Newman delineates the non-transferential nature of social therapy, by which he means that — unlike traditional therapy — it doesn't use transference as a vehicle for "cure." This doesn't mean that Newman denies transference. Far from denying it, he demonstrates that it's not limited to therapy; it happens every day, all the time — it is the normal means of adaptation under capitalism, the means by which we make sense of the alienated commodities we produce. Since under the current mode of production we are alienated from what we produce, we infuse those productions with powers and qualities different from and above us.

That fetishization, Newman maintains, extends beyond things to human relations — we transfer the qualities of others to the people we are actually dealing with. Thus despite the much touted secularization of society under capitalism, we are socialized to relate not only to commodities but to other human beings in an essentially religious way. And this ability to "transfer" allows people — as it did in Germany in the early '30s — to transfer their loyalty and belief systems almost overnight.

In the course of explaining the pervasiveness of transference, Newman also lays out in this essay the essential socialness of emotions, which is itself a challenge to the myth of traditional psychology that feelings are individualized, private, unique.

Fred Newman and I have been collaborating on the theoretical underpinnings of social therapy since 1979, I as a developmental psychologist, he as a Marxist methodologist.

During all those years, Newman would always say he didn't understand what developmental psychology was, although he knew what development was. Indeed, for years he had been building environments in which people (especially people whose development had been arrested by the oppressive and destructive conditions of our society) could develop emotionally, intellectually, culturally and politically. But developmental psychology always seemed bogus to him. As a social-scientific enterprise, it had little to do with real development — the activity of tool making, of using what exists to make something new and *other* than what is predetermined by what is.

It was not until Newman and I were asked in 1988 to write a book on the Soviet psychologist/methodologist Lev Vygotsky, that he began to study Vygotsky's writings in depth; they are, among other things, a brilliant expose of the pseudo-scientific nature of traditional developmental psychology. Our understanding of Vygotsky's contributions, of developmental psychology as a discipline, of human development and social therapy, have all been influenced by the writing of this book, *Lev Vygotsky: Revolutionary Scientist*, from which "Vygotsky's Method" is excerpted.

Lev Vygotsky was a leading psychologist/methodologist in the early years of the Soviet Union, a time when the practical tasks facing the first socialist country were enormous. The brief period from 1917 to 1930 — when Stalin put an end to it — was a time of intensely creative activity directed toward the development of a new human being. The overthrow of oppression and inequality and the first steps toward building a mode of production based on use, not on profit, opened up the possibility of building new modes of human interaction, the possibility of new, nonexploitative ways for human beings to relate to each other. Within this context Vygotsky asked: What is the essence of a human being, anyway? What kind of psychology would help *all* people develop to their fullest productive creative capacity? How could science, especially psychology, contribute to socialized, collective development?

"Vygotsky's Method" (an early version of Chapter III of *Lev Vygotsky: Revolutionary Scientist*, to be published by Routledge in 1992 as part of its Critical Psychology series) discusses in great detail the methodology that dominates late capitalism (pragmatics) and the revolutionary methodology of Marx, Vygotsky and Newman (practice). It intersects the debate among educators, psychologists and other social scientists about whether Vygotsky was merely a socially oriented psychologist whose work can "reform" traditional psychology, or a revolutionary scientist whose life-as-lived was dedicated to building a truly human psychology and whose contributions have the potential to change the entire enterprise of psychology.

Our position is that he was a revolutionary scientist. In the book we present "our Vygotsky," who is both the "tool and result" of the revolutionary activity that Newman leads — the production and distribution of social therapy. Our understanding of Vygotsky's methodological breakthroughs and his psychological insights about how human beings develop, learn, think, play, speak, etc. is a product of the community, movement, and clinical and educational psychology we practice.

First delivered on October 23, 1987, "Crisis Normalization and Depression: A New Approach to a Growing Epidemic" was originally a lecture in an annual series of lectures on "Politics and

Psychology" given by Newman.

Those talks, which constitute the remainder of this collection, are, in effect, case studies of contemporary emotionality — and what can be done about reorganizing their debilitating effects. Each examines the social/historic process of production through which a particular emotion or set of related emotional constructs has been produced.

In this essay Newman (following Szasz and others) takes on the perniciousness (and pervasiveness) of definitions: how they limit the ways in which we think of ourselves and others, how they limit who we are and who we can become. In particular, he takes on the definitions of mental illness — definitions that have much more to do with the needs of the insurance companies than with the needs of those suffering mental anguish.

Connecting the emergence of depression as the normal emotional state of vast numbers of people in contemporary society and our society's loss of connection to history, in "Crisis Normalization" Dr. Newman puts forward for the first time the idea of history as the cure.

Psychologists, including Newman, agree that depression is triggered by or related to a sense of loss. But Newman demonstrates that loss itself depends on the private property relations established by capitalist society. To experience loss you must first experience possession. But in history there *is* no loss — every change is part of the ongoing process of human beings constantly organizing and reorganizing their social/economic/political relations. In capitalist society when something changes, what you see is loss. In history what you see is social process. In society you experience loss; in history you experience transformation.

In moving the examination of depression — or any emotion — beyond the parameters of traditional psychological definitions (and past the limited boundaries of society), Newman challenges the myth that psychology is an attempt to cure people of emotional disease. If you think the moon is made of blue cheese, the rocket you build to reach it will be different from what you'd build if you thought it was made of rocks, soil and minerals. If you understand depression as the normal state rather than an abnormal or pathological one, then the approach you take to curing it will be very different. The approach social therapy puts forward is rekindling the individual's (and the society's) sense of history.

"Panic in America" is one of the clearest case studies of the historical evolution of an emotion. It was first delivered in December, 1988 as part of the "Politics and Psychology" series — at a time when pop psychology was being flooded with books on "anxiety attacks" and workshops on "panic disorders." Newman takes great care here to distinguish between anxiety (an adaptive emotion linked to the rise of capitalism) and panic (a dysfunctional state ever more prevalent during the current period of capitalist decay). The piece is fascinating for its documentation of the changes in emotionality wrought by the last 150 years.

But Newman is not interested in mere documentation. His interest in exploring panic, as in everything he does, is to discover how it is possible, given current social limitations, for human beings to express their revolutionary capacity to adapt to history — to reorganize the totality of their lives, to make meaning. And here is where the distinction between anxiety and panic becomes important to Newman. For if anxiety is adaptive and panic is maladaptive, and if anxiety has transformed into panic, then, Newman argues, we need to produce our own anxiety. We need to adapt not to a society which induces panic but to history.

When Newman first put forth this thesis I found it disturbing, a challenge to some of the most basic understandings of my own day-to-day emotional life. Along with almost everyone I know, I walk around feeling anxious and thinking that's problematic. Newman, contrary to this prevailing wisdom, was talking about creating new anxiety! To choose revolutionary activity, to choose to develop in a society that is no longer conducive to development, to "live in history" as he would put it, is profoundly anxiety provoking. Newman's point — not only of this talk, but of his life-as-lived — is that collectively we have to organize this anxiety so that people can adaptively function in history, i.e., can engage in revolutionary activity.

As always, Newman hits hard here at the psychological establishment, exposing the philosophical and political underpinnings of the prevailing therapeutic models of contemporary psychology — models from which the very concept of "cure" has been exorcised. He demands more for our species than the empty existential choice to merely exist (to survive, to live one day at a time, etc.) — the most contemporary psychology dares to promise.

I am a professor of psychology at Empire State College of the State University of New York, where I've been teaching working adults from all class and ethnic backgrounds for 12 years. Of the thousand or more students with whom I have worked, there is hardly one who has not either: (a) been in a drug or alcohol rehab program or had a family member who has; (b) been involved in Alcoholics Anonymous, Narcotics Anonymous, ACOA (Adult Children of Alcoholics) or similar groups for so-called co-dependents; or (c) been in prison for drug use or a drug-related crime. Such is just one measure of the extent of the addictions industry.

It is this industry of devastation — and the psychology that rationalizes and perpetuates it — that Newman addresses in "The Myth of Addiction" and his "Addiction Response." In the social role of addict, recovering addict, co-dependent, etc., Newman finds one of the most dehumanizing examples of the use of defini-

tions (labels) as a means of social coercion. He demonstrates that these labels — which have no scientific basis and serve no purpose other than to stigmatize and marginalize and make impotent those so labeled (and to make billions of dollars) — are literally killing people. The addictions industry, which is, after all, but a subdivision of the psychology industry, is making a great deal of money from the death of poor people. Multi-millions are made from pumping drugs into poor communities and then many millions more are made from "treating" (as distinct from curing) those affected by the drugs.

First delivered on April 27, 1990 at Columbia University's Teachers College as a talk entitled "The Politics and Psychology of Addiction" to an audience of hundreds — including many social workers, drug rehab counselors, "addicts" and former "addicts" — "The Myth of Addiction" was like a match thrown into a pool of gasoline. Newman's claim that there is no such thing as addiction immediately elicited passionate, angry, grateful and confused responses both from people at the talk itself and from those who read transcripts of it in the months that followed. It created the conditions for a much needed dialogue.

While the specific content of the responses varied from the enthusiastic embrace of Newman's thesis to passionate defense of psychology's definitions of addict and addiction (often by the same respondent!), a pattern was clearly discernible in the wide array of both formal and informal responses. The initial response was, "Addiction can't be a myth! People are suffering from it." Then, "You're right! It is a myth — it's a way to make money! It avoids the social conditions which make people drink or take drugs." And after that — "It *is* a myth, but…"

Almost everyone, from Harvard professors to working class former drug users, agreed that addiction is a multi-million dollar industry coining people's suffering into gold. But Newman in his

"Addiction Response" pushes beyond this fundamentally reformist agreement to expose the underlying philosophical and methodological basis/bias of the pseudo-science called psychology. Using the dialogue generated by his "Addiction" talk, Newman expands on his argument as to why it is that "addiction" refers literally to *nothing*. Further, he dissects the Eurocentric, white supremacist assumptions at the root of psychology in general and of addiction in particular, and in so doing posits revolutionary activity as the only "cure" — not for addiction which does not exist, but for the *myth* of addiction.

Among those in attendance at Newman's talk at Teachers College back in the spring of '90 was Jim Horton, the residential manager of the 32-bed Point Breeze Drug and Alcohol Residential Program of Philadelphia's Horizon House. With him was a busload of the program's clients. What has happened to Horton and the residents of Horizon House since then is a testament both to the power of the social therapeutic approach to drug use and the accuracy of Newman's analysis of addiction and the addiction industry.

Horizon House, founded in the 1950s, is a private mental health/mental retardation corporation that receives millions in city, state, and federal funding. In 1988 Horton began introducing social therapy into the program and it eventually became Point Breeze's primary treatment modality. The impact was startling. Over 85% of the graduates from the Point Breeze program remain drug and alcohol free (the national average is less than 7%). Half of these graduates have gone into the helping professions, as drug and alcohol counselors or to other social service positions. The other 50% are enrolled in GED programs and have secured employment.

At least as significant, the clients have developed through the process of creating the environment in which it is possible for them to decide for themselves the kinds of activities they want and need — they have created new wants and needs.

What was the response of the multi-million dollar Horizon House to this success, which on the one hand was remarkable and on the other hand involved only a tiny handful of the nation's African American and Latino poor who desperately need such services? In August, 1991, Horton was suspended and his program dismantled. A month later, he was terminated on the basis of a series of unsubstantiated charges — a measure of how much dread there is of any exposure of the myth of addiction.

"Community as a Heart in a Havenless World" — as Newman dubbed the topic of the evening in the opening minutes of his talk "The Politics and Psychology of Community"— was delivered to a full auditorium at Washington Irving High School in lower Manhattan on November 9, 1990. It was more than a talk — it was a practicum. To Newman a living community, one intent on transforming the society of which it is a part, is not — can not — be defined, since definition itself, as well as this or that definition, is determined by the very society being challenged. Community is, instead, an *activity* — a collective, self-conscious activity (self-defining, Newman says) that creates the environment in which individuals can contribute to the reorganization of the total society.

Newman's community is an extension of Vygotsky's Zone of Proximal Development (ZPD), not a place but an activity where/how human development takes place. To emphasize community as activity, as a ZPD, Newman organized those in attendance not simply to listen to him *talk* about community, but to pour into the street in front of Washington Irving High on that cold November night shouting "*We* define community."

The closed community divided along racial or ethnic lines, the sect, the cult, the gang, the exclusive neighborhood — responses to increasing alienation, atomization, violence and social decay — are dead-end reaction formations attempting the impossible — to provide a haven in a heartless world. In the face of these closed, socially determined communities formed to *keep out* and *conserve*, Newman counters with the open, historically-determined community formed to *include* and *transform*, to provide *a heart in a havenless world*.

One of the self-defining activities contributing to the creation of the heart of the world is social therapy — which is nothing if not the building of community. That building activity, unlike anything the myth of psychology has come up with, is curative.

THE MYTH OF PSYCHOLOGY

1

THE PATIENT
AS REVOLUTIONARY

It is thrilling to be here in Cuba. In many ways, my own development — both politically and as a group psychotherapist — has paralleled the development of the revolution in Cuba. Since 1959 — when I began graduate school and the people of Cuba began socialism — I have devoted almost all of my intellectual energies, as well as my practical energies, to the study of two things: psychology and revolution. I have done almost all of that practicing and studying in the United States, from California to New York, north, south, east and west. I've traveled on many different paths, and viewed these matters from many dif-

"The Patient as Revolutionary" was first delivered as a talk entitled "The Psychopathology of the U.S. Left," at the Congress of the Interamerican Society of Psychology at the Karl Marx Theater in Havana, Cuba in June 1986.

ferent perspectives. I want to share just a little bit of that journey so you'll have some sense of the practical-critical methodology that I bring to this discussion.

I received my doctoral degree in the philosophy of science and the philosophy of history from Stanford University in California in 1963. I began, some 28-29 years ago, to study the scientific validity (or invalidity) and the methodology of the social sciences and history and, most particularly, the validity (or invalidity) and methodology of psychology. That was before I was a Marxist. I share *that* with you because my belief that bourgeois psychology is a myth — that it is based on profound methodological errors, that it is essentially an intellectual and bourgeois (ruling class) biased methodological fraud — came long before I studied Marxism carefully. Actually it's more accurate to say that I became a Marxist out of the realization that psychology (and much else in bourgeois society, I must add) is a fraud. I say this at the beginning so that those of you who are listening (or reading) won't think that my critique of psychology is based purely on the fact that I am a dedicated Marxist and therefore *dogmatically* committed to the fundamentality of politics and not psychology. Psychology has always struck me, from the very beginnings of my philosophical investigations, as a pseudo-science.

In the course of the 1960s, while teaching philosophy at the university, I (like many others) became involved in radical politics. It was at that time that I began to study, as well as to participate in, the political process, in the revolutionary process, in the process of social change. There are those who might say, understandably, that the U.S.A. is a rather bad place to study revolution. But that's where I was so that's where I studied. In the course of the 1960s and the 1970s, my political activism caused me to be dismissed from one university after another in the United States. I sought, therefore, to find another profession. Life is filled with many ironies. An irony in my life has been that, coming out of an academic background in the philosophy of science, as someone who specialized in critiquing psychology, the profession that I came to in the 1970s was psychology. I became first a drug counselor and then a psychotherapist.

I therefore had to deal, in some way, with this transparent contradiction: I was now working in a field which I took to be, without a doubt, an intellectual fraud. To be sure, many people in bourgeois society engage in activities which they take to be frauds; it's the story of all too many working people's lives. But I was eager and able to engage this personal/political fraud. So I began an extended examination of what it would mean to develop a clinical psychology, to construct a psychotherapy, which did not embody the fundamental contradiction of orthodox psychology.

So far as I can see (I saw it this way in 1959 and I see it still as we're approaching 1989), the attempt to construct a paradigm, an explanatory model for human behavior, for social activity, for the processes which we identify as human life based on the model of the natural sciences, creates a hopeless contradiction for the entire field of psychology. You see, if we look, even in a very superficial way, at the origins of the model of the natural sciences which has dominated the capitalist world these past 300-400 years, we discover that Galileo and others were able to identify *a proper object of study* for the natural sciences, in particular, for physics. And that by virtue of that *ontological* breakthrough, they were able to create a new science, to revolutionize the feudal, pre-scientific (Aristotelian) world view. Put simply, Galileo was able to recognize that physics' proper object of study was not *things at rest* (as defined by the Aristotelian framework), but *things in motion* and, ultimately, *motion itself. Not things at rest, but things in motion, i.e., motion itself.*

On the basis of that quite extraordinary ontological discovery Galileo, together with many others, of course, constructed a model and a practice of natural science — essentially a mathematical model — which has proved to be remarkably explanatory and developmental albeit, in the final analysis, reactionary in the hands of the white male supremacist international bourgeoisie in terminal crisis. Over a period of hundreds of years, that natural science paradigm — which proved so efficacious in the development of technology and the transformation from feudalism to first mercantile and then industrial capitalism, in navigational and military advances, in industrial advances — that model became the model of *all* science. Even more, it became the model of understanding, of explanation, itself. Science, defined by this mathematicized naturalistic model, has become the paradigm for all human understanding. It should come as no great surprise, therefore, that there has been, over the course of this century, an attempt to apply this scientific-now-commonsensical model of understanding to human behavior.

Now while it is certainly true that the Galilean discovery of motion as the object of study was fundamental for the creation of his *Two New Sciences* (the treatise which introduced the *modern* sciences of mathematics and physics) and subsequent mathematical paradigms — while that was certainly valid for *nature* — the treatment of human activity as fundamentally analogous to the motion of matter in space and time (no matter how many qualifications you make, no matter how liberal you may be in saying, "Of course we appreciate the difference") is an error of inestimable magnitude. To use a model of comprehension or understanding (physical science) which is so rooted in the mathematicized conception of the natural world is fundamentally to distort what human beings are; it is, ultimately, to treat human beings as structurally analogous to the objects of study of the natural sciences.

In the 1960s I attended many conferences on this very topic. I was very very naive, very innocent. I assumed, after many conferences, that we had put this issue to rest. Philosophical fool that I was, I thought we had successfully buried psychology by analytically destroying its foundations. But I have learned that things like psychology, things like capitalism, things like exploitation, racism, sexism, homophobia, are very difficult to bury. They do not die easily. Moreover, they often die much sooner than they get buried. So psychology goes on! In fact, as in a bad horror movie, it thrives. In fact, it grows.

Let me make a jump here. What I had told people I would talk about today is the psychopathology of the United States left. Let me make clear first of all what I *don't* mean by that. I don't know if you know this, but in the United States, in my country, politically reactionary and backward as it is, they actually give grants to show that revolutionary behavior should be understood as *deviant*. So when I speak of the psychopathology of the U.S. left, I don't mean for a moment that leftists or Marxists or Leninists or revolutionaries are crazy people. Nor do I mean that we revolutionaries are unusually or disproportionately sane! *Rather I want to suggest that the U.S. left — despite all of its anti-psychology rhetoric — has transformed into a sectarian pseudo-psychology movement.* I think the modus operandi of the U.S. left is, in effect, to attempt to alter the subjective state of oppressed peoples and working peoples. Its "tactic," in the final analysis, is what is called "consciousness raising."

Never in the history of our species has a consciousness *ever been "raised."* But the United States left languishes in a totally impotent state by virtue of its having been transformed into a pseudo-psychological operation (consciousness raising) and is no longer concerned, as a revolutionary movement must be, *with the activity (and the duty) of making revolution.* So what has happened, ironically, is that this mythic pseudo-scientific manipulation called psychology, this essentially fraudulent activity, the attempt to transform people's minds understood as physical objects (or physical motion) — what might best be called coercion — has reshaped the U.S. left. Profound opportunities exist in the United States for the development of a broad movement, a mass movement of working people and oppressed minorities (the possibility of that exists in the United States today, in my opinion, more than at any time since the 1930s). But nothing is effectively organized, because the progressives (the honest ones, at any rate!) have become sectarian "consciousness raisers."

Over the course of the past 10 or 12 years, I have been associated with a group of people who have developed the largest independent Marxist therapeutic center in the United States. I'm here with some of my colleagues — Dr. Lenora Fulani and Dr. Lois Holzman and others. We have developed an approach, social therapy, which we identify as Marxist. At a meeting yesterday an audience member asked, "Why do you call your approach Marxist? After all, many people identify the origins of psychopathology as social. Is it only Marxists who know that?" I agreed that it is not just Marxists who know that. But the issue of whether social therapy is Marxist therapy does not turn on whether we recognize the causes of psychopathology to be social, but rather on the recognition *that human beings are capable of radically reorganizing social structures, that human beings are fundamentally capable of creating and reorganizing the social environment which creates and develops pathology.* The conception of a human being that underlies our Marxist therapy is that people are not fundamentally passive or inert, not fundamentally overdetermined by our environment, but are in a dialectical and contradictory relationship to that determining environment; that is, a human being is someone who has self-consciously helped to build (with her or his labor power) the very environment which causes pathology. That strange characteristic of our species must be a fundamental presupposition of any Marxist therapy.

In social therapy, we treat people from many different communities: middle class people (the usual patient population), working class people, Black, Latino, white, farmers, many people. They come to our offices, thousands of people each year, because they are in pain, because they have emotional problems — they come for the same reason that they would come to see any therapist or counselor. These are ordinary people. *We relate to these people as revolutionaries!* Our assumption about the fundamentality of who a human being is, of what a person is, our Marxist presumption, is that people, organized into various social groupings, are fundamentally identifiable as a social force capable of transforming their environment radically. People are not simply to be understood as basically adaptive to societal norms, though to be sure we all adapt to varying degrees. There's no question that we can adapt to societal norms — sometimes all too easily. But to presume *adaptiveness* to be the essence of a human being yields a therapeutic approach which is totally, qualitatively different from what you get if you presume that a person is *fundamentally* a revolutionary.

Let's talk about the difference between relating to someone as fundamentally adaptive to a societal situation as opposed to relating to someone as fundamentally a revolutionary who is capable of radically transforming a social situation. We're not talking about whether the patient, client, whatever, becomes politically active. We're talking about how effectively we can treat psychopathology if we relate to people as capable of transforming the world — i.e., history — as opposed to relating to people as simply adapting to existing society and its roles. If we change that basic premise, what are the effects, scientifically speaking? What are the effects in the group therapeutic situation? So far as I know we are the only ones in the United States who are treating people from the vantage point of this radically different perception of what a human being essentially is. And we have effectively "cured" thousands of people, in many cases after every other clinical treatment has failed.

What do we mean by "cured"? We mean people who have spent decades destroying themselves with alcohol and drugs giving them up. We mean people who have spent decades and thousands of dollars at traditional treatment centers but remain incapable of functioning in society at all, becoming productive, powerful and capable of emotional gratification. We mean people who have gone through between 10 and 30 years of orthodox treatment and by their own accounts (as well as by the accounts of the outrageous testing which goes on in many institutions of psychology) have been unmoved by any psychological treatment declaring themselves "better."

We have treated thousands with this revolutionary model. People ask, "Why do you think it works?" One reason it works, we believe, is that the root cause of a great deal of pathology has to do with people's difficulties in adapting to society. People's problems are in part *caused* by their difficulty in adapting to society. Therefore it is sometimes exceedingly difficult, if not impossible, to "cure" them by counting so heavily on their capacity to adapt. If people come to you, as a therapist, and somehow or another their adaptive capacities have been impaired, or if people come to you and they simply have no desire to adjust (I think here of Dr. Martin Luther King's marvelous quotation about how the people who he thinks will have to change the world *are the maladjusted*), it seems very odd to us that traditional therapists so frequently and typically count on them to do the very thing that they don't know how to do or don't choose to do in order to improve!

The approach that we're taking does not require people to be more adaptive to society. It does something else. We talk about helping people to adapt not to *society* but to *history*. We make a distinction between society and history — between society as a particularly organized form of the historical process at a particular extended spatio-temporal moment, and history as the continuum

A much less restricted perspective with more opportunities for "identification with", esp, i change.

of that social process. We seek to find ways to help people not to adapt to society, but to find their adaptive location in the broader social continuum identifiable as historic process. But to adapt to history rather than to society is, in its essence, revolutionary, because (and as) it is to express the human capacity to radically reorganize the totality of the social environment. So what we seek to do is to help people to develop further what we take to be a fundamental human characteristic — that revolutionary essence of our species. We attempt to reach that revolutionary essence, that fundamental sense of self as capable of *being* in history, by transforming it. Therefore, in adapting to history — which, after all, *leads* society — people are in a better position to do something about how they relate within society. History leads development in the sense of the discovery of the renowned Soviet psychologist/ methodologist Lev Vygotsky that learning leads (is in advance of) development. All too frequently, the price that you have to pay for adapting to society — I'm talking about U.S. society in particular — is to be sufficiently alienated so as to be totally distanced or removed from or estranged from history. So the contradiction of traditional therapy, if you will, is that even when it works to help people to adapt to their society, if it's a reactionary, racist, sexist, homophobic, backward, alienated, classist society like the one I come from — and to varying degrees all of modern society! — if you develop a therapy which simply adapts people to that, then you do so only at the price of people being further removed from history, which means people being further mis-identified as who we are fundamentally as a species. *To make people societally sane, using traditional therapy, you must make them historically crazy!*

it would seem to be recognition of history a process

speeching meaning

knowing history

obvious

identification within, not adaptation to it.

Modern science arose from the bringing together of the science of physics and the science of mathematics, and a political economic *base* which needed that mixture for continued human development. Traditional psychology, together with its companionpiece, traditional economics — the two new pseudo-sciences of the last several hundred years — must be effectively rejected. We must find a new science and organize a new political economic basis in order to "treat" the psychological problems that now stand in the way of continued human development. I am not suggesting, by the way, that psychological problems are in the mundane ordinary sense of the word fraudulent. No. Our world is filled, sadly, with people who have serious psychological problems. I am suggesting that traditional psychology has done precious little, if anything, to deal with them. I am saying that we must find some new paradigm (or anti-paradigm) — a *new way* — to deal with the psychological problems of our species. The paradigm or anti-paradigm? The new way? Revolution!

I think revolution needs to be the substitute for psychology. I think we should change the name of our psychological association to the "Interamerican Congress For Revolution." Now a lot of people say "That's terrible! It would make the whole thing political!" It would *not* make it political — it would make it scientific! It is *currently* political.

As currently organized, traditional psychology — not simply at this congress, but all over the world — is fundamentally an anti-scientific, secularly religious political operation. If we were, in fact, to take a step forward out of the dark ages and create a new approach, a new social science which truly dealt with people's emotional disorders as well as with issues of pedagogy, with issues of socialization, with all the issues that psychology is concerned with, we would discover scientific revolution.

Now, having said that, how do we carry out scientific revolution? How do we address social problems from the vantage point not just of some set of slogans, but from the scientifically organized activity of revolutionary change? One of the ways we do that, in my opinion, is to insist that we not simply speak of revolution to revolutionaries. We don't only speak of clinical psychology to psychologists. It would be very strange if we had created a science of clinical psychology where a precondition for coming to see a therapist would be that you were a devotee of psychology. Our patients come to us for help. They have problems, they're in pain. We don't require that they be "committed to psychology." Now if we are truly to make the shift from traditional, pseudo-psychology to revolution, we must do the same thing. We need to say, "Please come into my office, I'd like to help you. What we do is revolution. Have a seat."

"Is this some kind of joke?" you ask. No. Because by *doing revolution*, you are using a scientific approach, a model, which fundamentally rests on a certain conception of a human being as capable of transforming totalities. And we cannot minimize for a moment how fundamental that is to the carrying out of revolution and how fundamental that is to people being able to be cured. Because cure is a social revolutionary phenomenon when it is not an adaptation to society, when it takes place in history, in the world, not in reactionary society.

We have practiced this radical approach for almost two decades. The difference in responses to it is, as you would expect, very radical. What does that look like? It looks like people first of all saying, "What are you *doing*? What is the meaning of this? I *insist* that you relate to me as a passive recipient of your goods and services. Fix me up! I am a consumer. I wish to be fixed by you." "It can't be done," we say. "We cannot fix you. We cannot cure you." "Well, if you cannot cure me, why have you hung up that shingle?"

People say, "I simply wish to be cured of my pain! I simply wish my pain to be relieved! Why can't you do that for me?" "Because we can do something for you that can change your life, that will develop your emotionality, that will reorganize your 'psychology,' we can do all kinds of things for you, but we cannot cure you insofar as you insist that you are a commodity that is going to be effectively, coercively altered by something called traditional psychology." And a profound struggle ensues.

To wrap up. Going back briefly to the U.S. left. Here's an incredible irony. The U.S. left is forever telling me and others with whom I work very closely throughout our country that "our problem" is that we do psychology rather than politics. And we respond to them by saying your problem is that, in the name of politics, you in fact do bad, mythic, coercive, bourgeois pseudo-psychology.

I have spoken on just a few occasions to the orthodox U.S. left. I have said that one striking characteristic of the U.S. left is that they have no idea of how U.S. society functions! Never in the history of a left wing movement anywhere in the world has a grouping of leftists or so-called revolutionaries sought to revolutionize or change a society knowing so little about how it works. Their view, in the most arrogant, chauvinistic, exceptionalistic tradition of the United States, is to think that all one has to do is *raise the consciousness* of working people, or poor people, of oppressed minorities, and somehow this coercive pseudo-psychological activity will produce revolution. As I said before, in my opinion, consciousness is not raised. I do not think there has ever been a single known case of the raising of consciousness. I might sound like a vulgar materialist to you all, but I think buildings are raised, I think sometimes money is raised, I think children are raised, a lot of things are raised — but I don't think consciousness is raised. The conception of consciousness being raised, which dominates the U.S. left, is that an intellectual activity, a private mentalistic activity, is the precondition for carrying out revolutionary social activities. But as a matter of fact, it has been proven everywhere that exactly the opposite is true. In fact it is the active reorganization of social life which is

Begin Here↑
Just Do It?

the precondition for the *transformation of consciousness*. Marx taught that in the first pages he ever wrote. It is fundamental to the understanding and activity of revolution and for the psychology which I am calling revolution.

We speak of social therapy as revolution for non-revolutionaries. This radical Marxist conception — that the fundamental or essential human characteristic is being capable of carrying out revolutionary activity (what Marx called practical-critical activity) — that's the foundation of anything which can be called or should be called a Marxist psychology. Ours is a radical insistence that we not accommodate reactionary society by relating to people — *any* people — as anything but revolutionaries.

2

TALKIN' TRANSFERENCE

One of the more thought-provoking compliments I've received as a therapist came from an old acquaintance, who was for many years the head of the clinical psychology program at Boston University. She said that she was certain that my talent as a therapist was related to the fact that I have received no formal training in clinical psychology. I was flattered, but not at all surprised. For the attitude underlying this compliment is not so uncommon among progressive or, indeed, simply relatively honest clinicians or folks in the business of training clini-

"Talkin' Transference" was delivered at a workshop on transference sponsored by the Institute for Social Therapy and Research on November 13, 1982, and first published in Practice: The Journal of Politics, Economics, Psychology, Sociology and Culture *(Spring 1983) Vol. 1, No. 1.*

cians. There is a recognition by many that the process that people go through in being trained to do therapy often has as its consequence the desensitizing of the trainees. This kind of charge has been made not only against the training of therapists, but also of social workers, doctors, lawyers, teachers; the training of many, many people in the "helping professions."

I want to raise this at the outset for a couple of reasons. One is that I think it opens up a critical problematic for us to engage. It raises the question of how the practice of therapy is taught and how the teaching of therapy is practiced. This is a question that the Institute has been concerned to address and that our theoretical, practical and political work has focused on. Our particular concern with and work on transference grows out of our critical posture, a posture that is not simply trying to find an alternative psychology, but (and this is perhaps somewhat facile) a posture that is trying to find an alternative *to* psychology. One of the questions that the Institute has been raising is what this whole enterprise called psychology is all about. We do know some things about it. It is, for some, lucrative. It is, for others, expensive. Those facts we have. But we are concerned to raise the question, in a variety of ways, of whether it is even remotely scientific; whether it is even remotely a value-free practice; whether it is even remotely a helpful activity. Indeed the community of official psychologists, the community of people who practice and write about and think about and theorize about psychology (never mind for the moment the thinking and writing of some of us *outsiders*) is profoundly conflicted on these matters. There is, of course, an extensive literature on such questions; whether therapy helps at all is a question that has been written about for a very long time. And it's to the credit, I think, of many in the community of psychologists that it self-critically engages itself. That's one reason I began with this anecdote. Another is to share with you from the very outset that psychological language, psychological jargon if you will, is not the jargon I'm comfortable with. I have other jargon that I'm more at ease with. I wasn't formally trained in psychology. My training, taken at Stanford University back in the late 1950s and early '60s, is in the philosophy of science and to some extent in the foundations of mathematics. That those obscure, esoteric topics have, over the last 25 years, turned out to have relevance to political, psychological and social issues is one of the great surprises of my life. Since the jargon of psychology is not what I'm most comfortable with, I'm hopeful that people who *are* trained in psychology will bear with me in the way I am formulating these matters.

RADICAL THERAPY

There has been a radical therapy movement for a very long time. The radical therapy movement of the '60s and early '70s, that many of us here are most familiar with, made some quite profound contributions in that it raised some questions about the beliefs, attitudes and ideas that were, if not explicit, at least implicit in many traditional forms of therapy. It openly raised the issue of what many took to be (I think correctly) the fundamental sexism of traditional, Freudian-influenced therapeutic approaches. It raised the issue of the fundamental racism of many forms of traditional therapy, and of the anti-gay attitudes and beliefs which were, if not explicit, at least very close to the surface of many, many variations of traditional therapy. It raised the issue of the fundamentally anti-working class attitudes and beliefs to be found in Freudian, neo-Freudian, and Freudian-influenced psychologies. Actually, it raised issues of anti-people (anti-mass) attitudes and beliefs (the bourgeois bias in favor of the individual) that are structurally central to all Freudian-influenced therapies. I personally participated in this movement to some limited extent and applaud it. I think that one of the lasting and significant contributions of the women's movement and of feminism is having pointed out the subtle perniciousness and bigotry of many forms of therapy. And that tradition remains even though it is not the dominant one. There has been over the last decade, I think, a conservatizing reaction in therapy and elsewhere, but this reaction has not negated the significance of the radical therapeutic critiques, and I think New York City and indeed, this country, now abound with trained therapists who went through a radicalizing process in the '60s and '70s and managed to break away from the training they received in their clinical programs. In the language of the '60s, they "unlearned and relearned." That's been of great value.

But what I want to talk about today goes beyond radical therapy. I think it's important to begin by stressing that this "going beyond" is neither a rejection nor a negation of that radical thrust, but rather a very important and in my opinion qualitative extension of it. The lessons and lasting contributions of radical therapy have been its substantive points, the kinds of things that I identified a moment ago. In addition to these, the '60s and early '70s were also filled with attempts to radicalize the *form* of therapy. Here, on my view, things became more conservative. There was the Primal movement, there was the Encounter group movement, the Marathon movement, Bioenergetics, Systems and Communications and Transactional therapy; and a whole host of attempts to speak not simply to substantive biases embedded in therapy, not simply to address the racism, sexism and homophobia of traditional therapy, but to come up with forms of therapy which were less authoritarian and somehow less likely usable for conveying these substantive and pernicious biases. There were positive attempts at doing this, as well as critiques of the explicitly backward, bigoted, prejudicial content of traditional therapy. These attempts at radicalizing the *practice* of therapy have, by and large, in my opinion, failed. My sense as a practitioner — granted that it's hard to do a sound, statistical analysis of this by interviewing every practicing therapist — is that even the therapists who were radicalized in the '60s and '70s are now doing a therapy which though content-wise is nowhere near as pernicious, sexist, and racist as before the radicalization period is, in many cases, in its *practice*, its method and in its presuppositions *insufficiently* radicalized, i.e., it is not revolutionized.

Most contemporary radical therapists do a kind of therapy which is cleansed of a lot of the more backward characteristics of Freudian therapy, but the *form* of it, the way it's done, is not so dramatically different from that of their colleague down the block who's still practicing orthodox traditional neo-Freudian therapy of some kind or another. One could debate whether that's in fact the real situation, but I'm convinced that it's a serious problem. What we have sought to develop is not simply a therapy rid as much as possible, given our limitations as socialized members of this society, of the most backward, bigoted and pernicious beliefs and attitudes, but also to discover and to practice a therapy which doesn't embody those kinds of attitudes and beliefs in its *practice* and *method*.

Having come at this whole problem — what the institution of psychology is, if you will — from a psychological (albeit lay psychological) point of view, let me come at it for a minute from a political direction. Then I'm going to try to put those two together and share some thoughts about the very tentative answers that we've come up with.

THE POLITICAL SITUATION

The period that we're living through in this country today, from our point of view, is a period of profound social destabilization and encroaching political reaction. (Actually some friends object to this, saying, "Why do you say 'encroaching'?" My conservatism as a scientist says it's encroaching; my gut sometimes tells me to say that it's here.) Things can and no doubt will get worse and surely we are already moving in that direction. The economic variables, the social variables, our palpable experiences, tell us that we're heading down the road to reaction. One no longer has to be a sophisticated Marxist, or even an unsophisticated Marxist, to appreciate this. In a circumstance of this kind, in a social-political situation such as the one we're now in in this society, and indeed internationally, it seems of particular importance to have still another hard look at some very critical questions that have been raised in the history of the working class movement, in the history of the progressive movement, that have yet to be answered. There are lots of those questions. Obviously we're not going to consider all of them today. We're barely going to make a stab at considering one of them in some depth.

The question that I'm raising, and a critical question that I think remains unanswered in the history of the working class movement which is particularly relevant to what's happening in this society, is a question raised by Wilhelm Reich in the late 1920s and '30s, in a context which though in certain important respects quite different from our own, has sufficient similarities to what's going on in this society to be at least *frighteningly worrisome*. During the takeover of the political control of German society by the Nazi regime, Reich raised this fairly obvious and critical question, as a Marxist, which he was at the time, as a practicing communist, which he was at the time, and as a well-trained and indeed a leading Freudian psychoanalyst, which he was at the time. He asked, How the hell could Nazism have possibly happened? He was not asking what the underlying socio-economic conditions were which created the *context* for the rise of fascism. From Reich's point of view, there were all kinds of *good explanations* from an abstract Marxist perspective. What Reich was raising was, *given* all of these explanations of the destabilization and inflationary madness of 1920s Germany, the underlying conditions of production, the international realities — an endless series of superstructural and base conditions — it still wasn't clear how it was that a mass of people, in many respects the most politically and culturally sophisticated population in all of capitalist Europe, could go from a seemingly sane and rational understanding to absolute madness in what was a matter of months. How could that occur?

When one reads the pamphlets that were distributed by Hitler and the National Socialists we see in them a distortion of reality, a mythology which is at once insane and patently ludicrous. And yet millions and millions of people were acting as if they believed it. Whether they did or not remains a kind of interesting question, but they certainly acted in ways which suggested that they had bought in, seemingly overnight, on this mythology, on this folk myth.

Reich of course was eager to engage in a thoroughgoing polemic with what he identified as the more conservative elements of the German Communist Party on their unwillingness to engage this question. From Reich's point of view, the dominant leadership of the German Communist Party (and Reich used to speak in these terms) were more than content to simply go out on the street and stand on their soapboxes and deliver very profound and analytically sound Marxist economic analyses of what was going on in Germany. And while the people around the soapboxes of the KPD were falling asleep, Hitler's fascist orators were standing on the other street corner delivering absolute unadulterated bullshit which was winning over tens of thousands to the cause of reaction. Reich took that to be a startling — not to mention frightening — reality. Clearly it *was* a profound problem the consequences of which are now known to us all. This was the question, in both a practical and a theoretical sense, that Reich was raising. How could that have happened? How could that not simply rapid but radical reactionary transformation occur?

Reich proceeds to give a whole host of answers. I have some difficulties with some of them. Reich's answers, as many here know, have ultimately to do with certain structural characteristics of the human mind. It seems to me, although I don't want to go into this in detail, that Reich ultimately exposes his Freudian bias. And as is so often the case in attempted Marx/Freud syntheses, Freud dominates — Popular Frontism! But the contribution of the *question*, the contribution of formulating and raising that problem, makes Reich, from my point of view, one of the terribly important figures in the entire history of the working class movement in this century. Whatever his answers might be and whatever people think of his later work, which many progressives have serious problems with, the political issue — raised, for example, in *The Mass Psychology of Fascism* — is very, very, very important. It's a central and profoundly motivating one to us at the Institute. Because from an economic vantage point and a social vantage point we view ourselves as living in a society in which the potential for the rapid development of mass radical ideology is great.

I believe and many of my colleagues (both at the Institute and not at the Institute) believe that this potential for a rapid, reactionary and radical transformation of ideology clearly exists. Many, of course, disagree. Many people hold to the view, as we well know, that, "It could never happen here." I have problems with that position, because I've read too many similar statements that were written in Germany in the late '20s that it could never happen there. This kind of rapid and reactionary transformation of basic ideology could never occur because (the argument went) of the cultural and political sophistication of the German population.

Similar arguments are used about this country and this society. The claim is made that the fundamentally democratic character of the U.S. rules out such a possibility. Now not only have we heard the "it can't happen here" argument about Germany and the U.S., we've in recent years heard that argument put forth about Chile. What was said about Chile, as we all know I'm sure, is that the likelihood of a fascistic takeover (it's now more than a likelihood, it's been a longterm reality) was slight because of the long and deep-rooted tradition of Chilean democracy. We saw how rapidly the CIA turned *that* tradition around. Now none of us has a crystal ball. None of us are able, so far as I know, to predict the future impeccably. But I cannot accept anyone who denies the relevancy of considering at least the strong possibility that that kind of occurrence could take place in the United States. Actually, I'm convinced it *is* taking place!

Reflect for just a moment if you will — if you can get yourself to engage in this kind of radical empathic process (a sort of Collingwoodish empathy: stepping out of yourself for a minute) — imagine us sitting together in 1964 and having a discussion as to the likelihood of Ronald Reagan being President of the United States in 1980. You remember 1964. That was the year that political reaction was, so some said, totally destroyed. Remember? Barry Goldwater was defeated. Some people were speculating that not only was it the end of political reaction, it might well be the end of the Republican Party. That's not so long ago. Many of us in this room were not only there, we were participating in those crazy discussions. We were saying things like that. But in fact Reagan *is* now the President. And as a Marxist, I'm convinced that that has to do largely with the fact that underlying social conditions change dramatically, and when they change dramatically, what was taken to be impossible at one point in time becomes not only possible, but in some sense, reasonable.

But it's not only that Reagan is in the White House, it's that many people in this society don't even take it to be so shocking. We are accustomed to and have been trained well to accept exactly this kind of "gradualism": "Well, so now Reagan's in the White House; next time around someone else will be in the White House." One of the most pervasive of American myths is that the great strength of this country is its capacity to move from *regime* to *regime*; nothing really changes dramatically, goes the myth. Political scientists, who are essentially one variety of apologist for bourgeois capitalist society, will say things like, "Wasn't it fantastic that we could have the Nixon fiasco, and make the transition through it smoothly and calmly?"

This is a particularly relevant piece of American mythology in light of the events of the last several days, with the press trying desperately to convince us that cataclysmic things *might well happen* in the Soviet Union because of Brezhnev's death. The *New York Times* took pains to do the same "Brezhnev Is Dead" headline on two consecutive days. They said it was because of a distributors' strike; they were afraid some people wouldn't get the news. It still seems to me very strange to run almost the same headline two days running. I believe they wanted to *make sure* that we knew that Brezhnev died. And also it's an occasion for a great deal of propaganda — that propaganda which has as one of its primary concerns to point out the inherent (God-given?) stability of the American system, which enables us to go from one extreme position to another position in a "gradualistic" manner, that is not in any way disruptive or structurally destabilizing of our society. Well, that is, in my opinion, much more myth than fact. For one thing our society went through a profound destabilization during the Nixon days. What does seem clear from that experience as well as many others is that the institutional arrangement and the ideological structure of U.S. society are capable, even in the face of very extreme social changes, of interpreting, translating, recharacterizing and recasting significant social developments in ways which make them seem continuous and non-revolutionary. To be sure it is the existence of a permanent government (the state) which makes this all possible. Hence there *is* something ongoing *vis à vis* the bourgeois state whose existence is denied by the bourgeois political scientists. It is a serious problem, however, for us to be lulled into thinking that the state of the state (no less the governmental structure) never changes. The message of this kind of propaganda is that you never have to worry about changes taking place in this country that are so profound they cannot be assimilated. The message is that America will always be able — institutionally, politically, ideologically — to fit things in, that some wonderful ideal called American pluralism will make it possible to avoid reaction or fascism (not to mention socialism!). The U.S. state will prevail. Pluralism is the ace in the hole that everybody's supposed to buy in on to alleviate our concern about a Ronald Reagan in the White House. The checks and balances system we all learned about in our junior high school civics courses will make sure nothing too extreme or too destabilizing occurs. So when we read stories about Alexander Haig and his interest in doing something that looked shockingly like seizing power during the last days of Nixon, we are taught to say, "Ah, that must be put out by some conspiratorial-type leftist. Couldn't really be true." But the quotes from Haig looked very convincing, and when you see him you sort of say, "Gee, I can imagine this fellow doing that." But then you semi-consciously invoke the myth of "checks and balances": "No, that couldn't be; something would always balance out his power."

The myth of checks and balances is now less convincing to many people in this country than it ever has been. It's less convincing for a variety of reasons. It's less convincing because of phenomena like Watergate, like Chile, like Vietnam, like Three Mile Island. "Couldn't possibly happen. Nothing could really go wrong." Over the past 20 or 30 years, after experiencing many Watergates and Three Mile Islands (and one Vietnam!), people are increasingly becoming unconvinced of checks and balances. It has been applied just too too often. Overworked. The myth, as well, is applied to the ever increasing possibility of nuclear war: "There couldn't be an accidental (or, for that matter, intentional) nuclear war because we have all kinds of checks and balances." In sum, it is a very specious, less than conscious myth designed to convince us, as similar myths were designed in pre-fascist Germany, that "it can't happen here." And while the myth has weakened, it nonetheless prevails.

What I've been formulating for the last few minutes is in very general terms the political context, the political concern, that motivates the Institute. I've taken pains to delineate both the psychological and the political concerns because the Institute and the theory and practice of social therapy are motivated by a synthesis of both. It also has another characteristic that is hard to understand.

What we're trying to do and to build at the Institute is not to create a new science; our concern is not to develop a new psychology or indeed even a new alternative *to* psychology that is somehow true and valid forever. One of the basic canons, one of the basic underlying methodological assumptions of science as it's practiced in bourgeois society, is that science is supposed to be true for all times — universal, they say. We have absolutely no commitment to creating a psychology which is true for all times and all places. In fact, we would be enormously impressed with ourselves if we could come up with something which had some relevance to this time, to this brief moment in the history of humankind in this society; if we could come up with something which is so integrated, so related to what's going on in the world right now, that it can be of help to, and can be politically and socially and psychologically valuable to as many people as ultimately participate in it. If we could create such an activity, such a practice, with such an accompanying theory, we would be more than delighted. We would have made a contribution.

CONASON'S CRITIQUE

Our concern, developed from all of the issues and events I've been discussing, has been to engage the practice of therapy, how therapy is done. And we've been all over the map in the many years during which we've been doing this. We've read lots, we've studied, we've tried things, we've been around for quite a while doing a lot of different things, and the attacks have been very helpful to us. They haven't been very pleasant, but they've been helpful to us in several ways. One of the things I've tried to learn over the years as a political person — as a Marxist — is that the people that you can, in some sense, learn the most from are the people who really can't stand you at all. When they don't like what you're doing, they're right up front with their criticism.

Take Joe Conason's abusive piece in the *Village Voice* last June. There are many things about me that Joe Conason dislikes — I know because Joe and I have talked about them on several occasions. As a matter of fact, the guy can't stand me — has a whole laundry list entitled "Things I Hate about Fred Newman, the New York Institute and NAP." But the thing he placed at the center of his six-page journalistic critique, "Psychopolitics," was the issue of transference. According to traditional and neo-Freudian theory, transference is the process by which the patient gets cured; supposedly, the unconscious feelings one has toward one's mother and/or father are transferred *onto* the therapist. Despite all of the faults Conason lists in his diatribe about me, the New York Institute and NAP, the guts of his attack was that what is most pernicious, most vicious, most terrible, most unethical and most bad about what the folks at the Institute for Social Therapy are doing is that they take advantage of people while (and here we might have an example of my lack of training in psychology) "under the influence" of transference. It is talked about, even in some of the official literature, as being like alcoholism or sleepwalking. So when you're under the influence, you're easily taken advantage of, more suggestible, malleable, etc., and so forth. Brainwashable!

Thus, Conason paints a picture of people just sort of showing up at the Institute's social therapy clinic blindfolded or in a daze. Now, of course, that's not true. But reading Conason's piece you'd think people were just mindlessly walking down the street one day and happened into the lobby of the Institute. Indeed there is a tone to Conason's article — an attitude — that denies from the very outset that human beings (other than journalists or "other" intellectuals) have the capacity to make decisions for themselves. One of the things we've talked about a great deal at the Institute is how that article, in the final analysis, is not nearly as insulting to the people doing therapy at the Institute as it is to the people *in* therapy at the Institute. It identifies these people as straight out idiots and buffoons, that they would just sort of come in and say "Here's my mind, do to it what you will." That's the picture that is suggested by Conason's formulation. Well, that's not been our experience with the people we see or with people in general. People in this society have become, as we talked about a minute ago, more and more questioning as a result of the events of the last two decades.

But independent of how you arrive at the NYI (most people arrive through a friend's recommendation or an advertisement), what Conason is saying is that the patient is upset, distressed, and has emotional problems when she or he arrives, comes into the office to get help, and in doing so something called transference happens. Something happens between the client or the patient — or whatever words you're comfortable with, the person who comes for help — something happens in the interaction between the person who comes for help and the person who is identified in that get-together as the giver of help, however that person may have been trained or not trained. According to Conason (and the orthodoxy), something takes place in the interaction between these two people (or if it's a group, between many people and the leader) which makes the person or persons getting help much more vulnerable and susceptible than usual, and that has to do somehow with something known as or identified by the word "transference."

Conason's critique motivated us at the Institute. It's not that we hadn't already been thinking about and writing about this concept of transference for a long time. But the *Village Voice* piece motivated us even further (and with a more concrete political imperative) to have still another hard look at what transference is. What is this thing that happens? It seems clear that if this process or activity called transference *is* going on, it must be happening in lots of other places. For example, it would no doubt happen between teachers and students, between any grouping of two or more involved in the dynamic or the dialectic of helper to helped. What is "transference?" What does it mean to be "under the influence" of transference? Well, as we began our reexamination as Marxists we began by confronting anew a question we had been on and off devoting ourselves to for the better part of 15 years.

ALIENATION AND TRANSFERENCE

As Marxists, we believe that capitalist society, the society in which we live and in which many other people live, is in some fundamental sense an alienated society. Now as Marxists, we don't take the notion of alienation to be psychological. We take it to be sociological. What we mean by that is that alienation is not simply a state of mind; it's not how people feel. Rather, it's how people *are*. And people get to be that way by virtue of how the entire system and activity of production (which influences more than simply the narrow acts of industry, but rather influences the total process of human production of human life in our society) creates a fundamentally alienated society. Some of the important ingredients of that perspective, from a Marxist point of view, are as follows. Capitalism as a social-productive system is primarily in the business of producing commodities. It is not, as a system, primarily in the business of producing stuff on the basis of what human beings need although, to be sure, there has to be some relationship between what it produces and what people need, because if it didn't there'd be no one around to sell their stuff to and nobody around to keep reproducing their commodities. Nonetheless, the fundamental motivation of reproduction in capitalist society is *not* primarily the activity of creating or producing for use, but creating or producing for exchange (which means, in the final analysis, producing for profit). That is, the stuff that's produced under capitalism, by and large, is produced in order to exchange it. What gets produced are commodities. These commodities are sold and distributed on the market in complicated ways which wind up benefiting some few folks to the ongoing disadvantage of many others.

Thus the basic unit, as it were, the stuff, or if you want to use some philosophical language (unfortunately my more preferred jargon), the *ontology* of capitalist society, is commodities, things that get sold in vast numbers (well, not as vast as the Ford Motor Company would like them to be sold right now). The point of it all is to create commodities which are exchanged profitably. But the production of commodities for the market and for exchange is a profoundly alienated social activity. As Marx points out, the activity of producing what we use for our own needs (not necessarily our personal needs but the needs of our species, our class, our families, of human beings) in accordance with a plan based on criteria having little to do with our own needs, but producing rather *for exchange* and someone else's profit, has the effect of separating, of distancing, in a very, very profound way, the *activity* of production from the *product* of production.

Put more simply, when folks went out into the woods and built their own houses, harvested their own food, built their own tables and chairs, made their own clothing and so on, for the use of either themselves or their families or communities, the relationship between the activity of social labor and what was produced by that social labor was organic and self-consciously recognizable.

But when folks under the complex division of labor and mass production techniques of capitalist commodity production go off to large factories and engage in little pieces of work, turning this particular screw, turning that particular screw; when secretarial workers go in and engage in one narrow activity hour after hour after hour; when clerks do nothing but ring that cash register; when the whole organization of this activity is designed to maximize the profitability of commodity production and exchange, the result of that is a profound alienation, meaning not just a state of mind, but meaning an actual organized distancing from the stuff that the world is made up of. So people find it more and more difficult to comprehend, in capitalist society, products of our own collective labor. The stuff that's created is, in the final analysis, the product of our collective labor, there being nobody else to make it. If we don't make it, it doesn't get made.

This alienation is both the product of and produces, if you will, a commodified society. It is a society in which there is a fundamental distance (*a dualistic dichotomy*) between the activity of producers and the product. And the product is a commodity. This defines not simply industrial activities. It turns out that in such a society *everything of value* (literally) gets commodified. Human beings are related to as commodities in the social, civic and legal contracts that make up life in our society. There is a commodification of all activity, growing out of and emerging from the fundamental commodification that is intrinsic to the way in which production and distribution are organized under capitalism.

A friend asked me recently to give examples of this. I suggested she think about children. Think how the laws are written about children: how they are treated as private property, how they are "possessed." Think about wives (which, in this society, we "have"), students at school (compulsory miseducation), and to be sure, workers. By and large, the entire population is related to as commodities. There is a dehumanization which is not simply psychological, but which is structurally endemic to the way in which this society carries out its daily business. *See Halmos - Friends as objects to be manipulated so as to produce for you some advantage.*

All this is fairly straightforward Marxist sociology, though I am sure there are Marxists who would disagree with the way I'm talking about it. Let's have a look at this commodified society of ours. A question that we at the Institute have been considering for a very long time, and that I personally have been considering for over 20 years, was rekindled in the light of Conason's "commodified" attack (commodified, I might add, by Rupert Murdoch, the owner of the *Village Voice* and one of the most reactionary "commodifiers" in all of the world). This is the question: given that we live in a commodified world, given that the stuff of the world is commodities of all various sizes and shapes, what must the human mind be like and what do *we* have to be like to *understand* such a world? This seems to me to be a scientific question of some significance: what kind of adaptation must the mind make, what kind of *mental socialization* must take place for human beings in order for us to have the necessary comprehension of this thoroughly commodified reality to get on with our daily lives, to simply make it through the day? I'm not even talking about intellectual sophistication. I'm talking about having enough practical understanding to be able to stop at the red light and move at the green one, enough understanding to carry out the daily activities which include, I must say, some rather sophisticated activities in an industrially advanced society. What must we be like and what must our minds be like to make any sense at all out of these commodities interrelating in these very strange and curious ways? The sophisticates have several special pseudo-sciences to make sense of it all including a paradigmatic pseudo-science called economics which purports to explain how commodities, how these totally alienated entities, relate to each other. But how must we ordinary people, carrying out ordinary life activities, understand in order to get by?

Marx gives us a very important clue in what is a most critical component of his major work on capitalist economics, *Capital*. In a very early section of the first volume, Marx introduces a notion called *fetishism*, in the sense of "the fetishism of commodities." What he's trying to do in this small section of *Capital* is to offer a characterization of what commodities are *from a psychological point of view*. Hence, this section is important in the development of a Marxist psychology. He takes the whole of the four volumes to explain what commodities are from an economic vantage point. But what Marx insists on right at the outset in the first volume of *Capital* is that there will be *no understanding* of capitalist society, of commodified society, by simply comprehending commodities *economically* (in a kind of economistic-reductionistic sense). There must as well be an understanding of commodities *ideologically* or, if you will, psychologically. What Marx teaches in Volume One is that commodities must be understood as entities which *functionally appear* very much like gods. They are the secular gods of capitalist society. They are not merely gods in the sense that people worship money, and worship, therefore, what the exchange of commodities can yield. They're not simply gods in that kind of metaphorical sense. They are gods in a much more literal sense. They are gods (godlike) in that their very existence, being, and character have the property of being structurally disengaged from the process by which they were created, while *appearing* otherwise.

One of the most important things to understand about gods is this: gods are relatively useless entities if people in a given society know that the god(s) got made up in someone's back room, by someone who said, "You know, what we need around here is a couple of gods on Mount Olympus to keep the folks under control." If masses of people were to know that this was the actual *origin* of the gods, the effectiveness of them would be diminished to nothing. That is, gods must, of necessity, be seen as having an existence independent of their actual social origins.

Marx notes that commodities have precisely this characteristic. They must be understood as absolutely independent of the social origins which produce them. So not only is it the case that society is, sociologically speaking, alienated, but the products of that alienated process, in order to be comprehended at all, suggests Marx, must be related to as godlike. Well, an important reason for and an important consequence of gods (and commodities) being treated as utterly separate from their social origins is that folks believing in them take them to be essentially unchangeable. In contrast, imagine the following exchange: "Do you know where that god came from?" "Where?" "That god was made up by those three guys with the beards who live up on the hill. They had a meeting this morning. I know, I was watching. I saw it on videotape. They had this meeting and they said, 'Well, we need Zeus, so let's get a Zeus figure together,' and they even had some discussions of what Zeus should look like." If people started saying this down at the bottom of the hill, it would really dramatically affect the amount of social control you could get out of your Zeus god.

The fundamental capitalist myth is that capitalism is coherent with reality and therefore, in the final analysis, is the most sophisticated and advanced form of society because it is an economic and social expression of people's fundamental human nature — greediness, nastiness and hostility. These are the characteristics of those (the capitalist class) who, in my opinion, have primary responsibility for the continued existence of a commodity organized society but not the characteristics of the people of the society in total. But that's the myth.

The myth states that commodities (the gods) are not the creation of a particular society at a particular moment in history, under the heavy influence of existing social conditions and a particular class, but that they are independent, godlike realities which we must "worship" in various ways. We worship them by relating to them as fundamentally unchangeable, and by holding to the belief that commodity society is the highest stage of human development. Now, what Marx points out relevant to our question of what your head's got to be like in such a society is this: people must be socialized, if you will, as *religious,* in order to have a necessary and sufficient comprehension of the social movement of these entities to get by. Marx speaks eloquently in the *Communist Manifesto* about how the myth of capitalism, as it arrives on the historical scene, is that it ruthlessly tears asunder all prior religiosity and metaphysics, and puts in their place hard objective science. Marx points out that that's nonsense. While it's true that it tears asunder *prior* metaphysical conceptions, it puts in their place a new and more sophisticated metaphysical and religious conception.

This religious conception lives on in the socialized reality of people who live in capitalist society. Our society is profoundly religious in this particular and very deep sense: it is a religious world view which is needed for the comprehension of the so-called secular or non-religious reality of commodified society. Contrary to the mass propaganda and the popular myth, the religious state of mind is a *necessary* state for the continuation of capitalism. Bourgeois science is at once in perpetual conflict with this religious view and methodologically built on a religious perspective — a valorization of fetishization — more structurally metaphysical than

People must Be socialized to accept the IRRATIONAL AND SPECIFICALLY THE MAGICAL DISNEYLAND

any prior system.

I would suggest that this relationship between how we have to be and how things are, this religious view which is set up to be oppositional to religion but is in actuality deeply religious — is *transference*. People have to be socialized to *do transference* in order to make sense out of commodified bourgeois society. One must essentially — not just accidentally, but essentially — attribute to these commodified entities characteristics which treat them as completely divorced from their social origins. We have to learn from the very earliest age to relate to the world not as historical, not as we participate in it, but rather as made up of the resultants, the products of these activities dualistically separated from their social-productive history. And if we are not effectively socialized in this particular way of understanding, we are not able to comprehend what's going on in capitalist society. We have to be raised up religiously. IE IRRATIONALLY, MAGIC.

So I want to make very clear that the Institute hardly denies transference. In fact, what we believe is that transference is a very, very normal occurrence — indeed it is the normal state of mind in contemporary society! As a matter of fact, one way to look at what people characteristically come to therapy for help with is that their transference mechanisms have been impaired to some degree or another. Their problem is that they're not doing transference so well anymore. Or, perhaps, they never did. It may turn out to be that they're somehow, for some complicated reasons, glimpsing reality. So they rush to see a doctor, the objective message being, "This terrible thing happened to me today. I had a look at reality. I've got to get help somehow to have the transference mechanism repaired." Our concern in social therapy is therefore not to deny the existence of transference; that would be ludicrous. It is rather to evolve a form of helping, a way of understanding and supporting, a therapeutic approach if you like, which is non-transferential.

But isn't that a contradiction? Doing transference is what you have to do to understand anything, so how could you get help from a non-transferential therapy? Then you couldn't understand anything! A very real political and psychological problem.

First, let's look at Reich's Freudian answer. Reich's understanding of how the radical and rapid transformation of ideology and understanding in Germany in the 1930s was possible is that there exists a three-tiered organic structure of the human mind, including, in his view, a totalitarian component. The rapid embrace of fascism by the masses of German people followed from the fact that in some way or another the totalitarian component was reached and activated by reality plus the Nazis, and it came to dominate social reality. As I said earlier, I find Reich's answer problematic for a variety of reasons; it is essentially an expression of Freud's character-analytic tradition which ultimately explains things in terms of the character of the mind as opposed to the character of social reality. But I want to raise this just to contrast it with the kind of answer that we're developing.

What we're suggesting is *not* that there is some fundamental structure of the human mind, a component of which is, for various social reasons, totalitarian or proto-fascistic. Actually, I think that's ultimately a dangerous point of view. What we are suggesting is that the capacity to make this rapid transition has to do with the fact that the traditional or the "normal" mode of understanding in bourgeois society is much more profoundly religious than is characteristically recognized. We are suggesting that psychologically, ideologically and economically speaking, the distance between capitalism in its stable or normal state, and fascism, which is an extreme form of decaying capitalism, is not so great. Only if one takes the mass psychology and ideology of capitalism in its non-fascistic state to be pure, scientific, or objective and non-religious, does one perceive a transformation to the fascistic mentality as shockingly extreme. I don't think it is so extreme. Nor Do I.

Transferential forms of therapy are eminently usable to brainwash the hell out of people. So there's a certain way in which I agree with Conason. Insofar as Conason is saying that *if* what we're doing is transferential therapy, then we're dealing with something very dangerous because we could utilize it to coerce, I agree. If Conason is arguing that or saying something like that (which he's not — I'm being very, very generous), I would agree. The fact is that what Conason is saying is that "all" therapy is transferential; therefore bringing in politics is dangerous because it's potentially a form of brainwashing or coercion.

The very point that we're making, however, is that our work for decades now has been and continues to be the development of a non-transferential — that is a *historical* — therapeutic approach. By historical I mean a therapeutic approach which insists upon identifying or comprehending reality historically — *as its social origins*, not from the perspective of its alienated products. Let me spell out what we mean by the historical as opposed to the transferential approach. It is no less an adaptational approach. Some people say, "Oh, you mean you don't help people adapt to the society, to the world?" No, we *do* help people adapt to the world. It's *you* that don't. ("You" being the traditional psychotherapeutic establishment and its radical cover). What you adapt people to is a transferentially understood social arrangement which is fundamentally alienated.

The kind of help that we intend to give, and that we try to give (and I think that we have been quite successful at giving), is helping people to deal with their emotional problems. People sometimes think when you come into social therapy that you have to have problems like, "I used to be a Trotskyist and now I want to become..." *No*, that's not the kind of problems we're talking about. People come to social therapy with their emotional problems, because they feel anxious, bad, a nervous wreck, not to have end-less leftist debates. People present these problems and our concern is to help them with these problems by helping them to adapt (I hate the word but let's use it for a minute because it evokes a certain kind of tension) but *not* to adapt to the alienated products of bourgeois society. We help them to become reintegrated (reorganized) into the social processes which are the social and productive *origins* of their commodified lives. Specifics, please.

People say, "Alright, show me 2½ minutes of social therapy," and they look and they say, "Well, it looks pretty much like traditional therapy to me." Well, in some ways it does look like traditional therapy. People talk about their emotional problems and other people respond. People are saying how they're feeling, expressing their opinions. What's different in both the practice and the curing that goes on in social therapy is the political and psychological imperative to cure people in the sense of helping them to gain a quite specific active, practical contact with the social origins of the products of bourgeois society, including their lives as a component of that social reality. That's not the same thing as tracing the psychological origins of the presenting problems from a Freudian or neo-Freudian perspective. A part of the process of identifying the social origins is identifying the social origins of the way in which we are socialized within the context of a commodified society. Understanding how it is that we've been socialized to understand what problems are is part of what has to be done to understand what the *origin* of the problem is. One of the main ways that we're socialized in this transferential way, in this commodified sense, is that we are socialized to understand how our problems are to be understood transferentially. Magically Transactionally.

Lois Holzman, director of the Institute, has recently published a particularly important paper called "Growing Up Explained." Lois is a developmental psychologist who has worked for many

years on child development and adult development. The primary
point of her paper, as I understand it, is that what is characteristically left out in understanding how children learn to explain is that
at the same time that children are learning how to explain this and
this and this, they are concurrently learning what things count and
what things don't count as explanations. They are learning a quite
specific conception of explanation, in addition to learning how one
explains why the pot got hot when you put it on the fire. So children are not only learning causal accountings and explanatory
accountings, they're concurrently learning a particular conception
of what it *means* to give explanatory accountings. Indeed, they are
learning that there is such a thing as explaining and, as well, that
there is such a thing as learning.

We learn to do, as well, the emotive analog to explaining. Not
only are we learning how we feel, and learning the language of
feelings, we are concurrently learning the epistemology of feelings.
We are learning what feelings are and how to understand feelings,
that there are feelings and that they are learnable. We're learning
the origins of feelings, again, not merely in terms of the specifics of
this feeling, i.e., if you run into a tragic situation you get sad. We
not only learn these specifics, we learn something about how it is
that feelings function. So in learning the language of feelings we
learn, as it were, the conceptuality of feelings. Part of what it
means to engage people's emotive problems is not to let people
accept out of hand that whole understanding and conception of
emotionality as it is transferentially socialized in contemporary
society, but to engage with them what feelings are, how we do feelings, and what feelings are all about. How we are "feeling-orga-
nized." We seek to understand not only the complex network that
produces anxiety, depression, and so forth, but to engage the
socialization of feelings, the entire social organization of the feeling
activity.

Feelings are very confusing things. We all know that. One of my first tasks in training to become an analytic philosopher was answering such stupid questions as "Where are feelings?" I thought questions like these were completely ridiculous at the time, and treated them as if in the abstract they were. There are these little exercises you do to obtain a Ph.D. in philosophy: Are feelings in the head? Are feelings in the ends of the fingers, in the heart? Where are they? These exercises were in some ways fun and interesting but I never thought they were of particular value. Well, it turns out they are of some value, because there are some meaningful ways of formulating these questions about feelings. I think there are some very important questions concerning the social nature of the whole way in which we organize and live feelings. From the Marxist point of view, we can ask what is the social basis, what are the origins, not simply of particular feelings but of the whole conception of feelings, the whole doing of feelings.

This inquiry is characteristically treated as irrelevant in the traditional therapeutic setting. "Everybody knows that. What we're trying to find out in traditional (real) therapy is how come you're so upset? How come you're so anxious? How come you're so depressed?" What is missing is the simultaneous engagement of the understanding of what depression is. Lois makes this point very beautifully, because in fact that's a critical component of the learning (socialization) of these feelings in the first place. That is, it isn't the case that kids get born with a bourgeois conceptual framework — "I got all the basic categories, just teach me the details." That is not how the learning process goes, Noam Chomsky and/or Plato notwithstanding. The actual process is one in which there is a concurrent evolution of the conceptuality together with the learning of the particularity of these relationships. Now, if this whole mechanism is in trouble, it seems not particularly sophisticated to point out that what has to be engaged is the entire socialization mechanism which produced this outcome. In a way it's analogous to where we stand on the whole damned society. That is to say, I don't believe as a Marxist that the society can be fundamentally transformed by merely understanding new ways of getting these commodities to relate to one another better. I'm not of the opinion that contemporary capitalist society can be transformed by a plan for some slight (or even relatively extreme) redistribution arrangements of the commodities. This kind of a plan leaves out history — it leaves out the entire social structure which produces commodities, and racism, and sexism, and poverty in the first place.

Social therapy is an attempt to develop a historical approach to helping people with their emotional problems. This is very hard to do — to help people to begin the practical process of engaging the total social origins of their emotive incapacitations. Now, some people say, won't that take a long time? Well, there's no reason to believe it's going to take any longer than the Freudians suggest. The Freudians maintain that to understand we have to go back and delve deeply into the human mind — to prehistoric myth, as it were. So, timewise, we're no worse off than they are. To be sure, no one is suggesting these processes are absolute. That is, there's no doubt that people get help at various stages of the process. That's true of traditional therapy and it's true of social therapy. We're not suggesting for a moment that one is only helped at the conclusion of this journey. It's not even patently obvious, from a psychological point of view, that there *is* a conclusion. OH ?

Indeed, it seems clear that the conclusion of the journey is not simply a psychological activity, but a broad social-revolutionary activity. No part of the theory and practice of social therapy suggests that there is some kind of conceivable basic change in this society which would be purely psychological. Nothing could be further from what we believe and what we are committed to. But that's not to deny that the question that Reich raised — the question of what is and what to do about the psychological accompaniment to alienated society — is a critical issue to be engaged as Marxists, as progressives, as *scientists*. It is frightening to me to think of the unwillingness in the scientific community, including the Marxist scientific community, to engage this question on the grounds that "it could never happen here," that this is the land of checks and balances, pluralism, openness, hard objective science, technology, etc. The scientific community can state, "There is nothing religious about our world view. It is pragmatic through and through." Well, pragmatism, as William James was ever eager to point out, is merely the religion of contemporary capitalism. Pragmatism is not an alternative to religion. It is deeply religious. It is time that Marxists and all progressives cast a critical light on that fundamentally religious world view in the way that Marx instructed us: "The philosophers [pragmatists included] have only *interpreted* the world, in various ways; the point, however, is to *change* it."

3

VYGOTSKY'S METHOD

The search for method becomes one of the most important problems of the entire enterprise of understanding the uniquely human forms of psychological activity. In this case, the method is simultaneously prerequisite and product, the tool and the result of the study. — **Lev Vygotsky**

In their most scientifically and philosophically lucid moments, Karl Marx and his follower Lev Vygotsky reject much more than an ill-formed (or non-existent) psychological paradigm. Their intellectual

"Vygotsky's Method" is an early version of Chapter III, "The Method of Practice: Vygotsky's Tool and Result" of Lev Vygotsky: Revolutionary Scientist *by Fred Newman and Lois Holzman, to be published by Routledge in 1992 as part of its Critical Psychology Series and is published here by permission of the publisher.*

challenge is to the entirety of Western *thought, including thought about thought*. Marx's writings both *assume* (in non-propositional fashion) and *imply* (also non-propositionally) the invalidity of the Aristotelean, the scholastic, the Hegelian and the 19th century rationalistic-empiricistic-positivistic-vulgar materialistic world views. Marx subjected the broad and varied families of concepts associated with these historically inter-connected *world views* to intense scrutiny, using the method he developed — dialectical historical materialism — to challenge the fundamental epistemic (how we know) and ontic (what there is to know) categories of Western cognition.

Most notably, Marx took on Kant's *Critique of Pure Reason* (out of which much of the assumptions of modern psychology grew), exposing it as no less metaphysical than any other "philosophy." Indeed, philosophy and world views themselves — dominated in his youth by Hegel and "the young Hegelians" — are radically challenged by Marx, especially in his early writings where he put forth the premises and process of the revolutionary methodology he was developing (cf., Marx 1964; 1978; Marx & Engels, 1973).

"But," every critic of Marx since 1848 has asked (some cleverly, some stupidly), "isn't Marx's method of dialectical historical materialism simply *another* world view, *another* paradigm, *another* philosophy? Isn't a challenge to philosophy, no matter how radical, still a philosophy?" The Marxian/Vygotskian answer to this apparent contradiction is *radically methodological*; it challenges *how we challenge* and introduces a qualitatively different (practice of) method.

For Marx and Vygotsky the *object* of study and the *method* of study are *practical*, not in the mundane common sense meaning of that term (i.e., useful), but in the Marxian sense of *practical-critical activity*, i.e., *revolutionary activity* (Marx & Engels, 1973, p. 121). The world historical environment is both spatially and temporally seamless and qualitative (as opposed to quantitative); it can only be comprehended by a *scientific practice* free of *interpretive* assumptions (premises). But this by no means implies that it is without premises! It is, on Marx's view, filled with the real premises that are "...men [and women], not in any fantastic isolation and rigidity, but in their actual, empirically perceptible process of development under definite conditions" (Marx & Engels, 1973, p. 47). *This Marxian method, the method of practice* (if not yet the practice of method), not only redefines what *science* (or any other world view) is to be; it redefines what *method* is to be.[1] Indeed, it redefines what *redefines* is to be! (With all due respect to Shakespeare, it even redefines what *to be* and *not to be* are to be!)

PRAGMATICS

While the question of method has concerned philosophers since Plato, it was not until the emergence of modern science in the 16th and 17th centuries that it took center stage in philosophical investigation. Sir Francis Bacon took method to be the key to knowledge as he attempted to subject the tools of observation associated with the newly developing modern science to philosophical scrutiny. Since Bacon's time, most traditional views on methodology treat (define) method as fundamentally separate from experimental content and results, i.e., *from that for which it is the method!* Indeed, it is considered unscientific to do otherwise. Method is understood and used as something to be *applied*, a functional means to an end, basically pragmatic or instrumental in character. In sharp contrast, Marx and Vygotsky understand method as something to be *practiced* — not *applied*. It is neither a *means* to an end nor a tool *for* achieving results. Rather it is, in Vygotsky's formulation, a "tool *and* result" (emphasis added). On this view, as Vygotsky tells us, the method is "simultaneously prerequisite and product."

But what does *this* provocative formulation of Vygotsky's

using a particular method (tool) yields particular results?

Is this machine is important to the progress of mankind, and if Newman is to explain it to us, then we are lost.

mean? Indeed, to what are we to appeal in determining what it means? In the language of the early Cole laboratory, what sense of "validity" (not to mention ecology) is (to be) understood in the search for ecological validity? After all, *validity*, like *truth*, *proof*, *method*, *inference*, *explanation*, *concept*, *paradigm*, etc., is but one member of a broad family of concepts which are the ontological and epistemological core of Western cognition itself and/or our *understanding* of Western cognition. Can we use these concepts to determine what *tool and result* means? And if we cannot, then what else do we have at our disposal?

Pragmatism, which has emerged as the dominant methodology of the 20th century, has spent a good deal of energy seeking answers to these questions. Developed in the United States and associated with Charles S. Pierce, C.I. Lewis (who were oriented toward the philosophy of science), George Herbert Mead, John Dewey and William James (all oriented toward psychology and sociology), pragmatism rejected the dichotomous terms of the two major philosophical traditions of their time: empiricism, which took the world and mechanical biological processes to be dominant, and rationalism and idealism, which took the human mind to be dominant, having enormous powers in determining the universe. The pragmatists made a bona fide break with the dichotomy of matter and mind by focusing their investigation on the *connection* between *thinking* and *doing.* The term pragmatism was coined by Pierce (from the Greek *pragma* — act or deed) to emphasize the fact that words acquire their meanings from actions. According to Pierce, meanings are derived from deeds, not intuitions. In fact, there is no meaning separate from the socially-constituted conception of its practical impact; a word or idea is meaningless if we cannot conceive of any practical effect relative to that word or idea. For James, the commercializer of pragmatism ("you must bring out of each word its cash-value"), pragmatism has no content, but is pure method. Oriented toward results and consequences — it is fundamentally instrumentalist — pragmatism does not specify any *particular* results. All formulations are only approximations, never final. Ultimately, the meanings of theories are to be found in their capacity to solve problems. *Sehr interesting*

The pragmatists' world view has become the quintessential methodological paradigm of late 20th century capitalist science; their answer to the fundamental problems of methodology, particularly of validity, is what dominates (not only philosophically but practically) in a world in which decisions are based by and large on instrumentalist reasoning. W.V.O. Quine, the Harvard University pragmatist and dean of American scientific methodologists, offers a sophisticated formulation of pragmatism's philosophy/methodology in his seminal 1950s work, *Two Dogmas of Empiricism.* Quine employs a "core-periphery" image, in which world view is depicted as a web-like network, with logical and other fundamental ontic and epistemic concepts occupying a core (central) position and immediate sensory experiences (or reports thereof) occupying the most peripheral locations. In between are the complicated practical/theoretical links which connect the two. The model is meant to illustrate several critical features of pragmatism: (1) the relativity of world views; (2) the relativity *within* world views (anything might be changed); (3) the interdependency of the varied elements of a world view; and (4) the *pragmatic* value of preserving the core (or elements closest to it) as opposed to the periphery. For Quine, perhaps the most eloquent of the pragmatist methodologists, decisions as to what alterations should be made to a current conceptual framework or world view in the face of new developments (both large and small) and/or the decision to retain or reject a world view altogether are entirely based on the pragmatic criterion of "efficaciousness." In an oft-quoted paragraph near the conclusion of *Two Dogmas...,* Quine succinctly sums up his own *methodological world view:*

> As an empiricist I continue to think of the conceptual
> scheme of science as a *tool,* ultimately, for predicting future
> experience in the light of past experience [emphasis
> added]. Physical objects are conceptually imported into the
> situation as convenient intermediaries — not by definition
> in terms of experience, but simply as irreducible posits
> comparable, epistemologically, to the gods of Homer. For
> my part I do, qua lay physicist, believe in physical objects
> and not in Homer's gods; and I consider it a scientific error
> to believe otherwise. But in point of epistemological foot-
> ing the physical objects and the gods differ only in degree
> and not in kind. Both sorts of entities enter into our con-
> ception only as cultural posits. The myth of physical
> objects is epistemologically superior to most in that it has
> proved more efficacious than other myths as a device for
> working a manageable structure into the flux of experience
> (Quine, 1961, p. 44).

On Quine's pragmatic account, then, the conceptual scheme of
science (which is, most would agree, the hegemonic 20th century
world view) is itself a *tool,* a tool *applied* to the "flux of experience,"
a tool deemed "superior" by appeal to a pragmatic criterion
(efficaciousness). It is, to employ an overused word, a tool that
"works." But *not,* make careful note, *a tool and result.*

SETTING UP THE DEBATE

What is a tool, anyway? And what is a conceptual framework,
schema or world view? And whatever shall we employ and how
shall we employ it in an effort to answer these kinds of questions?
What *method* do we use in finding answers to these most fundamental questions of *methodology?* From our brief discussion thus
far, it should be clear that Quine, Marx and Vygotsky, each in his

own way, appreciated the utter failure of 19th and 20th century empiricism to answer such questions and attempted to develop alternatives. For while *empirics* (systematic observations) are obviously critical in the process of determining *what is*, empiricism's philosophically sectarian belief that empirics *alone* can determine *what is* has failed to pass many valid tests including, ironically, the test of empirics — the claim that all things can be tested by empirics cannot itself be tested empirically!

The first half of the 20th century brought one last ditch effort by philosophers/methodologists to synthesize 19th century empiricism and idealism in the pseudo-scientific criterion of verifiability by the logical positivists of the Vienna Circle.[2] As well, pragmatism and practice — the only seriously viable *alternatives* to empiricism — took shape. Yet *revolutionary practice*, the methodology created by Marx, was being deformed even in its infancy by revisionist philosophers and politicians who would turn it from a method for transforming *all* of social reality into a theory for guiding economic development. Pragmatism and the capitalist system with which it is associated have fared better, if not well, during these ninety years. Thus, as we move towards the 21st century, a methodological confrontation between the well-funded (albeit deformed) method of *pragmatism* and its poor relative, the (deformed) method of *practice*, unfolds. Even as worse-for-the-wear capitalism now stands victorious over revisionist Stalinist communism in the domain of *realpolitik* here in the prologue to the 21st century, the most basic practical-critical scientific issues of *world view* and *method* remain essentially unresolved, with *practice* and *pragmatics* the only important players left standing in the (world historic) contest.

This debate between pragmatism and practice, between method as a tool *for* result (the pragmatic method) and method as tool *and* result (the method of practice), cuts across the *realpolitik,* nationalistic lines of contemporary international society. It does not fit into any neat categories, certainly not the recently deceased dichotomy between capitalism and revisionist communism. The debate is not societal — it is historical. There is good reason to believe that its outcome will determine and be determined by whether or not our species will follow a progressive or regressive direction in the years ahead.[3]

Of course, "tool" and "world view" are themselves quasi-metaphors which cry out for explication. But (following B. Russell, that most important British mathematician/philosopher of the early 20th century), explications are best done in the *context of their use* (Russell, 1914). Thus, the formulation of the issue in the use-context of "tool *for* result" vs. "tool *and* result" is already somewhat helpful in that the term and/or concept of *tool* is employed (used) in both contexts and so, in effect, is *result,* since (for all of its grandiosity) a world view is simply a result of the highest order! At the risk of seeming ridiculously reductionistic, we suggest that the difference may well turn out to be embedded in the critical distinction between the connectives "for" and "and."

PRACTICE

We begin our discussion of the method of practice, seemingly indirectly, by investigating *tool.* Even in its simple dictionary denotative use (definition), the term "tool" is exceedingly complex. In contemporary industrial society there are at least two distinctly different kinds of tools/meanings of the word "tool." There are tools that are *mass* produced (hammers, screwdrivers, power saws, etc.) and there are tools designed and produced typically by tool and die makers or toolmakers, i.e., tools specifically and uniquely designed and developed to assist in the development of other products (including, often, other tools). For not everything that is needed or wanted by humankind can be made by simply using (applying) the tools that have already been mass manufactured in modern society. Often we must create a tool which is specifically designed to create what we ultimately wish to produce. The tools of the hardware store and the tools of the tool and die maker are *qualitatively* different in a tool *for* result/tool *and* result sort of way. Hardware store tools, such as hammers, come to be identified and recognized as useable for a certain end, i.e., they become reified and identified with a certain *function* and, as such, insofar as the manufactured hammer as a social extension (a tool) of human activity comes to define its human user (as all tool use does), it does so in a predetermining sense. Marxists of all persuasions (and many others) accept that tool use impacts on categories of cognition. Tools *for* results are analogous to (as well as producers of) cognitive equipment (e.g., concepts, ideas, beliefs, attitudes, emotions, intentions, thought and language, etc.) that are *complete* (fully manufactured) and useable for a particular purpose.

The toolmaker's tool is different in a most important way. While *purposeful*, it is not categorically distinguishable from the result achieved by its use. Explicitly created for the purpose of helping to make a specific product, it has no reified manufactured social identity *independent of that activity*. Indeed, empirically speaking, such tools are typically no more recognizable (as tools) than the product (often a quasi-tool or small part of a larger product) itself is recognizable (as product). They are inseparable. It is the *productive activity* which defines both — the tool *AND* the product (the result).

Unlike the hammer (the hardware store, manufactured, tool *for* result tool), *this kind* of tool — the toolmaker's tool *and* result — has no *completed* or generalized *identity*. Indeed, it typically has no name; it appears in no dictionary or grammar book. Such tools (or, semantically speaking, such a *sense of the word* "tool") define their human users quite differently from the way hardware store tools, whether of the physical, symbolic or psychological variety, do. The inner cognitive, attitudinal, creative, linguistic tools developed from the tool*maker* type of social tools are incomplete, unapplied, unnamed and, perhaps, unnameable. Expressed more positively, they are inseparable from results in that their essential character (their defining feature) is *the activity of their development* rather than their function. *For their function is inseparable from the activity of their development.* They are defined in and by the process of their production. This is not to say that such *tools and results* are without functions. It is, rather, to say that the attempt to define *tools and results* by their function (as is the case with tools *for* results) fundamentally distorts what they are (and, of course, in the process, what definition is).

This issue of tools — and the distinction we are taking such pains to put forth — are of great importance to understanding Vygotsky's work and the understandings and applications of his work by others. For every Vygotskian of both the revolutionary and reformist variety notes how important the concept of tool is for Vygotsky. But which tool (meaning of tool) do they employ?

In his prologue to the English edition of Volume 1 of *The Collected Works of L.S. Vygotsky* (1987), the American psychologist Jerome Bruner addresses the matter of tools.

In the new lectures (lectures published since the appearance of Vygotsky's *Thought and Language* in 1962, to which Bruner also wrote an introduction, ed.) it is quite evident once again that *instrumental action is at the core of Vygotsky's thinking — action that uses both physical and symbolic tools to achieve its ends* [emphasis added]. The lectures give an account of how, in the end, man uses nature and the toolkit of culture to gain control of the world and of himself. But there is something new in his treatment of this theme — or *perhaps it is my new recognition of something that was there before* [emphasis added]. For now there is a new emphasis on the manner in which, through using tools, man changes himself and his culture. Vygotsky's reading of Darwin is strikingly close to that of modern primatology (e.g., Washburn, 1960) which also rests on the argument that human evolution is altered by man-made tools whose use then creates a technical-social way of life. Once that change occurs, "natural" selection becomes dominated by cultural criteria and favors those able to adapt to the tool-using, culture-using way of life. By Vygotsky's argument, tools, whether practical or symbolic, are initially "external": used outwardly on nature or in communicating with others. But tools affect their users: language, used first as a communicative tool, finally shapes the minds of those who adapt to its use. It is one of the themes of Vygotskian psychology and his six lectures are dedicated to its explication in the context of human development. His chosen epigraph from Francis Bacon, used in *Thought and Language*, could not be more apposite: neither hand or mind alone suffice; the tools and devices they employ finally shape them (1987, p. 3).

Plainly Bruner is correct in his speculation that it is his "…new recognition of something that was there before" rather than there being "something new" in Vygotsky's treatment of the self- and species-transforming effect of the use of tools, which in fact is basic, although not unique, to Marxism — as Vygotsky was well aware. While Marx himself did not develop a new psychology that made use of this recognition, Vygotsky went a substantial way toward doing so. Fundamental to his work was the specification to psychology of the Marxist socio-methodological principle of self- and species-transformation through the use of tools. *Tool and result psycho-methodology, or toolmaking, is precisely that specification.*

[handwritten margin note: AND AT LEAST PARTIALLY BY THOSE WHO ARE ABLE TO EXERT SOME CONTROL OVER CULTURE]

Vygotsky's tool *and* result method is purposeful in the Marxian sense, not (contrary to Bruner's formulation) in the instrumentalist sense. Vygotsky's rejection of the causal and/or functionalist methodological notion of *tool* or instrument *for* a purpose or *result* in favor of the dialectical notion of *tool and result* in the study of human psychology is new and revolutionary. Why does Bruner not see this? Only the (certainly unintended) opportunistic denial of Vygotsky as a Marxist *revolutionary scientist* (as opposed to a psychologist who quotes Marx) by Bruner and so many others could lead them to miss what Vygotsky *brings* to his research and, therefore, to miss his advancement of Marxism as a methodology and humanistic science — *the method and science of psychology as revolutionary practice.*

For both Marx and Vygotsky, revolution was the driving force of history. Marx observes: "...all forms and products of consciousness cannot be dissolved by mental criticism...but only by the practical overthrow of the actual social relations which gave rise to this idealistic humbug; that not criticism but revolution is the driving force of history..." (Marx & Engels, 1973, p. 58).

Vygotsky makes the following clear statement of what he takes the scientific revolutionary activity to be: "The scientific mind... views revolution as the locomotive of history forging ahead at full speed; it regards the revolutionary epoch as a tangible, living embodiment of history. A revolution solves only those tasks which have been raised by history: this proposition holds true equally for revolution in general and for aspects of social and cultural life" (quoted in Levitan, 1982).

Marx, by no means a psychologist, was concerned with the sociology of history and the science of revolution. One of his most significant discoveries — that the paradigm of human activity is practical — he took to be a socio-historical fact, not a psychological fact. His concern was the making of revolution. It remained for

Vygotsky, in his quest to develop a Marxist psychology — a revolutionary practice that would transform human beings in a post-revolutionary period — to discover the methodological/psychological tool *and* result approach which identifies practical-critical revolutionary activity as *what people do*. What the pragmatist Quine (and his follower T. Kuhn, whose positing of "paradigm shifts" as the central "structure of scientific revolutions" has become the major explanatory principle in the history of science; Kuhn, 1962) regard as the "rare" *revolutionary act* of changing an entire world view is, for the revolutionaries Marx and Vygotsky, the practical-critical activity *of everyday life*.

On our view, the implications of thus standing Quine and the pragmatists on their heads are profound. A synthesis of Marx's discovery of practical-critical, revolutionary activity and Vygotsky's tool *and* result methodology yields a new understanding of the psychology of human beings consistent with Marxian and Vygotskian principles. It remains for us and other revolutionary Vygotskians to sketch out and develop this new mode of understanding. *Good luck!*

Practical-critical activity (revolutionary activity) is that essentially and specifically human form of life, i.e., activity in which the overdetermining empiricist, idealist and vulgar materialist pseudo-notion (fetishized notion) of particular activity *for* a particular end (which in reality, i.e., society, is behavior) is "overthrown" in favor of real (human) activity — a transforming of the totality of what there is. Changing particulars vs. changing totalities is a distinction that is vital to understanding tool *and* result methodology and, therefore, revolutionary activity.

CHANGING TOTALITIES IN EVERYDAY LIFE

"The coincidence of the changing of circumstances and of human

activity or self-changing can be conceived and rationally under-stood only as revolutionary practice." — **Karl Marx**

It was the German philosopher/mathematician/physicist Leibniz who first made plain in the 17th century that, from a naturalistic or spatio/temporal point of view, changing a single "thing" (spatio/temporal point) entails changing everything ("the totali-ty"). Indeed, it is the common sense notion of a *particular* action or happening altering or changing a single other or even several other states of affairs — but not everything, the totality — that is *thor-oughly metaphysical* and illusory; it is an abstraction beyond any type of verification. This causal, "a *for* b" paradigm (derived from and inextricably linked to tool for result methodology) has been outgrown in the physical sciences, yet persists within so-called common sense and the so-called social sciences. Why? Obviously the answer is exceedingly complex and to spell out the circum-stances and process of its overthrow is beyond the scope of this chapter — indeed, of this book. Yet the overriding reason seems clear and simple. In modern times, an understanding of physical phenomena no longer demands that a moral (ideological) and/or economic (political) account be implicit or explicit in the explana-tion, as was the case in pre-feudal and feudal times when Aristotelian and scholastic physical science did just that. It was not until this demand was revolutionarily overcome — by the rising bourgeoisie's need for knowledge that was quantifiable, measur-able and right here on earth and by the radical discoveries of Copernicus, Galileo and others — that the natural sciences were mathematicized, technologized and, thereby, fully liberated from the feudal constraints of teleology and God. To this day, the so-called social sciences remain fettered by deistic dogma primarily because these pseudo-sciences are, historically speaking, little more than handservants of the dominant (and false) ideology (political, legal, cultural, moral, etc.) which on the one hand requires *account-ability* and *responsibility* (the law must know, for example, what was done — *in particular* — and who — *in particular* — did it), and which on the other hand eschews revolutionary activity (the concept and, especially, the *practice*). Hence, Marx's theoretical insistence that *revolutionary practice* is the "peep stone" required to comprehend the *ordinary* dialectical practical-critical activity of *people changing circumstances which are changing them*, i.e., activity, and Vygotsky's advancement of that conception with the development of *tool and result* psychological practice are still seen as esoteric, rather than as the 20th century analog to Galileo's revolutionary *Two New Sciences.*[4]

But do we human beings engage in revolutionary activity? What does "the practical-critical activity of everyday life" look like? Doing something in particular, a, to bring about a certain particular end, b, is *real enough behavior* relative to our *societal* definitions and identity, but is, *historically* speaking, *illusory*. We are employing here the critical distinction (not a dichotomy!) between society and history as human "life spaces." As human beings, we all live simultaneously in history (the open-ended, indivisible totality of human social existence) and in society (the name given to a specific spatio/temporal institutional configuration within history). All societies adapt their members to this dual location and dual identity, but there is variation between differing societies in the degree to which the adaptation is just to society or to history as well. Modern liberal/religious industrial societies, the ultra-pragmatic United States in particular, adapt their citizens to society to such an extent that most people do not even know that they are in history (or even the world for that matter!) or that history is something one can adapt to! Indeed, elsewhere we have made the argument that the single most powerful cause of neurotic psychopathology in the contemporary U.S. is that Americans are deprived of any historical identity (Holzman & Polk, 1989). Life is lived from one day's 6 o'clock news to the next — what we might well call radical chauvinism![5] Adapting to history means engaging in the revolutionary activity of changing totalities; adapting to society, in the case of the societies in which we currently live, means carrying out certain acts, behaviors, roles, etc., relative to the narrow confines of this particular time and place (moment) in world history. Thus, our day-to-day, hour-to-hour societally determined "activities" are not activity at all in the Marxian, historical sense. They are *best understood as commodified activities* (or behavior) and, just like economic commodities under the socio-economic-ideological system known as capitalism, they are at once real (societally) and illusory (historically).

Why is this so? Because the process of commodification totally misrepresents — radically distorts — by alienation the *actual historical process of production*. As Marx (1967) points out, commodification occurs under the domination of the process of producing for exchange (which means, in the final analysis, for profit), not for use. Virtually all of the things that get produced under capitalism — cars, houses, food, books, diplomas, ideas, feelings, etc. — while they may be useful to our species, are not produced *because* they are useful, but in order to be distributed and sold on the market. This activity of producing what we use in a manner which has less to do with our own needs as human beings and more to do with the need of some to make profit has the effect of separating, in a profound way, the *activity* of production from the *product* of production. This social phenomenon is what Marx termed alienation (Marx, 1967).

Such causal and societal, *a for b*, commodified "activity" is, employing Marx's language, best understood as *fetishized activity* (Marx, 1967, p. 71-83). Marx took pains to understand commodities not just economically but also ideologically and/or subjectively.

On his view, commodities are fetishized, i.e., their very existence and character have the property of being structurally disengaged from the process by which they were created, while *appearing*, in society, otherwise. In this, they are much like gods — created *by* us to be incomprehensible *to* us.[6] Just as the fetishized commodity appears (within society) to have an existence and a motion independent of the social process of production that gave rise to it, so societal *a for b* "activity" (behavior) is god-like and overdetermined, i.e., seeming to be lawfully (causally, functionally) connected independent of active human agency *and, even more, unchangeable.* For example, this book you are reading is, while useful (we hope!), a commodity; it was produced for exchange; it has the characteristic of being fetishized, i.e., it exists and is related to independently of the social process of production which gave rise to it (which includes the complex conjuncture of many processes of production, including but not limited to the process of production of human language, written language, printing presses, mass produced books, educational institutions, publishing institutions, the discipline of psychology, etc.). So, too, societal *a for b* "activity," or behavior — the things we do every day — appear to exist (and do so, societally) and are related to in a way that separates them from the process of their production — in particular, from the actual human activity which produced them. (We created these words using language created by people — historically speaking; the book was printed on presses built and operated by workers; etc.)

The seemingly lawful connections of *a for b* "activity" (behavior) independent of historical, active human agency is one of the primary ways that the religious notions of predeterminism, overdeterminism and, indeed, vulgar determinism in general have been incorporated into capitalist ideology and bourgeois scientific methodology. They have been paradigmized into the (bogus) category "causality" (or, in its modern dress, pragmatic functionality).

Kant, of course, went so far as to glorify causality as one of the *a priori* synthetic categories (conditions) necessary for the human experience itself. And even as traditional physical science has, during the two centuries since Kant, pretty much abandoned the notion of *cause*, this idea of *a for b*, means/end instrumentalism or functionalism remains within the syntax of "common sense" (even scientifically informed common sense) and, therefore, in the pre-scientific (pseudo-scientific!) study of the specifically human activity called traditional psychology — more accurately, what is traditionally called psychology.

While causality — as both an explanatory principle and a topic to be investigated — permeates all of psychology, it is perhaps most pernicious and distorting in developmental psychology. No less renowned a developmentalist than Piaget is little more (or less) than a supplier of evidence for the "psychological reality" of Kant's *a priori* categories of experience. For Piaget development consisted of the means by which the child, acting upon the world (in societal reality, behaving in the world), moves her/himself through stages in the acquisition and use of the basic human epistemological tools by which it is possible to understand "our" world. These tools are Kant's categories of experience — the concept of the object, relation, temporality, causality, etc. According to Piaget, the concept of causality develops slowly, and he made great use of what he saw as the child's lack of correct (adult) usage of causal terms such as "because," "so," etc., the primitive "why" questions young children ask and the animistic answers they give when asked "why" to provide evidence for both Kant's contention that the mind is structured to see causality and for his own stage theory of intellectual development. This he did without ever questioning the particular causal connections a specific culture has produced nor, what is methodologically even more problematic, the socio-cultural-historical notion of causality itself![7]

Thus, while the natural science community has shaped a methodology suitable to its own development in the process and practice of its own development, psychology grafted an 18th and 19th century naturalistic and pseudo-scientific methodology onto itself and, to this day, has not fully discovered the human methodology necessary for a uniquely human psychology.

On our view, the revolutionary social scientists, Vygotsky and Marx before him, have made the most significant contributions to such an effort. To complete our sketch of their "combined and uneven" work on this score,[8] we would do well to summarize the complex relationship between: (1) revolutionary (practical-critical) activity; (2) a *and* b (tool *and* result) as opposed to a *for* b (tool *for* result) methodology; and (3) changing particulars vs. changing totalities.

REVOLUTIONARY, PRACTICAL-CRITICAL ACTIVITY

Revolutionary practice or activity (not to be equated with the *particular* revolutionary activity of *making a revolution*)[9] is ordinary day-to-day, hour-to-hour human *historical* activity: it is a particular action, *a, changing the totality* of circumstances (historical "scenes") of human existence B, C, D,...[B, C, D,...] etc. The distinctively human quality of our species is its capacity to *practice revolutionary activity*, a capacity, as we have said, that is, unfortunately, only sometimes self-consciously manifest. Instead, our ordinary activity (so-called) is non-revolutionary; in fact, it is not activity at all. Rather, it is either societally determined *behavior* or the motion of natural phenomena (physical, chemical, etc.); it is, thereby, neither *uniquely* nor *specifically* human. What we are calling human activity, in all its infinitely complex variations, is always changing that which is changing, which is changing that which is changing, etc. It is changing the historical totality (or, more accurately, the many totalities) which is *determining* the changer. Indeed, this radically nondualistic dialectic-in-practice is what changing — i.e., activity — is.

Our species (and the individual members who comprise it) is distinguished from other species (as far as we can tell) by the fact that it is never fundamentally changed, qua human being, except insofar as (by its revolutionary activity) it fundamentally changes other things — the circumstances of its continued historical existence.

What, then, is the relationship between changing particulars vs. changing totalities and tools? Recall that the toolmaker's tool *and* result is that tool specifically created to assist in the development of something which we wish to create. Tools of this sort are *paradigmatically* "prerequisite and product" in that the creation of the product is not limited by the pre-existent, societally determined manufactured tools (language, thought or store bought) available for its conceptualization and its actualization.[10] Indeed, it could not be so limited, for the tool, *not yet made*, is a precondition for the product. It is not linearly *in advance of* the product either conceptually or materially. Tool *and* product of tool are therefore of necessity a produced *unity*. The toolmaker and the poet (by contrast with the users of manufactured tools and/or ordinary language) do not begin with tool for product and move to product; rather, the toolmaker and the poet create the unity (totality) *tool and product*, since tool is materially defined by product as much as product is defined by tool. (The product makes the tool every bit as much as the tool makes the product.) The toolmaker must create the totality *tool and result* just as the poet must create meanings as she/he creates the poem. Unlike the user of hardware store tools who is defined and predetermined by the particular behavior of using those tools which are made *for* a particular (and also predetermined) function, the toolmaker is neither defined nor predetermined. As the producer of the totality, *tool and result*, the toolmaker is a changer of historical totalities. She/he is engaged in revolutionary (human-historical) activity.

THOUGHT AND LANGUAGE

We have taken pains to explain the significance of Marx's notion of *revolutionary activity* as being central to an understanding of Vygotsky as a revolutionary scientist and of Vygotsky's foundational discoveries in psychology and methodology (in particular, tool *and* result methodology). Yet no less a thinker than Marx himself was vulnerable to the dominance of tool *for* result methodology and causal/functional models.[11] In an oft quoted section of *Capital*, Marx exposes a functionalist bias:

> We presuppose labor in a form that stamps it as exclusively human. A spider conducts operations that resemble those of a weaver, and a bee puts to shame many an architect in the construction of her cells. But what distinguishes the worst architect from the best of bees is this, that the architect raises his structure in imagination before he [she] erects it in reality. At the end of every labor process, we get a result that already existed in the imagination of the laborer at its commencement. He [she] also realizes a purpose of his [her] own that gives the law to his [her] modus operandi, and to which he [she] must subordinate his [her] will. (Marx, 1967, p.178)

The above statement delineates what Marx took to be the essential characteristic of *human* labor as opposed to *animal* labor (although many have used it — erroneously and opportunistically — as a justification for their own denial of revolutionary activity, to claim that Marx took labor to be the essentially human activity).[12] But Marx's description is wrong and seriously misleading in a tool *for* result, functionalist way. It is both philosophically (analytically) and empirically (descriptively) inaccurate. If the structure is "raised in imagination" *before* it is "erected in reality," i.e., if the process is linear, then what and where is the dialectic of this human process? If, as Marx teaches us, "life precedes consciousness," (not the other way around), then how is imagination to *precede* its actualization or materialization? To be sure, one might imagine Marx arguing that the imagining activity associated with any labor process could derive from a prior process and/or set of material circumstances. But this simply puts off our question; it does not answer it. For we should still wish to know if the process or circumstances that "yielded" the prior labor process had an imagining associated with it. And if not, from what did *it* come? This reification of *imaginings* and the reintroduction of purpose as a psychological construct allow the old philosophical/theological argument of first cause back into play even as the early methodological Marx had ruthlessly eliminated it.

As is so often true with Marx, the corrective to this mistake is to be found in his own writings. Yet we point out this misleading inaccuracy on Marx's part because it is useful in illustrating how we understand Vygotsky's revolutionary scientific understanding of *thought, language* and *meaning* as revolutionary activities.

For *in the beginning* the human species (anthropologically and psychologically) is neither word nor imagining, neither thought nor language — we are, Marx has said, without propositional or mentalistic premises. In the beginning is the *revolutionary activity* of reorganizing the totality or totalities of human circumstance. The unique quality of human labor is not to be found in the realization of preconceived purpose but in the *meaningfulness* (the practical-criticalness, the revolutionariness) of human activity. The bee may very well have *something in mind* before it moves ahead, and the human worker, particularly with advances in the use of computers in the labor process (but even before), may have *nothing in mind*. But the bee knows and cares nothing of meaning. Meaning has no meaning in the life of the bee! No doubt, there is communication among (perhaps even between) the bees and/or the spider, *but there is no meaning*. Animals communicate (some make honey) but they don't make meaning. For meaning is to be located precisely in the human capacity to alter the historical totality even as one is determined (in one's societal particularity) by it. Therefore, the activity of *making meaning* is an expression (to be sure, the fundamental expression) of *revolutionary activity*; it is the toolmaker (our species) making tools *and* results using the predetermining tools of the hardware store (including nature and language) *and* the predetermined tools of mind developed by them to create something — a totality — *not determined by them*. And it is the *meaning* in the emerging *activity*, not the preconceived imagining followed by its realization, which is *transformative, revolutionary* and *essentially human*.[13]

Vygotsky provides valuable insight into meaning making as revolutionary activity in early childhood in his discussion of concept development. He identified the pseudo-concept as a "critical moment in the development of the child's concepts, a moment which simultaneously separates and connects complexive and conceptual thinking" (1987, p. 142). In discussing the value of experiments which investigated pseudo-concepts, Vygotsky reveals the process of meaning making (concept formation) as the activity of utilizing what we call "the predetermining tools of the hardware store (language) and the predetermined tools of mind developed by them to create something not determined by them."

According to Vygotsky, concepts develop in a dialectical manner, not "freely or spontaneously along lines demarcated by the child himself," but neither can the adult simply "transfer his own mode of thinking to the child" (1987, pp. 142, 143). Rather, there is an internal contradiction in pseudo-concepts in that they look just like adult word meanings yet they are constructed in an entirely different manner from adult word meanings. A child's language (word meanings, concepts, generalizations, etc.), is produced using word meanings predetermined by the adult language, but the child's language is not the adult language: "The speech of those who surround the child predetermines the path that the development of the child's generalizations will take. [But] *It links up with the child's own activity...*" (p. 143, emphasis added). This activity produces the pseudo-concept, something new, something *not determined by the tools used to produce it.* The child's language learning activity is, then, one of *making meaning;* to use Wittgenstein's rich description, it is the activity of playing language games (Wittgenstein, 1953).

While there is no evidence that Vygotsky had such a formulation in mind, his arguments for the dialectical character of pseudo-concepts and the significance of experiments which reveal this process are strikingly supportive of precisely this understanding:

The experiment...allows us to discover how the child's own activity is manifested in learning adult language. The experiment indicates what the child's language would be like and the nature of the generalizations that would direct his thinking if its development were not directed by an adult language that effectively predetermines the range of concrete objects to which a given word meaning can be extended.

One could argue that our use of phrases such as "would be like" and "would direct"...in this context provides the basis for an argument against rather than for the use of the experiment since the child is not in fact free to develop the meanings he receives from adult speech. We would respond to this argument by noting that the experiment teaches more than what would happen if the child were free from the directing influence of adult speech, more than what would happen if he developed his generalizations freely and independently. The experiment uncovers the real activity of the child in forming generalizations, activity that is generally masked in casual observation. The influence of the speech of those around the child does not obliterate this activity. It merely conceals it, causing it to take an extremely complex form. *The child's thinking does not change the basic laws of its activity simply because it is directed by stable and constant word meanings. These laws are merely expressed in unique form under the concrete conditions in which the actual development of the child's thinking occurs* (1987, p. 143, emphasis added).

On our view, Vygotsky's practical-critical understanding of Marx's radical non-propositional historical monism (whose premises are "men [and women]...in their actual, empirically perceptible process of development under definite conditions") made it possible for him to discover that the uniquely human character of thinking and speaking is that it is the revolutionary activity of making meaning.

Vygotsky speaks further about the inseparability of the human capacity to *make meaning* (to engage in *revolutionary activity*) from *speaking* and *thinking*. He makes plain that thinking and speaking are not linearly, causally, teleologically, purposefully or functionally related; they are dialectically "unseparatable" by *meaning*. Unlike functionalist or causal linear theorists (such as Piaget, for example), Vygotsky (speaking and thinking dialectically) says that meaning "...belongs not only to the domain of thought but to the domain of speech...A word without meaning no longer belongs to the domain of speech. One cannot say of word meaning what we said earlier of the elements of the word taken separately. Is word meaning speech or is it thought? It is both at one and the same time; it is a *unit of verbal thinking*. It is obvious, then, that our method must be that of semantic analysis. Our method must rely on the analysis of the meaningful aspect of speech; it must be a *method for studying verbal meaning"* (1987, p. 47).

The study of thinking/speaking as activity exposes the meaning making essence of humankind and, thereby, the revolution-making essence of our species. Thinking and speaking do not make us human. Rather, thinking and speaking are *uniquely* human in that their dialectical unity derives from the ability of the species to *make meaning*, which is nothing more nor less than the ability to *make* revolution, to *make* tools (*and* results). *Verbal behavior* (the computer-like use of language as a tool for result by tool for result-determined thinking) may dominate societally fixed intercourse (precisely as exchange value in general dominates within an economically commodified society). But the sometimes manifest ability to use such tools *for* result to *create* meaning and thereby reorganize thinking/speaking and much else (indeed, *everything* else) is the essentially human, essentially revolutionary activity. In its absence, there would be no thinking/speaking at all. As Wittgenstein took great pains to teach us, the essence of language is not that *it* refers but that people refer (and do much else) using it (1953). *What is fundamental is the activity.* Unsegmented and timeless history in which we all live makes possible the uniquely human activity of transforming all of history at any historical moment.

Those who seek to study human activity by somehow eliminating the experimenter are indistinguishable from those who would study birds *as if* they could not fly. One can do so but only at the cost of no longer studying birds. The "proper unit of analysis for an ecologically valid psychology" is, at least as the Vygotskian-informed Rockefeller researchers noted, "...not the individual, but the 'person-environment interface' or 'the scene'"(Cole, Hood, McDermott, 1978). But while "the scene" takes into account the socialness of the human being, it does so in a way which hardly distinguishes the human being from the bee or spider. And while Cole, Hood (now Holzman) and McDermott are splendidly sensitive to the overdetermining categories and language of society and sometimes they are even concerned with the "history" of these and other institutions of society and the genetic analysis of people functioning within them, they are seemingly oblivious to the truly activistic (as in *revolutionary activistic*) nature of human beings in history and, therefore, to a truly historical method for psychology. Hence, while their approach is social and, perhaps, even radically so, *it is not historical.* For the object of study in a truly historical psychology is the revolutionary activity of our species. And this, in our opinion, is what a uniquely human psychology — a Vygotskian psychology — must be. Those social and functional approaches which fail to treat *revolutionary activity* as their object of study fail, thereby, to study human beings as human beings.

Vygotsky's overriding scientific concern was to study people *as* people, not as something other than people. He shared with Freud, a revolutionary (albeit conservative) scientist, the drive to discover the uniquely human. For Freud it was the unconscious mind and the social need to *repress* it. For Vygotsky, like Marx, it was the fundamentality of revolutionary activity and the social need to *express* it. (Which is why, by the way, there can be no Marx/Freud "synthesis.")[14] Marxian psychology is Vygotskian, for both Marx and Vygotsky treat *revolutionary activity* as human activity. All else is naturalistic or behavioristic revisionism.

While many who have studied thought and language have sought to explicate the complex and dynamic relationship between the rule-governed component of thought/language and the creative component of thought/language, in our opinion only Vygotsky and Wittgenstein (among the major thinkers) have done so as truly *revolutionary* activity theorists. While Wittgenstein may not take *revolutionary activity* as fundamental (indeed, it is not totally clear that Vygotsky does so self-consciously), he (at least the later Wittgenstein) most certainly takes *activity* to be that which forbids the deadly dualistic separation of thought and language and of language and what, presumably, language is *about*. In doing so, he was engaging in *the study of meaning making as ordinary revolutionary activity*.

As life in society/life in history is the ongoing total dialectical environment (scene) of human existence, so, then, is verbal behavior/revolutionary activity the ongoing thought-language (thinking-speaking) environment (scene) of human learning and development. A Marxian developmental, clinical, social, and educational psychology must be thoroughly located within the society/history scene and totally directed toward the study of the verbal behavior/revolutionary activity scene.

The tool *and* result study of thinking/speaking (which on Vygotsky's account is, after all, "semantic analysis") must incorporate a Wittgensteinian approach to semantic analysis; most particularly, it must employ Wittgenstein's notion of "language games."

I shall in the future again and again draw your attention to what I shall call language games. These are ways of using signs simpler than those in which we use the signs of our highly complicated everyday language. Language games are the forms of language with which a child begins to make use of words. The study of language games is the study of primitive forms of language or primitive languages. If we want to study the problems of truth or falsehood, of the agreement and disagreement of propositions with reality, of the nature of assertions, assumptions and questions, we shall with great advantage look at primitive forms of language in which these forms of thinking appear without the confusing background of highly complicated processes of thought. When we look at such simple forms of language the mental mist which seems to enshroud our ordinary use of language disappears. We see *activities*, reactions, which are clear-cut and transparent (1953, p. 17, emphasis added).

Language games help us see clearly the *activity* of language and thought, i.e., the revolutionary process by which language and thought are produced, by which meaning is made. The "confusing background" mentioned by Wittgenstein is societally transfixed semantics and syntax which do more to hide thinking/speaking *as activity* than to expose it. Revolutionary activity is, on this account, itself a game which, in Wittgenstein's words, bears only a "family resemblance" to other games. It is the revolutionary game of making new meanings which shows the social *activity* of language/thought through the "mist" of societal and metaphysical meaninglessness.

NOTES

1. The phrase *method of practice* puts the focus on method, while the phrase *practice of method* puts the focus on practice. The practice of method, therefore, emphasizes doing something different relative to practice, rather than reifying a different method. What we call the practice of method (Holzman & Newman, 1979), is the re-initiation of practical-critical, revolutionary activity. The practice of method is not a new method to be practiced, but a method which is a practice (in Vygotsky's words, "a tool and a result").

2. Founded in the 1920s in Vienna, logical positivism was a self-conscious attempt to synthesize idealism and empiricism that was highly influenced by developments in science and mathematics, especially logic. The logical positivists attempted to construct a universal methodological criterion of verifiability which would serve as a contemporary scientific first principle to answer our most basic questions about the world and how we understand it, and resolve our most puzzling metascientific riddles. But logical positivism failed on its own terms (for example, its verification principle

could not be verified!) and with the rise of Nazism its members — many of them Jewish and/or progressive — left Vienna and scattered to British and American universities.

3. No less a political personage than Francis Fukuyama, an advisor to the Bush administration, has written that we are now living through the end of history (Fukuyama, 1989). This is the ultimate victory of pragmatism!

4. For an excellent discussion of Galileo's discoveries and their social-polit-ical-scientific impact, see Butterfield, 1962.

5. Newman (1987) points out that this deprivation of historical identity leaves us vulnerable to both reactionary political change (fascism) and psychopathology (e.g., depression). In speaking of the American experi-ence, Newman says, "Our sensibility, such as it is, is mediated by an incredible barrage of words and images carefully shaped in such a way as to not simply create a certain picture, but to explicitly create a certain sense of alienation from the sources and objects of that picture. That is, to destroy our sense of history. There is ample evidence to suggest that as a people, we have not simply been alienated from the historical process of work and production but we have been alienated from the historical pro-cess of our own historical development. We have been denied the *possibili-ty* of history as well as the actuality of *history*...The 'me-ness' of American culture goes beyond any single generation...The question [Wilhelm] Reich raised in Germany in the 1930s was how was it possible to transform the ideological responses, values and attitudes of a mass of people in so short a period of time. How could that have happened? How could German fas-cism have happened? That is an important question for us, for obvious socio-political reasons. It is also profoundly relevant to personal depres-sion, because one of the factors of personal depression that must be engaged if we hope to help anybody with it is: How could this have hap-pened 'just like that'? How does someone go, in the face of a serious loss, from being a relatively stable 'coper' to someone who is essentially disem-bodied? How does this radical breakdown occur?...What I believe, and what we've come to see in our social therapeutic work, is that our *normal* social interaction is so profoundly alienated and lacking a sense of *histori-*

cal connectedness that relatively minor changes in the actual process by which information is communicated and disseminated can create total transformation overnight. The absence of a sense of history leaves us extremely vulnerable" (pp. 20-22).

6. "A commodity is therefore a mysterious thing, simply because in it the social character of men's labour appears to them as an objective character stamped on the product of that labour...[with commodities] the existence of the things qua commodities, and the value-relation between the products of labour which stamps them as commodities, have absolutely no connexion with their physical properties and with the material relations arising therefrom. There it is a definite social relation between men, that assumes, in their eyes, the fantastic form of a relation between things. In order, therefore, to find an analogy, we must have recourse to the mist-enveloped regions of the religious world. In that world the productions of the human brain appear as independent beings endowed with life, and entering into relation both with one another and with the products of men's hands. This I call the Fetishism which attaches itself to the products of labour, so soon as they are produced as commodities, and which is therefore inseparable from the production of commodities" (Marx, 1967, p. 72).

7. Hood (now Holzman), Fiess and Aron (1983) present a radical Vygotskian critique of Piaget and Piagetian research into the development of "causality." Another critic of Piaget's ahistorical bias is Buck-Morss (1975).

8. We discuss this in Chapter IV of *Lev Vygotsky: Revolutionary scientist* (in press).

9. "One is capable of historical transformation as an individual only insofar as one is *involved in* (more accurately, *is*) the activity of changing society in a self-conscious manner. This should not be taken to mean that one must be a revolutionary in order to change; being a revolutionary is working to change society in a very particular way. But, while being involved in the activity of self-consciously changing society is not identifiable with

being a revolutionary, it is identifiable with having revolutionary con
sciousness, or with revolutionary, practical-critical activity in the sense
Marx explicates in the *Theses on Feuerbach*" (Holzman & Newman, 1979,
pp. 22-23).

"*Revolutionary activity* is not to be equated with 'the activity of making
a revolution.' Obviously making the revolution is a revolutionary activity
(albeit a very special societal/historical one) even though not all revolutionary activity is making the revolution. Less obvious but even more
important is that in the absence of the ongoing *historical* activity of *making
the revolution* the societally-located, practical-critical revolutionary activity
will eventually be transformed into reform. Studying 20th century revolution makes this plain" (Newman, 1989, p. 6).

10. There has been over two decades of opposition to Kuhn's paradigmatic
position on paradigms, as first laid out in Feyerabend's (1978) book on
anti-paradigms.

11. While there are significant differences between and among causal models and functional models, it can be argued that, generally speaking, the
functional is the historical outgrowth of the causal. Our justification for not
examining this causal-functional distinction-for-itself is that we hope to
show the whole causal/functional nexus to be a thoroughly unsuitable
paradigm for delineating the essential human method necessary to comprehend essentially human activity.

12. For example, Cole et al.'s *Mind and society* (1978), the second publica-
tion of Vygotsky's writings in English, opens with this very quotation.
Wertsch (1985) is also subject to this error, as can be seen in the following:
"Whereas Marx clearly emphasized the emergence of socially organized labor and production as the key to distinguishing humans from animals, Vygotsky considered the emergence of speech to be equally important. In this connection he made his most important and unique contributions but also departed in significant ways from the ideas of Marx and
even Engels" (p. 29; see also p. 32).

Wertsch's choice of words is important; after all, given that Vygotsky was investigating the developmental relationship between speech and thinking, it would make sense that he would emphasize semiotics and communication. But Wertsch sees this stress as a deviation, not merely a placement of emphasis. In this he reveals a position on language and communication that is, to our understanding, in opposition to Vygotsky's Marxian analysis.

Wertsch, like many Vygotskian researchers, falls into two traps. One is following the tradition of Western philosophy, psychology and linguistics, which treats language and communication as outside the realm of socially organized labor. (Note the opposition Wertsch sets up between "socially organized labor and production" and "the emergence of speech.") Language is understood to have a special status; it is thoroughly reified and treated as if it were not produced, as if it were not a socially produced cultural artifact, growing out of the complex development of human production and organization, but as somehow following some natural course. Language is most often discussed as if its ontogenetic and phylogenetic emergence occurs in some *interplay* with social production, not *as* social production. But for both Marx and Vygotsky, language is a product of socially organized labor! Over and over Vygotsky insists that signs, speech, meaning, etc. (the host of meaning and communication concepts) are tools, not metaphorically, but materially, meaning that they have been produced by human labor. All too often, this critical fact is lost in discussions of Vygotsky's claim that signs are psychological tools, as they are wrenched from their history of social production and appear as if from the air, all ready to be used. But human beings are not just tool users; they are tool*makers.*

Wertsch's second mistake derives directly from Marx's functionalist deviation. Here it is worth noting that Vygotsky does better on this point than either Marx or Wertsch. Vygotsky identifies "...labor as the fundamental means of relating humans to nature..." (1978, p. 19) rather than as a way of distinguishing humans from animals. In so doing, Vygotsky is free to view thinking/speaking as the "fundamental means of relating humans to humans." Here there is no "departure" from Marx and Engels (except insofar as Marx and Engels depart from Marx and Engels!). The unifying principle connecting Vygotsky's correct formulation about labor and his recognition of the fundamentality of thinking/speaking is, of course, *revolutionary activity* which relates *humans to humans to nature*. It is for this reason that we avoid the traditional distinction between "dialectical materialism" and "historical materialism" in favor of dialectical historical materialism.

13. Those, like Lichtman (1977), who argue that Marx's conception of humankind denies any essence at all are both right and wrong. For *the absence of any essence* in the Platonic or Aristotelian sense *is*, seemingly contradictorily, itself the distinctly human essence. The continuous creation of essence by revolutionary activity *is* the essence/non-essence of our species. Human beings are essence makers, toolmakers, revolution makers, meaning makers.

14. Almost from the beginnings of the first socialist state and the beginnings of psychology, there have been attempts to synthesize Marx and Freud. Some of the more notable (influential and/or interesting) discussions are those by Vygotsky's student and colleague Luria (1978), the noted Soviet philosopher Volosinov (1987), those of the Frankfurt School (e.g., Adorno, 1951; Habermas, 1971; Fromm, 1973), and various psychologists, philosophers and social critics (e.g., Brown, 1973; Jacoby, 1976; Lichtman, 1977), and of course Reich (1970).

4

CRISIS NORMALIZATION AND DEPRESSION

No one — as far as I can see —
has ever offered a fair, reasonable, succinct, incisive, or valid
definition of depression. We are trying to find scientific answers to
questions about something that we have not even reasonably identified. I am not denying that there is such a thing as depression.
Obviously the pain, torture, and torment of depression is all too
real. What I want to speak to here is not the reality of depression,
but rather the scientific (or unscientific) nature of *our approaches to*

*"Crisis Normalization and Depression: A New Approach to a Growing
Epidemic" was delivered on October 23, 1987 as the annual lecture of the East
Side Institute for Short Term Psychotherapy and first published in* Practice: The
Journal of Politics, Economics, Psychology, Sociology and Culture *(Winter
1987) Vol. 5, No. 3.*

depression. James C. Coyne, the editor, in the general introduction to the book *Essential Papers on Depression*, points out that there are still very live debates on what depression is. Not simply on what causes it, how to cure it or suppress it, but on *what it is.* He points out that, according to the standardized symptomatological analysis of depression and depressive disorders, two people could both be diagnosed as depressive while sharing absolutely no symptomatological characteristics. As a traditionally trained methodologist I am offended by that; it seems *prima facie* outrageous. But — and this is even more problematic — despite Coyne and all nineteen authors reprinted in his book pointing out the imprecision and ambiguity in defining depression, all of them move almost immediately (and, so it seems, inexorably) to offering a definition! Having stated that the empirical and analytical evidence makes plain that we lack and cannot give an adequate definition of depression, their discussions offer still more definitions to add to the long list of unsuccessful definitions that have already been developed in this field.

I do not wish to add my name to the long list of definition mongers. I believe that the search for definition is methodologically problematic. What I want to try to develop here is what it means to evolve an approach to depression which doesn't have, amongst its presuppositions, the need to offer a definition of what depression is. I want to talk about why definitional approaches are less curative, less useful, less helpful — in fact, function negatively — relative to the treatment received by people we see in the "nondefinitional" short term, social therapeutic approach.

A curious feature of our language (noted by many) is the humor sometimes obtainable by flipping subjects and objects in phrases or sentences. More often than not, such a flip produces both humor and insight. I'll give you an example of what I mean. A much more precise title for Coyne's *Essential Papers on Depression* would be *Depressing Papers on Essentialism*. These are indeed very depressing papers on essentialism! They all attempt to give not only a definition of depression but an essentialistic characterization of the human being as a precondition for discussing depression. "Depression must be understood as the common cold of psychopathology," we are told. Exactly right. After all, depression, in one form or another, strikes not just handfuls of people, but millions of people. The estimates given center around 1 out of 5 people. That figure is likely an underestimation, referring only to people who have received some kind of treatment. The number is surely higher since there is a continuum of depression. Indeed, it is often debated whether depression, *qua* clinical category, is actually an extension of depression as we know it in ordinary life. It is hard to do therapy for more than ten minutes without treating people who suffer from depression. And many of us here, I am sure, have gone through severe bouts of depression ourselves. *Being depressed*, then, seems almost an element of the definition of *being human*. *IN America.*

The *DSM-III* [*Diagnostic and Statistical Manual of Mental Disorders (Third Edition)*, the official categorization of psychological-psychiatric "disorders" published by the American Psychiatric Association] criteria for major depressive episodes further this question. Here is the definition (officially of depression, unofficially a partial definition of human being): "Loss of interest or pleasure in all or almost all usual activities and pastimes, characterized by symptoms such as the following: sad, depressed, blue, hopeless, down in the dumps, irritable. Must be persistent but not necessarily the dominant symptom. At least four of the following symptoms must have been present nearly every day for a period of nearly two weeks (in children under six, at least three of the first four): (1) Poor appetite or significant weight loss, when not dieting, or increased appetite or significant weight gain (in children under six, consider failure to make expected weight gains); (2) Insomnia or

DSM-III DEFINITION.

hypersomnia; (3) Psychomotor agitation or retardation, not merely subjective feelings of restlessness or being slowed down (in children under six, hyperactivity); (4) Loss of interest or pleasure in usual activities or decrease in sexual drive not limited to a period when delusional or hallucinating (in children under six, signs of apathy); (5) Loss of energy, fatigue; (6) Feelings of worthlessness, self-reproach, or excessive or inappropriate guilt, either may be delusional; (7) Complaints or evidence of diminished ability to think or concentrate, such as slowed thinking or indecisiveness not associated with marked loosening of associations or incoherence; (8) Recurrent thoughts of death, suicidal deviation, wishes to be dead or suicide attempt." It goes on. So must we. Let's try to move beyond definitional approaches.

LOSS

Most of the articles in Coyne's anthology associate the catalyst for depression, of both the short-term and chronic variety, with *loss*. In some of the approaches, for example, psychodynamic approaches, felt loss of a deeper nature is what is triggered by the immediate loss. In more social approaches and in some of the cognitive approaches, the loss is not so much a triggering as it is the direct object of the depressed response. Across the various approaches runs the theme that the loss associated with depression has more than the normal or usual impact on the individual who suffers it. So whereas we are characteristically able to deal with losses (or so the story goes), in the case of depression (either of a short-term or long-term variety) we are unable to *cope* with the loss. It either triggers something of a much greater and deeper magnitude than would seem reasonable given the actual weight of the object or person or whatever is lost, or in cases of profound loss there is some standard of what an appropriate response is (e.g., after an appropriate period of mourning, of sad or depressed reaction, one should begin to come out of it) which is violated.

Some experts suggest that loss is primarily emotive, some that loss is more cognitive than emotive, others say that loss is more interpersonal than either cognitive or emotive, and still others actually say that loss is chemical. The idea which comes across in these varying approaches to depression is that there are some kinds of loss which provoke or induce an inability to cope, and that this inability to cope is not specifically a sadness nor a feeling blue. Rather, the feeling state identified with depression is more appropriately identified as *the lack* of a feeling state. What cuts across many of these statements and points of view is that the essence of the depressive state is the experience of helplessness, to some extent a non-feeling, i.e., a seeming inability to any longer be responsive.

GLUE

Coyne's book includes a most interesting paper by Ernest Becker which gives a personal-social characterization of depression and loss. According to Becker, what is actually lost in depression is that sense of meaning which is the social-psychological "glue" that ties together the disparate experiences of human life. Whatever the immediate cause, what we lose, internally or interpersonally, as we move into the depressed state is any sense of connection between the various life activities, what Becker calls not the objects but the games. Becker notes that we do not only lose objects. What actually gets lost in a moment of crisis is the *interconnecting mechanism* of all the various objects of our lives. Without the interconnecting mechanism, what we come to experience are discrete, *objective,* separate life experiences. Separate games are played, but the games *themselves* lose meaning because they lose the interconnected set of rules (not necessarily formalistic rules) which ties them together. Such a loss produces a profound sense of pointlessness, of sociocultural meaninglessness. And so as the depression takes hold, it becomes very difficult to escape from, because no amount of object replacement, if you will, is sufficient. Because no matter how many new things you put back in, they remain unconnected.

As I understand Becker, what is common to both the experience of depression and the approaches to the experience is this loss of the capacity to cognitively, emotively, psychologically, culturally, politically "keep the whole damned thing together." There has essentially been a breakdown of framework and meaning. With this breakdown, one becomes weighted down with a sense of helplessness ("learned helplessness") because the life experiences which previously may have been nourishing, developmental, meaningful, and significant, no longer have that impact. The depressed experience is compounded by the fact that one is now going through life *epistemologically* aware of doing the same things one had always done (and, in the past, derived nourishment and pleasure from) but now these experiences give no pleasure. The depression, then, deepens due to what is effectively a kind of "learned helplessness." In place of the ability to take experiences and fit them into an overall framework which is growthful, productive, and makes you feel human, cared for, capable, and alive, increasingly these same kinds of experiences now contribute nothing to your sense of self-identity. You become dead in life. You go through the motions. You might perform well — many, many depressed people perform very well. In some cases people don't even know that they are depressed. They say "Oh, that's how I thought life was! I didn't know that was a sickness! I didn't know that could be cured." In the midst of a rather severe depression many years ago, I could see that my life experience for some 15-20 years before was not all that dramatically different. I came to see that depression (almost as severe as what I was then experiencing) was what I had thought of as the normal state of life.

ANTI-DEFINITION

These observations (some based on Becker's paper; others on my own clinical and personal experience) are a good starting point for a non-definitional approach to depression. Remember, we are not looking for a definition in order that we might have a clinical characterization suitable for appearance in *DSM-III*. Let us begin by rejecting the need for definition at all and by considering that depression, *far from being an abnormal state, is perhaps a normal state*. The two new assumptions (or anti-assumptions) are interconnected. For if depression is normal as opposed to abnormal, then straightaway we don't have to look for a definition of the disease. Looking for definitions, moreover, is the very social process by which we effectively deny that depression is a normal state. So this assumption that depression is a normal state profoundly alters one's approach to the whole issue. Let us then take depression to be by and large a normal process in the context of our culture, with, perhaps, chemical accompaniments and varying degrees of behavioral, cognitive and affective variations. Let us begin to develop a specific and concrete psychological approach to depression as normal. By this I am not suggesting for one moment that we should not seek a cure. For we must break out of the abnormalist paradigm which insists that we only cure disease! It's high time that we appreciate, on social, psychological, cultural and political grounds, that we had better start curing normalcy. Normalcy is about to kill us all. I do not mean that metaphorically; I mean that literally. We are dying (physically and emotionally) because of what is normal in contemporary society. Depression is one critical element of normalcy in our culture. Ours is a profoundly depressed society, not simply on Wall Street, to say the obvious, but on Main Street. (I believe there is a connection between these two, but I will leave that for another night.)

Once again let us change the initial premise of our investigation from searching for a *cure for a disease*, to searching for a *cure for a normal state*. This of course has serious socio-economic implications. For example, if you put up a shingle which says, "Only Normal People Come Here," no one would know whether to come or not! People might come in and say, "I'm terribly ill," and you'd reply, "Well, to tell you the truth, I don't treat illness." I do not treat illness. Because much of what has been conceptually and socially defined as illness makes it, in my opinion, fundamentally incurable. A lot of people fail to appreciate the perniciousness of definition and categorization, fail to appreciate the perniciousness of language, and fail to appreciate the extent to which we have all been socialized by language and categories, including the categories of emotion, cognition and disease, such that if we persist in functioning within these categories, it is questionable whether we can ever make it out of them.

Starting from our quite different assumption, our *anti-paradigm*, if you will, how do we relate to folks who come to see us and lay out all of the symptoms described in the literature on depression? People tell us, "I feel sad, disempowered, listless, helpless, I don't know what to do with my life, I'm thinking about committing suicide…" Those are very real things said by very real people, and they should not be denied or doubted. Millions of people feel this way, and some few come to us seeking help, and one cannot make fun of the people who are suffering, who are in pain. What do we do then, when people come to us depressed?

HISTORY

The writings of Becker about meaning that I mentioned earlier come closest to some of the things that we in the social therapy movement have been developing for many years. Moreover, it is not because of how close they come that I brought them up; it is because of the profound differences. I believe, as Becker does, that there is a serious loss that occurs in depression, which means a very serious loss that occurs in normal life in our culture. What is that loss; what name shall we give that loss? I think that what we have lost (and what we are continually losing), and what is directly related to the epidemic of depression in our culture, is best identified by the word *history*. Now history is a provocative word. A lot of people immediately react by saying, "You think 'depression' is imprecise — what about 'history'? I mean this is the catch-all word of all of history! So catch-all is it that we even have to use it to say how catch-all it is. How can you possibly think that the notion of history is going to be useful in presenting a new approach to the treatment of depression?" Well, let me try.

American culture, more than any other, has profoundly and dramatically lost a sense of history. Far from being a radical statement, this is the standard analysis of many people across the political, social and cultural spectrum. Over and over again it has been pointed out that the American sensibility runs roughly from the six o'clock news to the ten o'clock news. "What happened?" "What is historical?" "What is really going on?" The answer is what is momentary; it is whatever is presented in the media, largely on television. Our sensibility, such as it is, is mediated by an incredible barrage of words and images carefully shaped in such a way as to not simply create a certain picture, but to explicitly create a certain sense of alienation from the sources and objects of that picture. That is, to destroy our sense of history. There is ample evidence to suggest that as a people, we have not simply been alienated from the process of work and production but we have been alienated from the historical process of our own historical development. We have been denied the *possibility* of history as well as the actuality of *history*. People like Richard Sennett and others have noted the narcissism of American society. But the "Me Generation" is more than generational. The "me-ness" of American culture goes well beyond any single generation.

All over the world, people are astounded by the historical deprivation that is characteristic of our culture. We read in the European press of Europe's fears of the Reagan administration. To be sure, part of that has to do with his programmatics. But it also has to do with the fact that Europeans quite correctly are fearful of a major power, to which they are beholden in a life and death sense, being run by someone whose paradigm of reality is the grade B movie or six o'clock news. Many people are concerned about a population, a President and a culture which overidentify war, for example, as something that appears on television, which identifies profound social problems as images in a movie. We have, in many ways and for many reasons, evolved as a culture so thoroughly alienated from history as to make us profoundly vulnerable, in a momentary situation, to deep-rooted depression.

I am not suggesting that the more traditional elements discussed in classical papers and research on depression are irrelevant. However, I am urging that none of what is said makes a whole lot of sense unless we locate these analyses in some sociopsychological understanding of our particular culture, specifically our deprivation of history. In the absence of a historical sense we are enormously vulnerable to profound depression. Does this happen to individuals? Yes. Does it happen to masses of people? Yes. Is it of great concern? Certainly.

FASCISM

The work of Wilhelm Reich on the mass psychology of fascism is worth considering for a moment. Fascism can best be understood as a profound form of depression. That is not to trivialize it. The significant question that Reich raised in Germany in the 1930s was how was it possible to radically and fascistically transform the ideological responses, values and attitudes of a mass of people in so short a period of time. How could that have happened? How could German fascism have happened? That is an important question for us, for obvious social-political reasons. It is also profoundly relevant to personal depression, because one of the factors of personal depression that must be engaged if we hope to help anybody with it is how this could have happened "just like that." How does someone go, even in the face of a fairly serious loss, from being a relatively stable "coper" to someone who is essentially disembodied? How does that radical breakdown occur?

The study of how that occurs at the mass level is much more informative of how it happens at the individual level than the other way around. The study of mass psychology is much more informative of individual psychology than individual psychology is of mass psychology. Freud, and even his radical follower, Reich, did not fully appreciate this. They effectively believed that mass psychology is best modeled by an examination of the individual psyche. But it is clear, at least to me, that it goes the other way around.

How did this mass social transformation called Nazism occur? Reich gives a complex, characterological answer which I can only summarize here. He argues that there are three levels to people's characterological make-up. One element is fascistic, implying that there is the capacity for fascism in all of us. I do not accept that model. What I believe, and what we've come to see in our social therapeutic work, is that our *normal* social interaction is so profoundly alienated and lacking a sense of *historical connectedness* that relatively minor changes in the actual process by which information is communicated and disseminated can create total transformation overnight. The absence of a sense of history leaves us extremely vulnerable. And this was very much the situation with German culture and German society in the 1920s.

APPLICATIONS

And so when someone comes into my therapy office what I try to do is find some way to bring this person who is in pain and, most likely, depression, into history — to get her or him out of society and into history. The person says, "I'm depressed. Life means nothing to me. I don't want to go on. I don't care about anything." I say — and this is not a cognitive response although you will perhaps think it is — "How do you know?" "How do I know? What do you mean how do I know? *This is how I feel*." "How do you know you feel this way?" "Well, I feel this way because this is how I feel. I've felt this way for months. This is how I feel." "How do you know you feel that way?" People often become furious. "Are you saying I don't feel this way?" "No, I'm not saying that." "Are you saying I'm lying to you? What is it you're saying, anyway?" "I'm simply asking — how do you know that that's how you feel? Who told you that? Where did you learn that? How did you learn to talk that way? What makes you think that the words you're saying to me right now mean what you want them to mean? What do you and other people get from talking that way? I want to study the history of this way of talking. I'm not just talking about your personal history, I'm talking about you as a person in this society and I want to know *that* history." As this process unfolds, I insist that we simultaneously also learn the history of this very process that is unfolding between me and my "normal patients."

This process, while in varying degrees cognitive, emotive, and social, is not characterizable as any of these processes. Rather, it is a process of *investigating* if there is another sense of identity aside from the overdetermined societal sense of identity. This societal sense of identity, in my opinion, is the ultimate source of the depressed state. *This is not the same thing as saying that depression has social origins.* To be sure, it does. The point is that the whole mode of our emotional organization, both its *normalcy* and its *abnormalcy*, is effectively organized by the categories, life interactions, and social roles of one super-*ahistorical* culture and society.

If we take depression as a *normal* as opposed to an *abnormal* state, then looking for the source of depression *in its particularity* means looking for the historical origins of the total social experience which leaves us vulnerable, in the face of particular historical stimuli, to an unraveling best described as losing our sense of identity because of having lost our sense of location in society.

In *Anti-Oedipus* (a very good book which I completely disagree with) the French psychoanalysts and philosophers, Guattari and Deleuze, say that, in the final analysis (pardon the pun), Freud's greatest contribution was that he gave the madman social validity, a societal location; that what Freud did for the insane was to offer them a social contract, and say, "We have a place for you. You're not a devil, you're not a demon, you're not extra-societal — you're merely insane. And we shall enter ("we" meaning the psychoanalyst and the patient) into a social contract which gives you a relationship to society. Having that relationship, you are now able to function in a more stable fashion whether or not anything else of any significance happens in these interactions, be they five or six or seven days a week." What is fundamentally curative, Guattari and Deleuze argue, is that contract. I believe this is by and large correct. I think that this contract with the maladjusted is of profound importance. R.D. Laing once said that the good news about psychoanalysis is that most people who practice it do nothing resembling what is contained in its theories for, if they did, they would do terrible damage to people. It is the contract that does the good work.

Now, if we want to move beyond therapy whose effectiveness is totally contained in its liberal contract, then we have to change the depressive person's relationship not *within* or *to* society but *within and to* history. The distinction I am making here is the distinction between adaptation to society through a reorganization of one's relationship to society and adaptation to history through a reorganization of one's relationship (or a group's relationship or a nation's relationship) to history. History cures depression.

What does that mean? My colleague Lois Holzman and I have been doing research on these matters for the better part of a decade. In an article we wrote about three years ago called "Thought and language about history," we pointed out that in our culture both thought and history have been profoundly overdetermined by language. Others have observed that. Some people, including distinguished social scientists (e.g., the communicationist school in Palo Alto, California) go so far as to say that in point of fact, we should talk only about language usage because language usage is the closest approximation we have to both thought and history. They mention that any attempt to reach thought or history *directly* is ill-fated, that the study of human existence, of interpersonal behavior, of subjectivity, of life, is best accomplished by the study of communication.

The attempt to reach history, then, is inseparable from the attempt to understand the ideological limitations of a linguistically overdetermined socio-pathology. The questions, "What is language?" and "What is language usage?" are not abstract, but questions about a social process which involves the very rich and complex phenomena of making sounds, making inscriptions, making marks, putting them together in certain ways, forming them verbally, etc. What is this extraordinary social process? And to what extent has this process emerged in such a way as to become identifiable with life itself and with history itself? In many respects, the process of reaching history is best understood as the process of self-consciously creating a new language — actually, an *anti-language*. Many people say that this is part of the Freudian tradition.

Too ABSTRACT.

Isn't there, after all, a sense in which a new language is created in the process of psychoanalysis? Yes, but it is designed specifically to translate from one societally-bound language into another societally-bound language. What we are talking about here is the creation of a language (anti-language) whose specific function is to reach the historicalness of our social being.

We are, of course, in history right now, you know. Being in history, if you'll permit me this word, is our "natural" state. The unnatural state, the pathological state, the abnormal state, is being in the limited location that is society. In the case of our particular society and its particular developmental route, this fundamental abnormality translates into a depressive population. There will be no cure for depression in the absence of breaking down all the ideological connectors to society.

THE PHENOMENOLOGY OF HISTORY

Let me conclude by sharing a few thoughts about the phenomenology of history. Out here in history, we are not vulnerable to loss. Nothing is lost here in history. All kinds of things are lost in society, but nothing is lost in history. It is not at all clear, in fact, what "loss" would mean in history. To be sure, in history there is something other than loss, which to a large extent is what keeps people out of it. In history what we have is continuous change. Development. Social process. Growth. *Dying, Decay* But not loss. Society violates basic laws of "historical thermodynamics"; it is filled with loss. Straight-out loss. In its social laws, it actually allows for the total annihilation of objects. It destroys people. It destroys products. And it destroys them relative to their societal location, because society is specifically organized so as to maintain a certain set of social relationships between classes, between groupings, between individuals, and it maintains these relationships in such a way as to require loss. I believe that most people, including experts on depression, think that loss is as natural as sunrise, that we never can do away with loss. So what they are always looking for is some cure for depression based on the fact that loss is a God-given, eternal truth. There will always be loss, and therefore we must treat those who are unable to cope with it. But what would it mean to have an approach to depression which actively engaged the issue of whether or not there has to be loss? What would it mean to help people, to cure people, by finding a way to bring them into history wherein there is no such thing as loss? Well, this might sound simplistic but I think that if we can do away with loss, we can do away with depression. No loss, no depression.

A person comes into my office and says, "I feel blue, depressed, suicidal."

"Why?"

"I have suffered a great loss."

"How do you know?"

"How do I know I have suffered a great loss? I have lost a loved one. She's dead. She's gone. She's left. That's a great loss. What do you mean how do I know?"

"I appreciate all of that pain, I appreciate that experience, I appreciate your feelings. I empathize, I sympathize. But why do you persist in identifying it as a loss?"

"To me it's a loss!"

"How did it get to be a loss?"

"To me it is a loss. It is my personal loss."

"It may be your personal loss, but it is after all not your personal *conception* of loss." Does this deny the validity of the emotional response? Not at all. Rather, it speaks to the organization of emotionality, which is specific to the societal definition of who we are. And it raises, going back to the issue of definition, why it is that we have to accept these definitional, categorical locations at all, and how fundamental this question is to what we call depression.

This historical approach is most powerful when a person is in crisis, whether or not you wish to categorize that as depression. There more than anywhere must we challenge the societally over-determined affective-cognitive self-understandings. In its crudest form, short term crisis normalization therapy looks like this: A person comes in and says, "Everything just fell apart. The stock market, my family, the world, it all fell apart." And in the loudest possible voice, one has to work up the gumption to say, "How do you know? What makes you believe that? Where did that happen? What gave you that idea? What the hell are you talking about?" As a social therapist, one takes the risk of having the patient think that you are out of your mind. But the question is a profoundly important question. "How do you know that? How do you know you're in crisis? How do you know you're incapable? How do you know that you can't cope?" That is not said in the form of a pat-on-the-back — "You really can do it, kid." Maybe you can't do it; in fact, the presumption of being in crisis therapy is that you can't do it. But the question is how do you know that? Why do you think that way? Why are those your emotive responses? You must as a social therapist directly question the organization of emotionality when someone is in crisis because if you don't, you will be leaving her or him in the situation of potentially being permanently locked into no longer having the capacity to cope, no longer having any sense of meaning, i.e., in what we have identified as the experience of societal identity being totally demolished. And the cure for that is not to help someone relocate or adapt, but to find a new place. History is the name of that place.

Amongst the traditional approaches I found the various biochemical approaches to depression the most compelling. I hope you are not shocked. From the vantage point of attempting to define depression, they were the least pretentious. That is, the authors (in

Coyne's anthology) at least had the decency to say that what they were doing was simply discovering what they took to be techniques for dealing with symptoms. One might not like them; I myself have some very serious questions about them. They at least admit that we should not confuse our capacity to help people with having identified the source or the cause of a problem. In one particularly insightful paper (in Coyne's collection), it was pointed out that the effectiveness of aspirin for the simple headache should in no way be taken to imply that aspirin deficiency is the cause of headaches. I think that is an important insight not only for biomedical approaches but for all approaches. All that I have said tonight should not suggest that we have the correct definition, causal analysis, ideological location, or understanding of depression. Do not make of me a definition-monger. In fact, what I am saying is that holding to a definitional paradigm is problematic. We are not suggesting that the "aspirin of history," if you will, is giving a causal accounting of depression. What we are contending is that we have discovered a very effective aspirin — in history — which we call the short term crisis normalization approach.

5

PANIC IN AMERICA

Soren Kierkegaard discovered anxiety in 1844. He announced his discovery in a little book called The Concept of Dread. *Translated into English 100 years later, it is a classic of modern existentialism. Obviously anxiety existed before Kierkegaard, and indeed anxiety disorders have been known throughout history...Nevertheless, Kierkegaard is credited with the first description of anxiety as a vague, diffuse uneasiness, different from fear in that no apparent danger is present, and pervasive, allowing no escape.* — **Donald Goodwin,** *Anxiety*

"Panic in America" was delivered on December 2, 1988 as the annual lecture of the East Side Institute for Short Term Psychotherapy and first published in Practice: The Journal of Politics, Economics, Psychology, Sociology and Culture *(Spring 1989) Vol. 6, No. 3/Vol. 7, No. 1.*

Some may laugh at the claim that anxiety was "discovered" in 1844. I have something even more bizarre to tell you. One reason that it was discovered in 1844 is that it didn't come into existence until 1843! Kierkegaard was simply quick to notice what had just happened. Anxiety, you see, is a product of modern industrial society. Of course people had anxieties before 1843, but anxiety as a sweeping social experience is a modern phenomenon.

Goodwin says that, unlike fear, there is nothing good to be said about anxiety. Fear has a certain utility, an adaptive function, namely, it keeps us away from those things that could do damage to us. But, says Goodwin, anxiety has no socially redeeming or adaptive characteristics. Goodwin notes that some people say that a certain amount of anxiety can be helpful; creative people will sometimes tell you that if they're not anxious they can't write or dance or sing and so on. But creative turmoil notwithstanding, according to Goodwin and many others, anxiety is not a good thing and whatever we can do to get rid of it is worth doing.

I strongly disagree with Goodwin. Anxiety, I believe, is an adaptive emotion. Historically speaking, anxiety comes into the picture relatively late because it is basically an emotive or attitudinal adaptation to alienation. And alienation comes into the picture at a relatively late date; it comes into the human experience as an historical fact — not merely as a private subjective response — at a certain historical point when the social process of production becomes qualitatively and quantitatively separated to a critical degree from the product produced, i.e., when production for exchange becomes the hegemonic mode of production.

Prior to the middle of the 19th century, human production was primarily production for use; in the ensuing 50 years there was a profound global industrial transformation. More and more the world became dominated by production not of the things that we need or, more accurately, not based on what we as a species need, but by the production of commodities, production for sale or exchange. And anxiety emerged as an emotive/attitudinal adaptation to this social-historical phenomenon known as alienation which, in turn, is a social consequence of the total domination of commodity production.

The paradigm of anxiety created by Kierkegaard — and this characterization is carried into *DSM-III* — is a fear carried to a certain qualitative extreme. Specifically, it is a fear that is ultimately objectless. It is a fear, a trembling, a palpitation, a sweating — whichever language you prefer — connected to something not clearly identifiable or even capable of being identified at all. It's not the fear of falling off the cliff that you happen to be walking across, nor the fear of the about-to-fall frying pan teetering on the shelf above your head. No. Not these "objective" fears, that is, fears of objective actualities or possibilities. It is an objectless fear. The ideological, social, cultural, and economic transition to the alienated mode of production for exchange — commodity production — brings with it as an emotive, attitudinal, subjective adaptation a new kind of relationship between emotions and attitudes and the objects (or lack thereof) that give rise to these emotions or attitudes.

Put it this way: In a society in which production is fundamentally for use, there is much object-based fear. Goodwin quite correctly points out that the pre-industrial, pre-anxiety age (most accurately, the pre-commodified age) was very frightening — in some ways far more frightening than life under industrial capitalism. The fundamental paradigm for that fear-dominated culture was religious. The fear paradigm depicted the relationship between the individual and God; the quintessential fear in pre-alienated society was that one could be, might be, struck down — instantaneously or ultimately — by the deity. Fear was paradigmatically comprehended as a terrible and terrifying impingement on the individual by an identifiable object. *THAT IS NONETHELESS A FIGMENT OF THE IMAGINATION PRODUCED TO EXPLAIN WHY perceived EVENTS OCCUR.*

The gradual transition of society and culture from an anthro-pomorphized religious/theological world view to a com-modification world view brought with it a profound emotional and attitudinal transformation. The "deity" was now more subtly and invisibly located in the very ordinary objects and activities of everyday life. The deity became a fetishized (in Marx's language) commodity, no longer "on high" or radically other than its produc-er but something we as producers constantly participate in the pro-duction of. Feuerbach made plain the contradictions of an ideology in which a priest-produced or priest-created deity is related to as totally separated from — as indeed the creator of — those who in fact produced Him. Marx made plain the contradiction of an ideol-ogy (and a society) in which the class of producers continuously creates via their estranged labor a social and ideological force which imprisons them. God himself was no longer merely reified. He became commodified as the nexus of human life more and more became cash and profit.

In such a world, the identifiable source of our difficulties is paradigmatically less apparent than in the pre-capitalist epoch. For all of the pain and terror of pre-alienated society — and no one should ever glorify it — it was at least relatively plain what the source (or in God's case at least the name of the source) of the fear, the pain, the trembling and dread was. The transformation that began "in mid-March 1843" (so to speak) demanded that the source of our emotive and attitudinal reactions, the causes of our fears, be increasingly invisiblized. Moreover, that invisiblized source is the product of our own ongoing social activity — orga-nized and alienated labor. God was not murdered. He was merely stood on his head and continuously produced on an assembly line! Anxiety emerges, as I see it, during the second half of the 19th cen-tury and well into the 20th century as an emotive/attitudinal adap-tation to a profound transformation in the organization of human industry. In a world in which the fetishized commodity dominates, it is necessary to have an emotive and attitudinal adaptation to objectless fear. Its name: anxiety.

THE AGE OF PANIC

Our present century is many things. Some, like W.H. Auden, have called it the Age of Anxiety. Freudianism, likewise, is many things and, no doubt, helps many people. But from a social-historical point of view, it is, frankly, an apology, a rationalization. For it fails to identify the historical cause of anxiety — not to mention other pathological states. Rather it offers us an ultra-psychic rationalization to account for anxiety disorders. But as the 20th century moves far beyond anxiety, science, including Freudianism, becomes less and less capable of dealing with the emotive, social, and cultural crisis that is brought into being by commodification-gone-mad.

For while anxiety effectively functioned throughout the second half of the 19th century and well into the 20th century, anxiety now fails as a social-adaptive mechanism precisely as the system of commodification and social alienation known as capitalism winds its way down some very frightening roads. In the course of this century, alienation, anxiety, and commodification turn on themselves (commodification is commodified, alienation is alienated, anxiety is made anxious), and what emerges is pre-fascism, capitalism without progress. Under pre-fascism, explicit or implicit, anxiety is increasingly unable to function adaptively. Why? Because as the extremes of the capitalist mode of production manifest themselves, as pre-fascism or non-progressive capitalism becomes dominant, it is increasingly difficult for anxiety — the object-less fear — to play its adaptive role. It is precisely because the objective and fearful realities of pre-fascism are so transparently the recognizable object of emotive and attitudinal reactions that the mechanism which is socially shaped to help people adapt to an objectless fear is, almost by definition, no longer adaptive. *"Appropriate"*

When capitalism (both as a system of production and as an ideology) gives way to pre-fascism (both as a "capitalistic" system of production and as a reactionary ideology); as our century — once an "age of anxiety" — draws to a frightening and panicked conclusion, the pre-capitalist object-fear returns to haunt us — only now at a quantitative and qualitative level unthinkable in feudal times by virtue of the destructive capabilities generated by several hundred progressive years of alienated and anxiety-riddled capitalism. The natural disasters and disorders of the pre-capitalist period are now joined by and, moreover, are overshadowed by a human capacity for producing disaster on a worldwide level unimagined in the God-fearing world of, say, the 12th century. It is not only the possibility of nuclear holocaust that objectively haunts us. Destruction of the earth's environment, massive and seemingly unchangeable (by the current means) poverty and disease, violence of a pervasive sort primarily perpetrated by those in power but reacted to in violent desperation by masses of people not in power, anti-humanistic values manifest in a drug-dominated international social environment, political corruption and decadence that make Machiavelli look like Mr. Clean — these and more have sent the once-atheistic powers-that-be (capitalist and communist alike) back to God! Meanwhile, the masses of the earth's population, unable to adapt to good old capitalism/communism with either the middle class or working class version of anxiety, are more and more panicked!

The middle classes — the helping class, and its vanguard the "helping professionals" — ever out of step with historical class dynamics, ever seeking to rationalize the irrational, seek to update or reform the anxiety paradigm even as anxiety gives way to panic. The 19th century-born philosophy and psychology of fear, trembling and anxiety is thereby transformed here in the 20th century into a theory of hopelessness known as contemporary Existentialism.

SISYPHEAN TASKS, SISYPHEAN MYTHS

The 20th century existentialists, still followers of Kierkegaard but aware of the rise of pre-fascism (if not its causes), maintain that all the human being can really do in such a disastrous world is to make the choice to exist. The symbol of the modern existential man or woman is no longer the downtrodden, suddenly Godless peasant. Rather it is the pathetic "activist" identifiable in Camus' *Myth of Sisyphus*. Sisyphus rolls this big rock up the hill until he reaches the top, whereupon the rock rolls back to the bottom. Sisyphus walks down, and...pushes the rock back up. And therein, according to the existentialists, lies the only available "cure." The non-adaptive adaptation to post-industrial society is no longer anxiety but hopelessness. The only cure and the only freedom is the freedom to exist. Essence — a reason for being, an ideal that we might aspire to, or even anxiety — is replaced in late 20th century existential thought with the idealization of mere existence.

What does it mean to choose existence over essence? And what does all this philosophizing have to do with *DSM-III* or with how to treat people who come to us for help with anxiety disorders? A good deal. For the basic therapeutic models in late 20th century society are existential. What do I mean by that? Whether the treatment is chemical, ego-psychologistic, psychoanalytic, or other, the paradigm of orthodox treatment is existential. And it is rooted in the belief that all one can do in contemporary society is make an empty choice to exist. The very concept of cure has faded out of the psychology business much as the concept of cause once faded out of the physics business. The notion that there is something resembling genuine rehabilitation or even the possibility of development for "healthy" people, the possibility of progress, the prospect of a better world and/or a better person — all of those progressive conceptions, 19th and early-20th-century to the core, have been depressed, repressed, stepped on in favor of a survivalist, insurance company-designed existential paradigm. So while Sisyphus might sound a little bizarre, rock rolling is what's happening when people are treated — as they increasingly are — with drugs for most contemporary psychic disorders. If you think that Sisyphus' trip up and down the mountain is so profoundly different from or any less existential than the life of the poor client (working class or middle class) who is permanently drugged, whether they be healthful (legal) or unhealthful (illegal) drugs, then I think you're fooling yourself. It is fundamentally an existential model of treatment. The *DSM-III*-based symptomatological categorization of psychic distress, and the biochemical treatment wedded to it, is nothing more than the commodification of anxiety, depression, phobias and so on. On that Goodwin and I do agree.

This elimination of essence in favor of existence, together with what I would identify as the illusion of choice, this hopelessness, proves to be in some respects a successful "cure" for extreme post-anxiety syndrome, i.e., panic; it is a response to pre-fascism. You see, we no longer live in the Age of Anxiety; we live in what is rapidly becoming the Age of Panic. What is the social basis of this panic? What does panic mean? We are a species now almost totally maladapted to the objective reality of alienation gone mad. Anxiety no longer works. Panic, as opposed to anxiety, is not a subjective adaptation to an alienated, commodified society. Quite the contrary, it is that most painful of human states, viz., not having the capacity to adapt to a system which is objectively dysfunctional relative to the needs of our species, individually or collectively. Think of what it means to be living in a world in which the objective conditions are totally incompatible with human development, indeed with human existence, and at the same time having no subjective adaptive mechanisms other than hopelessness (its ultimate form — choosing to exist) to deal with the situation. Result: no more anxiety, and in its stead, hopelessness and/or panic.

At the beginning I noted that some people don't have a good word to say about anxiety. I didn't go along with that. I would, however, agree that there's nothing good to be said for panic. Panic has no adaptive function. It is, rather, the name of that moment in the subjective history of our species when adaptive mechanisms have pretty much completely failed. This is, after all, a very emotionally disturbed world. Michael Dukakis and George Bush notwithstanding, there were issues in 1988, serious and profound issues. But they cannot be reduced to slogans and sound bites. If we want to talk seriously about crime in America we have to talk concretely about what produces crime — the economic, social, and mass psychological state of America. American society as constructed is a crime-producing society. Hopelessness produces crime.

TREATMENT MODALITIES AS SOCIAL POLICY STATEMENTS

There is no such thing as a treatment modality which is not an expression of social policy. I don't care if we have an individual practice; I don't care if we never read a newspaper; I don't care if we never look at television — our treatment modalities are expressions of social policy. And the philosophical underpinning of the social policy statement that now dominates orthodox psychotherapeutic treatment is effectively an existential policy of control and survival.

One of the ironies of the varied attempts over the last 20 years to treat people's drug-related problems is that the rhetoric of these typically drug-dominated programs is filled with the word "choice." "You can say no," they say. Well, perhaps Nancy Reagan can say no. (I can think of at least one time when she should have said no and didn't.) But the option of saying no is not so transparent for the vast majority of the people of this city and this country. It sounds very high-minded to say "just say no." But it's not apparent what it even means or if it's even possible to "just say no."

I have no love of essences, philosophically speaking. But I do have a problem nonetheless with the elimination of essence by existentialism in that it is a classic case of throwing out the baby with the bathwater. Because in throwing out essence what they basically destroyed was history. You see, the real choice, the empowered or social therapeutic choice, is not between existence and essence, but between a Sisyphean model of hopelessness and social control, and a model of human empowerment.

What is the social therapeutic approach? People come into therapy and in one way or another they ask us for drugs. Sometimes they don't say they're looking for drugs. Sometimes they want drugs without drugs. People say, "Give me a cure. Give me something. I need a fix. I don't care if it's verbal or chemical; all I want to do is continue to exist. I choose existence; I choose survival." The social therapeutic approach refuses to give into that perfectly reasonable request. In fact, what we say is that the way to deal with pre-fascistic-based panic is to create anxiety, a new kind of anxiety. We have to collectively work to create anxiety in order to be able to adapt. Anxiety is adaptive; panic is not adaptive. "Are you saying," some might ask, "that you want to help people create anxiety so that they can adapt to society?" No! We can't adapt to contemporary society. Indeed panic is the very subjective indication that anxiety is not adaptive to society because of the current state of society! We help people to create a new anxiety so that they can adapt not to society but to history, and to history directly. Now that raises the issue that living unadapted to a society in which life is no longer sustainable — living in history, that is — is profoundly anxiety producing, and we have to collectively organize that anxiety so that people can adaptively function in the historical setting.

Rx: HISTORY

People come into therapy and they say, "Can you help me to

adapt? I have palpitations and sweaty palms, so I looked in *DSM-III* — I have panic disorder! What do you have for panic disorders?"

"We produce anxiety here."

"You produce anxiety?"

"Yes, we collectively produce anxiety so that people can adapt to that which it is possible to adapt to in contemporary society."

Don't think of this abstractly; think of it concretely. Let us go back to a very marvelous statement made by a very marvelous leader. Dr. Martin Luther King, Jr. said, "Today, psychologists have a favorite word, and that word is maladjusted. I shall never be adjusted to lynch mobs, segregation, economic inequalities, the madness of militarism, and self-defeating physical violence. The salvation of the world lies in the maladjusted."

That is both a morally and scientifically sound position. The option that we now face — and this is a key issue in mental health — means adaptation to a society which we cannot adapt to and, further, adaptation to it would effectively mean taking moral positions which are antithetical to how many of us feel about human life.

So what then is the choice in the face of this extraordinary dilemma? Do we try to adapt or help others to adapt to an utterly rotten and sickened society? (If you don't believe that's how society is, that's another issue and a different debate.) Or do we remain hopelessly panicked and unadapted to anything? Those are roughly our choices. The social therapeutic approach is to help people of different class and racial backgrounds, straight, gay, people of different genders, to create the anxiety necessary for an adaptation to history. To bypass society. By bypass, of course, we do not mean to escape from it. No, not to escape from it! Indeed the issue is that society has escaped, has abandoned, us! No, we are not advocating that we race off to Vermont and collect maple syrup or even elect socialists! Rather, the issue is to understand the extent to which our emotional disorders are rooted in this malfunctioning relationship between our subjective equipment of adaptation and the objective conditions of our culture. *AND our EXPERIENCE IN IT.*

Does this deny the physiological component of mental disorders? No, not at all. Does it deny the behavioral or the psychodynamic? No, not at all. It doesn't deny any of that. It merely says that all of those features must be located within the sociocultural facts of human emotionality and human pathology. That all of these other components are effectively ordered and organized by our culture in its current moment.

I want to close by sharing something of great importance to me, a poem by the Guatemalan political activist and poet, Otto Rene Castillo. As I was preparing this talk, this poem came to mind once again. I want to commit an "aesthetic" sacrilege of sorts; I want to change a word in the poem. I don't think the author, a Guatemalan revolutionary murdered by the fascists in 1967, would object. The title of the poem, as Castillo wrote it, is "Apolitical Intellectuals." I want to change the name in this reading to "Apolitical Psychologists." Here's how it goes:

> One day
> the apolitical
> psychologists
> of my country
> will be interrogated
> by the simplest of our people.
>
> They will be asked
> what they did
> when their nation died out
> slowly,
> like a sweet fire,
> small and alone.

No one will ask them
about their dress,
their long siestas
after lunch,
no one will want to know
about their sterile combats
with "the idea
of the nothing"
no one will care about
their higher financial learning.
They won't be questioned
on Greek mythology,
or regarding their self-disgust
when someone within them
begins to die
the coward's death.

They'll be asked nothing
about their absurd
justifications,
born in the shadow
of the total lie.

On that day
the simplest men will come.
Those who had no place
in the books and poems
of the apolitical psychologists
but daily delivered
their bread and milk,
their tortillas and eggs,
those who mended their clothes,
those who drove their cars,
who cared for their dogs and gardens

and worked for them,

                and they'll ask:
"What did you do when the poor
suffered, when tenderness
and life
burned out in them?"

Apolitical psychologists
of my sweet country.
You will not be able to answer.

A vulture of silence
will eat your gut.
Your own misery
will pick at your soul.
And you will be mute

             in your shame.

I read this poem not to attack my colleagues in the helping professions, but rather as a way of insisting that there is no neutrality in the pseudo-science or mythology known as psychology. It is moral, political, and social through and through. And in my opinion, a treatment approach which requires denying that fact is not psychology but straight-out social coercion. I shared this poem because it's so meaningful to me and to many others.

Social therapy is ultimately not terribly profound. In fact, it's little more than an organized refusal to leave the oppressive, pre-fascistic social realities of our culture and our society out of the theory and practice of providing help to other human beings. And it's little more than a relatively small grouping of people who relate to human beings wherever they may be — in hospitals, schools, private offices, communities — with this same perspective. That's the "essence" of social therapy. More importantly, that's the history and practice of social therapy.

6

THE MYTH OF ADDICTION

I think I feel a little bit defensive about this talk. Let me tell you why.

The way these talks work is that the staff members of the East Side Institute for Short Term Psychotherapy come up with a topic that they think would be important for me to talk about, to add a social therapeutic point of view to something that's hot. So this year Dr. Hugh Polk, the director of the Institute, came up to me

"The Myth of Addiction" was delivered as a talk entitled "The Politics and Psychology of Addiction," on April 27, 1990 as the annual lecture of the East Side Institute for Short Term Psychotherapy and first published in Practice: the Magazine of Psychology and Political Economy *(1991) Vol. 8, No. 1. "Addictions Response" was published for the first time in the same issue of* Practice.

and said, "The hot topic this year is addiction. There are big grants going out to researchers in the addiction field. Everyone's writing about it — it's the word."

And so Dr. Polk and Bette Braun, director of training, pointed me in the direction of a whole body of literature which I began to study. Well, after a while I realized I had a certain problem — which is why I feel defensive tonight.

You see, two years ago I gave a talk on depression — apparently depression was hot two years ago — and after having perused the literature I saw that, while I didn't agree with a lot of the literature about depression, I had a critical contribution to make as a social therapeutic theoretician. While I had all sorts of criticisms of the traditional theories and attitudes about depression, after reading as much of the literature as I could, I wound up believing that there was such a thing as depression and that's what they got!

Last year I was told that the big topic was panic. I got all the literature, read through it very carefully, had severe criticism of a lot of the positions on panic and its correlate, anxiety. I gave a real radical talk on the subject — I called it "Panic in America" — but at least when I finished reading all the literature I still believed that there was something called panic and something called anxiety. So I didn't feel so bad when people came to hear me talk, because they got what they paid for!

Now here's my problem this year: I read through a huge pile of books and scholarly articles. I watched films. I read the writings of social workers, respected psychologists, distinguished psychiatrists. And here's the strange thing that happened: *the more I read the more I came to believe that there is no such thing as addiction.*

I notice the silence in the room! "What!!? No such thing as addiction?" you're saying to yourself. Now, I know that what I'm putting out is a tough position. I know that Nancy Reagan said that there is such a thing as addiction. I know as well as you all do that there are billions of dollars made in the addiction industry. I know that the word appears all over the place. I know that lots of people, including our young people, our people in the communities who are so *heavily* labeled, branded and stamped by that term, have themselves come to believe in addiction. But you see, I don't think it follows that there is such a thing as addiction. And that's why, as I mused over alternative titles for tonight's talk, what kept running through my mind (I am addicted to thinking up names for things!) was "The Myth of Addiction or the American Addiction to Myths."

I want to talk about how profoundly addicted to myths, mythically speaking, this addictive society is. Take a look at this big word on the banner up here on the stage — Addiction. In the language of philosophy, this big word refers to nothing. I think it *damages* profoundly, but it literally refers to nothing. Let me tell you why I think that, and why it's so important to clear this up and make this statement.

THE BIRTH OF THE ADDICTION INDUSTRY

In 1968 I gave up university teaching in philosophy or, rather, university teaching gave up on me. I had been giving my students all A's because I didn't want to participate in having young people sent over to Vietnam to be cannon fodder for a bunch of people who fight all kinds of wars for mythical reasons. We know the real reasons — but they put forth mythical ones. So these young people would come into my class and I'd say something like, "OK, let's get it straight here. Everyone's got an A. You've got an A whether you come or you go or you stay or you write or you don't write. Frankly, I don't care, I'm giving everybody an A here. Now if you want to talk about some philosophical issues we can do that, and if you don't that's fine, too."

Well, I didn't do that for very long at any one school, as you might well imagine. I was fired all over the country — I think in my best year I went through seven schools. I finally walked out in 1968. Of course I didn't quite know what I was going to do — I thought I wanted to become an organizer though I hadn't the foggiest idea what that meant. So in '68 I did what a lot of people were doing — I went to a lot of rallies, I went to meetings, I tried to figure out what to do with a Ph.D. in philosophy if you didn't use it to teach at school. And of course I was broke, but I had spent a lot of my life being broke; it wasn't altogether new to me. I knew how to be broke.

But when you're broke, eventually you've got to find some work to put a few bucks in your pocket so you can get to be broke again. In early 1970 I picked up the paper looking for work. And there was an advertisement there — I think it was in the *New York Times* — for a "drug rehabilitation counselor." It looked like something I should apply to. New York State gave a test to become a drug rehabilitation counselor. I took the test, and I passed it with flying colors. I got a very high score, and since I knew nothing in the world about drug rehabilitation, I already knew the field was slightly suspect! I was hired by an outfit called the Narcotics Addiction Control Commission, set up by the Rockefeller Drug Program, and they sent me across the East River to the Queensboro Rehabilitation Center to be a drug rehabilitation counselor.

Well, when I got there I discovered that the Queensboro Rehabilitation Center was in fact a prison. They didn't *call* it a prison but it was one nonetheless. The people got to live there by copping a plea to go through a nine-month program rather than spend two to three years in a prison. But the Queensboro Rehabilitation Center was a prison — it was a lock-up prison. It came complete with six by eight detention cells and beatings by guards. In short, it had all the accouterments of a prison because it *was* a prison.

In the context of this prison they had something which was euphemistically called the Therapeutic Program. This was right before the moment when methadone came in, so they were still playing with '60s concepts like "rehabilitation." I remember those first days very, very vividly. The first day I arrived with the usual trepidation and fear of a first day on the job, not to mention the strangeness and oppressiveness of the prison environment, not to mention that I knew nothing about drug rehabilitation! I was sent up to the fifth floor and introduced to 50 African American, Latino and white working class young men, sitting around a large game room. The guards started banging and shouting out, "All right! Gather up here! The new social worker is here! (ha! ha!)" and they said to me, "Here are your men. Rehabilitate them!"

So we all sat down, and these men started checking me out — a perfectly reasonable, indeed more than reasonable, thing to do. It was all happening very, very quickly. As a matter of fact they weren't even talking to me; they were talking to each other about things they knew about their shared experience — but it was *transparently* obvious that they were talking about me. One didn't need any training at all to figure that one out — you can tell when you're being talked about.

It became apparent after a relatively short time that one young man — a very tall, powerful looking man who was to become a very dear friend of mine and who was later killed on the streets of New York — was obviously the leader. So after about five or ten minutes, I addressed him. His name was Leonard. I said, "Leonard, how's everybody doing here?" And he answered, "We're doing great."

"Are you sure?" I said.

"Yes," Leonard said. "We're fine."

"Well, I hear what you're saying," I replied. "But — you know you're in a prison."

"Yeah, we know that."

"You know if you try to get outside this place and you get about three steps they're going to bust your head open with that bat over there?"

"Oh yes."

"You know that you'll be locked up here again and again and again because the rate of return to this place is 97%, so what you're looking at is a lifetime of being locked up here in this place, stuffed in a six by eight detention cell if you open your mouth, slugged in the head if you try to walk out of here, unable to make a move without fear of state reprisal...What the *hell* do you mean by telling me that everything's going fine? This ain't 'fine!'"

Well, in the next eight weeks we organized a worker and residents job action. We went to Albany, we went downtown to Broadway, we got the press in, we tried every kind of action to expose what the hell was happening at that place because it was a prison and a corruption pretending to be a rehabilitation center. It was a complete lie! And we failed — methadone and the whole addiction phenomenon were on their way in. The medicalization of the social problems of America had started.[1] Goodbye to the old 19th century understanding of addiction as some kind of moral turpitude. No longer would it be the case that addicted people were evil people; this was going to be progress special for the 20th century! We were now going to introduce a medical model to cover over the realities of social problems.

Methadone was on its way in. Addictions were on their way in. You see, the real meaning of the story of Leonard, this very dear brother, was how rapidly everybody on that floor had become so-called "addicted" to what they were supposed to do in the therapy game. That game got picked up and learned as quickly as any other game. It wasn't addiction! It was just what people learn to do when they're in situations where they have to make certain kinds of moves in order to respond "appropriately" to the particular social oppression of a given reality!

THE UNITED STATES OF ADDICTION

The addiction business is not a small business! I'm not making this up! Take a look at this stack of books I've brought here! This author, this scientist with a real Ph.D., he said it, not me. I could show you all these quotes, from all these doctor types and many of them say the same thing: this is a multi-billion dollar business! This is an addiction *industry!* It's *well* documented. I was *shocked* when I found out how many folks — learned folks, experts in the field — *know* that there is no such thing as addiction.[2] I thought I was some kind of weirdo! But it turns out that everyone knows this is a hoax, a lie. What's shocking to me is that *despite* the fact that folks know it's a phony sham, we don't get to hear about that out in the communities. It's a *very well kept secret in America today* — it's a very well kept secret that *there is no such thing as addiction.*

Somewhere around the tenth day of my journey into the addiction literature, I came upon a *New York Times* bestseller, a book that takes it all the way: *When Society Becomes an Addict.*[3] The thesis? Everyone is addicted to something! You're addicted to drugs, to love — there are even people who are said to be addicted to people who are addicted to something. In all the books I went through, I never found a single book that talked about people being addicted to money. But everything else is covered! They got 40 million of this particular type of addict, 30 million of these, 70 of those, 90 of this other type adding up to a figure that's three times the population of the country!

Here's an interesting item from one of the journals I read, *Journal of Substance Abuse Treatment.* A man named Howard Shaffer did a test called "Frequency of Disease Ratings for the Complete 80 Item List."[4] He wanted to find out what things this sampling of people thought were diseases and what were addictions. The list included all kinds of bizarre things. For example, it included not only asthma, measles and muscular dystrophy, but also jogging, cubism, Taoism, metabolism — all kinds of things. Cubism got 4.2%! Yes, that's right, 4.2% of the people thought that cubism is a disease. (I think I might have been one of them actually, but that's another issue!) Muscular dystrophy won, with 94.8% of the sampling.

Here's an interesting one: 35.4% of the people took racism to be a disease. I think it's interesting because it shows how effective the medicalization of America has been. If this test has any validity at all, what it suggests is that one out of every three Americans no longer identifies racism as a fundamental social problem, but regards it as a disease, on a par with pneumonia or heart disease. What a convenient rationale for not implementing the programs necessary to do something about the *social corruption* that is racism!

Here's another one: 22% think that lesbianism is a disease! Homosexuality: 33.3% of the people think it's a disease. The history of the last 20 years shows quite vividly that those political, social and community leaders who have no intention of facing the hard realities of the crisis of America have been eager to find an ideological solution to what is a hard material human problem.

Someone whom I very much respect, a radical theorist named Sylvere Lotringer, said many years ago: "One does not cure neurosis [we could substitute *addiction*, or *illiteracy*, or *poverty*]; one changes a society which cannot do without it."[5] On all too many occasions over the past 20 years I've been asked to speak about education in America, and I invariably begin those talks by saying something that people are initially shocked by. I point out that *from the point of view of those who are responsible for it, the educational system is working just fine. In fact, it's a total success.* They could not *live* with a more successful system! They could not turn out bright young students prepared to go on to college or to enter the labor force when there are no educational programs out there to further train them, no jobs to sustain them.

Illiteracy in America grows by leaps and bounds every day, yet there are societies in the world — indeed some very poor societies — which have cured illiteracy *virtually overnight*. Why can't this country cure illiteracy, or poverty, or addictions, or mental illness? The answer is that, in terms of those who have primary social control — those *real people* who run this society — there is no particular reason to do so!

Here's a news item about William Bennett, the drug czar, one of the real people who runs this country, about his appearance at a news conference in Orlando. The reporter said, "You talk about a stronger country, Mr. Bennett. But our inner city schools, hospitals, clinics, churches are more in decline than ever before. What can we do to solve the problems of these communities?" And America's drug czar, reactionary to the core, replied, "If these institutions are failing we should take the children away, out of the community, from their families, and put them in special programs." So he pretends to be a humanist looking out for the kids who are being abused. But what about the families, the communities that are being abused? This is America's drug czar! This is America's social policy expert!

The failure of the American school system, the failure of the drug programs, the failure of the community health programs, these are not natural catastrophes. A lot of us in New York remember when they decided to remove all the people from the mental institutions and put them in the communities. That decision was the explicit creation of what is now known as "the problem of homelessness." Were there not homeless people before? Yes, there were. But it never was state policy before. It was a *problem* before. When the people in charge closed down those institutions and brought those people into the communities but refused to fund community support programs in any serious way, homelessness was created as a social policy in New York City. And now people are making big bucks and giving big talks — some of the same people who created the mess in the first place — by saying we have to address this problem of homelessness. It's a fraud and a sham, a lie. And the worst of it is that people are suffering and dying from it. Some people like Bennett and his Democratic Party friends are saying it's a "disease" and "epidemic," a "crisis." No! *You're* the disease! You're an epidemic!

As I was walking up here thinking about how defensive I was going to be about this talk, I began to think about the '60s, and about people like Thomas Szasz who back in the '60s were saying things like, "There really is no such thing as mental illness."[6] Szasz would argue that those terms were invented, by and large, because the insurance companies demanded them. He said that there are no scientific criteria for identifying schizophrenia or depression or lots of other diseases.

That humanistic tradition lost, for all kinds of reasons. I was part of that tradition. I didn't agree with Szasz completely. "Listen. I think your argument is faulty. What you're saying has great merit, but the truth of the matter is that there are people who are mentally ill and it is problematic to deny that." I remember one talk where Szasz argued that the criteria we have for identifying someone who is mentally ill could apply to virtually any person and so therefore it must be that there is no distinguishing characteristic of the mentally ill. I thought, "Thomas, there's a little problem with that reasoning, since if everybody had cancer and therefore we couldn't distinguish between those who didn't and those who did, it wouldn't follow that nobody had cancer."

I had some problems with Szasz, but in general we walked on the same road that a lot of people walked on in those days. What we said was that there had to be a political, therapeutic, community-oriented solution to the problems that face the people of this country. We stood up tall and pointed out what everyone knows is true — that the single most effective drug rehabilitation program in the history of the United States of America was carried out almost overnight by the Black Panther Party. The Panthers and the Young Lords had a higher rate of "cure" for people who were using drugs than anybody in the entire world. Do you appreciate, when you think of the multi-billion dollar rehabilitation industry, what the figures are in terms of the number of actual people cured? Do you know that today they claim a cure rate of 6-8%? And they lie all the time — those are inflated figures. People are not being cured! Alcoholics Anonymous has become a major force in American social-political life and by its own admission *it does not cure many people!* It has influenced *masses* of people; indeed 12-step programs are one of the latest addictions.[7]

MYTHS AS SOCIAL CONTROL

I'm not saying, by the way, that people have not been helped by those programs. And I'm not saying that drugs and alcohol aren't potentially very, very harmful and destructive. No, those are real problems, disastrous problems. *And we can't afford these phony, mythic explanations!* The history of science, one of the fields that I have studied, is *filled* with the creation of mythic explanations which function as social coercion, as a way of avoiding looking at the actual social causes of human problems. And it's particularly true of societies in advanced states of decay. As Greek civilization was going under, they started increasing the activities of the Greek gods. The Greek gods during the heyday of Greece used to sit around doing pretty much nothing. They just hung out — everything was cool. But as Greece started declining, the gods got busier. If something happened down here, somebody would say, "Whoops! I think that's a big fight between Jupiter and Juno over there on the mountain." They had to account for these things going on down here. *[handwritten: AND IT COULD NOT BE ATTRIBUTED TO SOCIETY.]*

So there's a long history of people in power creating myths to socially coerce. Addiction? Though there is no such thing as addiction, it is a very good topic to be talking about.

I know there are some people out there who are saying this is all very interesting politically speaking, but what's the scientific evidence for all this? Simply this: *there is no systematic, hard evidence in any research studies anywhere in the world that there is such a thing as physio-chemical addiction.*[8] In fact there is no hard evidence indicating anything other than the fact that social environment is consistently a key if not the key factor in whether or not people can or can't change their habits relative to the so-called opium drugs, or anything else for that matter. That's the hard *scientific* evidence.

Again and again it has been asserted that the two dominant characteristics, the classical characteristics, of addiction, particularly drug addiction, are: (1) having some kind of powerful reaction when you stop, typically identified as withdrawal; and (2) needing to take more of it in order to get the same reactions. But there is evidence everywhere that many people, not just handfuls but high percentages, kick hardcore drugs by simply stopping.[9] Zero withdrawal. Every major article, including the ones written by people who take the opposite position, admits that statistical studies accounting for how people actually kick drugs show that the single most frequent way is people saying, "I just stopped." There's a higher percentage of success among people who stopped because they decided to stop than any other single approach in the entire world.

This notion that addiction is a *success* industry is a myth; it is a *money-making industry!* It is a failure industry! AA is not a success program, except insofar as it is major business and has major political influence. The National Council on Alcoholism, the major cover association for folks giving help and advice to alcoholics, had the American liquor industry as one of its primary sources of support until 1982.[10] The liquor industry has no problem supporting AA. AA says alcoholism is a disease and that only a relative handful of people have it.

BUCKS AND BOONDOGGLES: THE ADDICTION INDUSTRY

It ends up that I share a position with Nancy Reagan. She says, "Just Say No." What does that mean, "Just Say No"? I mean, if you can just say, "No," it can't be a hell of an addiction, can it? The addiction mythology is filled with these kinds of contradictions. *This whole thing is a colossal boondoggle. It was made up!* I was there — in the prison known as the Queensboro Rehabilitation Center — when they decided to make the move, when they decided that it was necessary and profitable and possible to introduce into this country a major social control industry, because the times they were a changin', rather profoundly.

They talk rather glibly down in Washington and at major universities like Columbia about how this is a society with a chronically poor population. What is that supposed to mean — chronically poor? I think if it means anything it means a poor population about which nothing can be done — and that came about by virtue of this country's leadership. And now they've introduced all kinds of terminology and models and paradigms to justify their doing nothing about it. You see, the meaning of calling poverty or homelessness an addiction — the meaning of addiction — is that nothing can be done about it. That's what they say. It is a reactionary and reactive model which many know to be a fraud but which is presented to the American public with a credibility that justifies billions and billions of tax dollars for programs which are utter failures, and endless amounts of money being made and being laundered, which justifies Ronald Reagan and George Bush.

So no, I'm afraid that Ann Wilson Schaaf, who says that society is addicted, is wrong. I think she's saying society is addicted so we will either accept the fact that there is no cure, or *foolishly* think that there is a way to cure it using, as it were, a medical point of view. Society is not addicted; society is vulgar, racist; it is oppressive and destructive. It is inhuman, it is uncaring; it generates policies that miseducate; it generates policies that fail to respond to human needs. It does all of those things, but it's not addicted.

So I decided tonight I would raise again at this very critical moment this lost fight of the '60s and early '70s. Dr. Lenora Fulani, Dr. Rafael Mendez, Reverend Al Sharpton, young people all over the country, are beginning to raise some very old issues in some very new ways. Issues which those of us who were there remember from the '60s but are not the same as the '60s, because different people are raising them, at a different stage of our history, in different ways, making different statements. There is a wisdom to those who are now rising up, to our Black and Latino youth rising up and saying, in all honesty, and with firm commitment, "No Justice, No Peace." That's the slogan, it means something — No Justice, No Peace. No Addiction. We won't buy it. Can't fool us no more. Can't feed us this kind of stuff and expect that we'll believe it. We won't enter into trivial kinds of little debates. What we're saying is *the killing must stop*. The drugs must stop. And we won't stop the drugs by a nonsensical explanation that it's all about addiction, because we know what it's all about! We know who puts those drugs into our communities! We know who profits from it! We know where it comes from, that there are people throughout the world making billions every day and laundering it through major banks in this country! There was a report that came out just a few days ago about the major banks in this city and the role they're playing in laundering drug money. That's why there is no book about the addiction to money, because if they had a book about the addiction to money it'd point the fingers in the right places!

Our children aren't addicted, our children aren't bad, our children aren't evil; our children are being murdered. And our children are teaching us something that we have to learn. Those of us who attempted proudly to introduce some of these things back then and who failed must learn from those who are now leading the way and saying in a militant language that cuts through all of this nonsense — No Justice, No Peace! No more of those empty words, no more of that sham science. No, we won't take addiction as your nonsensical accounting for your deadly behavior. No, it's not that I'm addicted to being poor. It's that you're a filthy rich monster!

I'm very glad to have stayed around long enough to see these fights being restructured and being redeveloped, coming out of our working class communities, our African American, our Puerto Rican, our Chicano, our Asian American, our Native American communities. Our communities are beginning to raise this issue up, and all over the world I think people are raising up issues about myths — from Eastern Europe and Tiananmen Square, to Central America, Southeast Asia and Africa — people are saying we cannot afford these myths any longer! We are being murdered!

It will be good to stamp out addiction. I raise for you that political call. We must stamp out addiction because it is a fiction that is killing us. We must stamp out all of those mysteries, those myths, those rationalizations that have traditionally been used to destroy us. So, with appropriate defensiveness I hope you will not think ill of me for spending all this time and inviting you all here to hear me talk about something which doesn't exist.

ADDICTION RESPONSE

To respond to the outpouring of interest in Newman's provocation to the addictions industry and its consumers, Practice: the Magazine of Psychology and Political Economy *formed a special editorial board to put together an issue dedicated to addiction (more accurately to anti-addiction). The editorial board sent Newman's talk to social workers, drug rehab workers, former "addicts," research and clinical psychologists and psychiatrists. Nineteen responses, along with Newman's original talk and his "Response" to the responses, appeared in* Practice *(Vol. 8, No. 1).*

As Newman notes at the beginning of his "Addiction Response," in putting together that issue of Practice *something very rare was generated — an enthusiastic and authentic dialogue —* people talking about people. *The responses came from a wide range of people, including those to whom Newman refers specifically: James Mancuso, professor of psychology at the State University of New York at Albany; Howard Shaffer, Assistant Professor of Psychology at the Harvard Medical School; Dr. Ron Leifer from the State University of New York Medical Center at Syracuse; Wendy Deutelbaum, associate director of the National Resource Center for Family Based Services in Iowa City, Iowa; Doug Miranda, a medical aide at the Dimock Detox Unit of the Dimock Community Health Center in Boston, a former member of the Black Panther Party who is currently an organizer with the New Alliance Party; and Abukarriem Shabazz, executive director of Phase: Piggy Back, a Harlem-based drug free substance abuse company he helped to found 23 years ago. What follows is Newman's response to these responses.*

I deeply appreciate all of your insightful and passionate responses to my talk/paper on the myth of addiction. It is, in my opinion, very timely and extremely positive to have this dialogue about *addiction* and about *myths* and (as your thoughtful remarks make plain) much else that is interrelated with them. Moreover, it is encouraging to see these matters taken on by people with varied histories and points of view — i.e., pluralistically. What we are all really talking about, in my opinion, is *people.* Moreover, we are *people talking together about people;* about who we are, what we are, how we are to be understood, treated, explained; about how we live, whether we live and when and where we live. And it is terribly, terribly important, I believe, that people — indeed, masses of people — begin to self-consciously talk about people. It is that *activity* — people talking about (and hopefully related to that, actively learning and developing) who and what we are — that collective activity of self and collective defining — that must, as I see it, take on the increasingly hierarchical (yeah, I'll call it neofascistic!) *imposition* of definitions that is the repressive hallmark of contemporary *international* society — George Bush's new world order. In the spirit of both intensifying and broadening this activity of *people talking together about people*, let me share as honestly and succinctly as I am able some specific responses to your responses.

Professor Mancuso says that addiction is not a myth; it is not unreal. Rather, it is a real *construct* interconnected in complex ways with a network of constructs which, taken together, contribute to an *identity* and *even rats need a valid identity*. In the process of constructing his position, he analogizes *addiction* and *diabetes*; both are constructs, he says, which are real to those who *use* them. But isn't it the problem that constructs (whatever they are) are *used* differently by different people and that some of those *users* have the capacity to impose *their use* on others — *and regularly do so?* The child in a traditional public school may construct all sorts of mental (and physical) entities (both her or his identities and/or object identities) but the teacher, principal, school psychologist, have the authority to insist that their *use* is correct — with all that that entails. The teacher may be philosophically *out of line* but the child, typically, has little recourse. Likewise with the so-called "addict." We do not live in a constructivist radical democracy where everyone at least starts out with an equal opportunity for self or object identification. We live in a top heavy, white supremacist, patriarchal autocracy where official institutions characteristically *define* even what is possible to imagine, desire, conceive, etc.

The analogy between addiction and diabetes is, however, problematic even *from* a constructivist point of view. (I hope, by the way, that Professor Shaffer will see from these observations about Professor Mancuso's remarks that while he is correct to point out that I am not a constructivist, *I am, even less,* a realist. If the labels are of any use here, I am, in point of fact, a clinician who "follows" Karl Marx and Lev Vygotsky, the Soviet methodologist/psychologist, *revolutionary activity* practitioner/theorist who does not believe that the static, morbid, hierarchical epistemological categories *realism, instrumentalism* and *constructivism* are of any progressive human value at all. More on this later.)

To continue with *addiction* and *diabetes.* A sort of clinical post-Wittgensteinian ordinary language analysis of "addiction"and "diabetes" (an analysis of these words *in use*) seems to me to expose very, very important and *relevant* (to our dialogue) differences between them. Let us grant for the moment that both *addiction* and *diabetes* are constructs and let us leave aside for a second that the addict or diabetic is not, qua user of these labels, constructs, whatever, in the same hierarchical social location as the doctor, professor, teacher, judge, police officer, etc., qua user of the label. But even *qua construct in general, addiction* and *diabetes* are fundamentally different-in-use and disanalogous. For *diabetes,* the label, functions in our culture primarily as *classificatory,* and *addiction,* the label, functions in our culture primarily as *explanatory.*

Western civilization (talk about myths that destroy!) has a long and jaded history of both *classification* and *explanation.* And, to be sure, there are, and always have been, complex and varied interconnections between them. Yet, from the pre-Socratics to the present, it has proven useful, in my opinion, to distinguish between the claim that Earth, Water, Air and Fire, for example, are the elements that *make up* the world (a classificatory analysis generally attributed to Empedocles) and the Heraclitean contention that the world is to be *understood* by noticing that everything (whatever and however it might be classified) is *in a constant state of flux* (an explanatory analysis).

Diabetes belongs to a complex classificatory system employed by traditional modern medicine. I for one have serious questions about the relative validity of that medical system *in toto.* Indeed, I regard it as more mythic than scientific (in the positive sense of that word). But there are myths and there are myths. And a *classificatory* myth is worth distinguishing from an *explanatory* myth precisely because the critically important and *revolutionary activity* of *myth-elimination* demands that we see the differing ways in which myths operate.

Addiction does not, for the most part, classify. It functions to explain *why* someone has a drug or alcohol "habit." But in point of fact it explains nothing. It simply *reiterates* in pseudo-explanatory language that the person is in the "habit" of using drugs or alcohol or, even more precisely, that the person uses drugs or alcohol enough to be physically, psychologically, legally or socially problematic in this culture at this time. Addiction explains nothing. It is exactly analogous to the pseudo-scientific medieval "explanation" which attributed *dormative powers* to wine, which turned out to mean simply that some people fell asleep when they drank certain amounts of wine. Worth knowing that — especially if you were driving (or a passenger in) the ox-cart! But *dormative powers* explained nothing; added nothing; said nothing; was a myth. *Addiction,* like *dormative powers* and much else in contemporary society that passes for *psychological explanation,* is actually an attempt to give "scientific" credibility in an age when Western science dominates ideologically and, thereby, commands the dollars — public and private. But whatever you think of Western mathematical, physical and chemical sciences (I for one have serious doubts about a lot of it), Western social science, so-called, makes

Back to the Future (I, II and III) seem like hard-core truth.

Thomas Szasz certainly taught us all a great deal about *mental illness* when he made plain in his 1960s book *The Myth of Mental Illness* that the classificatory network of so-called "Abnormal Psychology" (sometimes called *DSM-III*) — and, in particular, the classification known as *schizophrenia* had everything to do with what the insurance companies, police, courts, asylums and prisons needed and virtually nothing to do with any valid scientific (not to mention compassionate) analysis of human emotionality and pain. But Szasz's focus — a totally valid one — was primarily about the *classificatory myth of mental illness.* What I was urging then and have continued to urge in theory and, more importantly, in practice for the past quarter of a century (as have many of you) was a more careful examination of the *myth of psychology.* For, in my opinion, it is psychology's pseudo-scientific *mode of explanation* (*addiction* being but one member of an extended family of mythic psychological explanatory concepts) which is even more pernicious and dangerous than psychology's mythic system of classification.

Psychology functions as a modern day, secular religion which, for the most part, *does not* create gods (merely *constructs* which *exist because they are believed* — "I think it therefore it is" is a bizarre modern day idealist variation of Descartes' equally bizarre *cogito*) but which creates pseudo-explanatory concepts like *addiction* — *as needed* — to get the grant or the patients or both. My concern is not so much the vulgarly faddish introduction ("discovery") of new diseases or mental problems (bulimia, anorexia, attention deficit disorder, pervasive developmental disorder and even "addiction" *when it is used* in a classificatory sense) but the pretense that psychology is an explanatory mode (or has one) capable of understanding these real human problems (whatever you call them) and, thereby, helping people with them as opposed to simply further classifying and labeling the already burdened consumer in our bloated commodified society. But psychology not only makes a lot of money; it is the historical ideological *rationalization for* human greed, i.e., *for* making a lot of money. Hussein Abdilahi Bulhan makes the point well in his valuable book, *Frantz Fanon and the Psychology of Oppression:* *Previously noted pp. XX-XXI*

From the fourteenth century to the present, Europe and its descendants have been embarked on an unprecedented mission of violence and self-aggrandizement throughout the world. Meanwhile, an intellectual debate on the human condition had been raging in academic circles. A discipline called "psychology" emerged by the sixteenth century, when Philipp Melanchthon, a friend of Luther, coined the term, even though the roots of this new discipline reach back to ancient civilizations. In time, the new discipline flourished and proliferated in various aspects of society. It developed its own concepts, won numerous adherents, evolved its own tradition, won a measure of respectability, and defined a jealously guarded turf. As Europe conquered much of the world, the European imposing as the only honorable model of humanity, the discipline of psychology too emerged as a powerful specialty and a scientific arbiter of human experience.

The discipline of psychology did not of course emerge in a social vacuum unrelated to Europe's history of conquest and violence. From its beginning to the present, the discipline has been enmeshed in that history of conquest and violence. This fact is all too often unappreciated and conveniently avoided. Yet for a discipline known for its commitment to unmask the repressed and for its profusion of studies, such neglect and avoidance of human history and the role of psychologists in that history are curious indeed (1985, p. 37).

In a forthcoming book, *Lev Vygotsky: Revolutionary Scientist*, Lois Holzman and I address this issue as well:

In modern times, an understanding of physical phenomena no longer demands that a moral (ideological) and/or economic (political) account be implicit or explicit in the explanation, as was the case in pre-feudal and feudal times when Aristotelian and scholastic physical science did just that. It was not until this demand was revolutionarily overcome by the rising bourgeoisie's need for knowledge that was quantifiable and measurable and existed right here on earth, and by the radical discoveries of Copernicus, Galileo and others, that the natural sciences were mathematicized, technologized and, thereby, fully liberated from the feudal constraints of teleology and God. To this day, the social sciences (so-called) remain fettered by deistic dogma primarily because these pseudo-sciences are, historically speaking, little more than handservants to the dominant (and false) ideology (political, legal, cultural, moral, etc.) which requires *accountability* and *responsibility* on the one hand (the law must know for example what was done — *in particular* — and, who did it, *in particular*), and which eschews revolutionary activity (the concept and, especially, the *practice*) on the other hand. Hence, Marx's theoretical insistence that *revolutionary practice* is the "peepstone" required to comprehend the *ordinary* dialectical practical-critical activity of *people changing circumstances which are changing them,* i.e., *activity,* and Vygotsky's advancement of that conception with the development of *tool and result* psychological practice is still seen as esoteric, rather than as the 20th century analog to Galileo's revolutionary *Two New Sciences.*

IF you can unders-the...

Vygotsky's extraordinary methodological discoveries (see, for example, *Mind in Society*) and Fanon's critique of psychology as a Eurocentric, white supremacist, male-dominated tool of social oppression and exploitation are nothing less than foundational for creating a non-mythic psychology. Fundamental to Vygotsky's work is the recognition that *activity* — not behavior, not consciousness, neither realities, instruments nor constructs, but *tool AND result activity* (history) — is psychology's *proper* object of study. But what is *activity*? It is, for Marx, Vygotsky and Fanon, human beings collectively *transforming society* by virtue of *making history*. In society we are locked into a hierarchy of roles which we adapt to (well or badly), sometimes by self-coercive constructs. In history *alone* there is activity. Indeed, more accurately history *is* activity, revolutionary activity; the activity of collectivities of people (in various group-determined shapes and forms) challenging *by their activity* the roles of society and *creating for themselves* an environment suitable for *continued human development*. Vygotsky calls such environments Zones of Proximal Development. Social therapists call them *therapeutic communities*. Shabazz calls it Phase: Piggy Back. Wendy Deutelbaum calls it family therapy that deals with "social oppression." Doug Miranda calls it the Black Panther Party before the law enforcement arm of *society* destroyed it. Marx and Fanon called it Revolution.

So, Dr. Leifer, you may now see that your insistence that I "admit" that "social therapy is political action not benevolent treatment" is too weak. In actuality, social therapy is not merely "political action" — it is nothing less than *revolutionary activity*. For it is only when people engage in historical *revolutionary activity* as opposed to *societally overdetermined behavior* that, in my opinion, they may continue to develop and it is only *continued human development* (led by, not independent of, learning, to use Vygotsky's famous formulation) that can "cure" — the individual, the group, the community and the species.

Let me be as clear on these matters as I am able in this limited space. People, in my opinion, do not *construct our own identities.* Collectively, i.e., socially, however, people can engage in *historical, revolutionary activity* (not, of course, necessarily the same thing as "making a revolution") which creates the new environment which can give rise to or *reignite* development at least partially free from the overdetermining adaptive constraints of society. Dr. Martin Luther King, Jr. addressed the matter of adaptation eloquently:

> Today, psychologists have a favorite word, and that word is maladjusted. I tell you today that there are some things in our social system to which I am proud to be maladjusted. I shall never be adjusted to lynch mobs, segregation, economic inequalities, "the madness of militarism," and self-defeating physical violence. The salvation of the world lies in the maladjusted. (Oates, 1982, p.99)

The building of constructs — or networks of them which supposedly yield an identity — is, in my view, but another self-destructive way of adapting to a society not worthy of adapting to. While it may appear to be an egalitarian response to our oppressive social order — a way of doing your own thing — it is, in fact, still another Eurocentric psychological myth. For the societal environment in which we "construct" (and the assumptions of constructivism) are as overdetermining of our mental "constructs" as the building materials available are determining of the bridge. The Cartesian and neo-Cartesian assumptions of constructivism are already exposed by Abdilahi Bulhan in his extraordinary work on Fanon:

> In our view, the limited and uneven advances of this psychology derive from the essentially *solipsist* character of this basic assumption, methods of inquiry, and sources of experiential datum. *Solipsism* is the perspective that only

the "self" exists or can be proven to exist. The dominant psychology is founded and imbued with the outlook that (a) the Euro-American world view is the only or best world view; (b) positivism or neo-positivism is the only or best approach to the conduct of scientific inquiry; and (c) the experiences of white, middle-class males are the only or most valid experiences in the world. The first of these I call *assumptive solipsism;* the second, *methodological solipsism* and the third, *experiential solipsism.* These three types of solipsism interpenetrate and influence one another. Together they form the foundations of Eurocentric psychology (1985, pp. 64-65).

To develop new materials and new assumptions we must revolutionarily reorganize by activity, not mental manipulation, the historical environment which gives rise to them. And to do that is to engage in the quite ordinary, though *uniquely human activity, revolutionary activity.*

My colleague Shabazz, who has done such extraordinary work at Phase: Piggy Back in Harlem for so many years, says he too disagrees with me — that addiction is real. And in supporting this claim he teaches us a good deal about drugs that are cut and the effect of using cut drugs on "withdrawal." I disagree with nothing that he says. But notice in his eloquent statements that he has no use for addiction — indeed, for the most part he doesn't use the term. Surely, drugs and in particular, heroin — cut and/or otherwise — can and do adversely affect our bodies, sometimes severely, sometimes to death. And surely the physical/mental experience in giving up these drugs (so-called *withdrawal*) will vary depending on various social, chemical and psychological factors. There is much disagreement on whether or what "withdrawal" is. But let us leave that fight for others. My contention that there is no such thing as addiction is in no way meant to deny the quite real horrors that are drug use and stopping drug use. In fact, it is meant to focus more clearly on the horror of that reality by eliminating the pretenses of a Eurocentric psychological pseudo-explanation which is what *addiction* really is. In much the way that we must debunk the rhetoric of Euro-American nationalist *patriotism* in order to see what war these past several hundred years really has been, so we must overcome our *seeming dependence* on *addiction* to see what drug use and abuse really are. Shabazz, a Black working class hero, explains a great deal and helps a good many. *Addiction*, a white middle class phony, explains nothing and helps no one.

NOTES

1. The medical model of addiction is a recent concept, the development of which runs concurrent with the application of medical models to a wide range of phenomena which had hitherto been understood morally, religiously or supernaturally. Harry G. Levine (The discovery of addiction: Changing conceptions of habitual drunkenness in America. *Journal of Substance Abuse Treatment,* vol. 2, 1985, pp. 41-57), using alcohol as a case study, traces the development of the current disease model as successor to the moral turpitude model of the Puritan and Temperance movements. Citing M. Foucault (*Madness and civilization: A history of insanity in the age of reason,* New York: Vintage, 1975) and D. J. Rothman (*The discovery of the asylum: Social order and disorder in the new republic,* Boston: Little Brown, 1971) on the subject of the medicalization of insanity, Levine notes that the application of the medical model was part of a trend, "...the medical model of madness, first established at the end of the eighteenth and beginning of the nineteenth centuries in Europe and the U.S., was in fact a medical model of deviance in general, a part of the world view of the middle class" (p. 52). Craig MacAndrew (On the notion that certain persons who are given to frequent drunkenness suffer from a disease called alcoholism, in S.C. Plog and R. Edgerton, *Changing perspectives in mental illness,* New York: Holt Rinehart Winston, 1969, pp. 483-501) goes further, stating that the disease model is a social, not a scientific fact. "...in officially proclaim-

ing that 'alcoholism is a disease' whatever else the proclaimers may be doing, they are not announcing a discovery of fact" and "the success of this latest venture in medical designation is a social-historical attainment, and not a scientific achievement" (pp. 495-496). See also S. Peele, *The diseasing of America: How the addiction industry captured our soul*, Lexington, Mass.: Lexington Books, 1989.

The appellation "disease," however, did not remove the moral judgments inherent in pre-20th century conceptions. Howard J. Shaffer (The epistemology of addictive disease: The Lincoln-Douglas debate. *Journal of Substance Abuse Treatment*, vol. 4, 1987, pp. 103-113) astutely notes that "the contemporary disease model of addiction can be viewed as the moral model metaphorically labelled" (p. 42). The medical community, speaking out of both sides of its mouth, simultaneously says that the addict has an unfortunate disease over which he or she has no control, while the social perception and reception of addicts is that they are weak, unesthetic, messy and to be kept away from.

2. Stanton Peele (Redefining addiction. *International Journal of Health Sciences*, vol. 7, 1977, pp. 103-124; and *Love and addiction*, New York: Signet, 1975, see esp. pp. 19-48) has compiled a comprehensive review of studies which disprove the alleged causal biochemical link for addiction. The evidence includes well documented cases of the absence of withdrawal symptoms upon cessation of administering opiates: abrupt cessation of opiate use upon change in social environment without any rehabilitation, therapy or painful withdrawal; and transfer of use from one class of drugs, e.g., opiates, to another, e.g., amphetamines. Norman E. Zinberg (*Drug, set, and setting*, New Haven: Yale University Press, 1984, esp. pp. 19-45) draws on research he and others conducted throughout the 1970s on drug-using populations which, while they may have been using "addictive drugs," did not exhibit the classic signs of addiction. These signs, according to the World Health Organization definition of addiction, include: (i) compulsion to obtain and take the drug by any means, (ii) tendency to increase the dose, (iii) psychological and physical dependence, and (iv) detrimental effects to the individual and society (Zinberg, p. 29). The mere existence of

substantial populations which are able to use "addictive drugs" in a controlled, non-compulsive fashion itself mitigates against the concept of addiction, at least regarding those particular drugs. The best known single group of controlled drug users is that of medical doctors. Peele (1975, pp. 26-27) also cites studies of middle class professionals who are controlled heroin users, and notes that current figures estimate that one in every hundred physicians is a controlled drug user. Zinberg argues that the drug (the biochemical entity), set (the psychological profile of the user) and setting (the social setting — the whole dynamic of social expectation and social shaping of the experience of drug taking, the cessation of drug taking and withdrawal) constitute a three-way interaction which determines the particular "look" of a case of drug use. Herbert Fingarette, a professor of philosophy at the University of California at Santa Barbara who has served as a consultant on alcoholism and addiction to the World Health Organization, asserts that while "the disease concept of alcoholism not only has no basis in current science, it has never had a scientific justification," and that "there is a consensus among scientists that no single cause of alcoholism, biological or otherwise, has ever been scientifically established," and notes that "the disease model of alcoholism is a harmful myth" and "a big business." (Alcoholism: The mythical disease, originally published in *The Public Interest*, 1988, reprinted in *Utne Reader*, Nov./Dec. 1988, pp. 64-69). See also J. W. Coleman, The myth of addiction, *Journal of Drug Issues*, vol. 2, Spring, 1976, pp. 135-141.

3. Shaef, A .W. (1987). *When society becomes an addict*. New York: Harper and Row.

4. Shaffer, H.J. (1987). The epistemology of addictive disease: The Lincoln-Douglas debate. *Journal of Substance Abuse Treatment*, vol. 4, p. 106.

5. Lotringer, S. (1977). Libido unbound: The politics of "schizophrenia." *semiotexte*, vol. 2, no. 3.

6. Szasz, T.S. (1974). *The myth of mental illness: Foundations of a theory of personal conduct*. (revised edition). New York: Harper and Row.

7. See E. Herman, The twelve-step program: Cure or cover? *Out/Look: National Lesbian and Gay Quarterly*, Summer, 1988; L. Collett, Step by step: A skeptic's encounter with the twelve step program. *Mother Jones*, July/August 1988; both reprinted in *Utne Reader*, Nov./Dec. 1988, pp. 52-63 and pp. 69-76, respectively.

8. See footnote 2.

9. The most striking example of this was provided in the early 1970s by American veterans of the war in Vietnam who, although they were "habitual" heroin users while overseas, returned to America and simply gave up their opiate usage with success rates better than the reciprocal of success rates exhibited by formal drug treatment programs, most involving methadone. See S. Peele, A moral view of addiction: How people's values determine whether they become and remain addicts, in S. Peele (ed.), *Visions of addiction: Major contemporary perspectives on addiction and alcoholism*, Lexington, Mass.: Lexington Books, 1988, pp. 201-233 and 221-222; N.E. Zinberg, *Drug, set, and setting*, New Haven: Yale University Press, 1984, pp. 12-14.

10. Fingarette, H. (1988). Alcoholism: The mythical disease, originally published in *The Public Interest*, reprinted in *Utne Reader*, Nov./Dec. 1988, pp. 64-69, esp. p. 66.

7

COMMUNITY AS A HEART IN A HAVENLESS WORLD

I've been looking forward to giv-
ing this talk, and that's a problem. When I'm looking forward this
much to giving a talk, I really get into it; I think about it. I wake up
in the middle of the night and it gets bigger and bigger and bigger,
and then I wind up trying to say so much that no one knows what
the hell I'm talking about. So I've decided to try to remedy that.
I've asked my very dear friend and distinguished colleague, Dr.
Lenora Fulani, to be up here with me so that she can periodically
say to me, "Fred, no one knows what the hell you're talking
about." Then, when I've finished, I invite *all* of you to tell me I

*"Community as a Heart in a Havenless World" was delivered as a talk entitled
"The Politics and Psychology of Community" on November 9, 1990 as the annual
lecture of the East Side Institute for Short Term Psychotherapy.*

don't know what the hell I'm talking about. But please bear with the sprawling quality. I'm very eager to share these thoughts with you.

Back in the 1970s an article came out that was very unusual because it actually had something to say. I don't have much confidence in articles, be they in learned journals, newspapers or wherever they might appear. I grew up in a working class family and got a Ph.D., so I have an appropriate distrust for the academic. But this article (it was actually a series of articles) was quite good. It was by Christopher Lasch — some of you may have heard of him (most of you probably haven't and that makes sense). It was called, "The family as a haven in a heartless world." The title itself suggested it could possibly be worthwhile, and it was. Lasch was talking about the crisis of the traditional family as part of the crisis of our society and about a new role that the family was playing in a world, a society, a culture, that had become completely heartless.

He pointed out that the family was more and more becoming a haven, a place to hide from the cruelty, the ugliness, the tragedy, the oppression, the pain, the torture of this society in which we all find ourselves living. We didn't decide this was the moment in history we were going to come around; that just happened to us. We are all here together in a world that can be very, very cruel for many people. For some, to be sure, it's more cruel than for others, but it's cruel not just for a handful, but for billions of our people.

So "The family as a haven in a heartless world" moved me because it addressed, in an intelligent and passionate way, this cruel world and the changing role of the family in it. But ultimately, in my opinion, the paper was wrong. I don't condemn it for that. Actually, a paper that's worth reading is something to be applauded even if it's completely wrong. When people attack the New Alliance Party, I always think: "Gee, even if everything that Lenora Fulani is doing, if everything she says, is wrong, she should still be applauded." Some people find that very strange. I think it's important to applaud not truth in the abstract, but the passionate efforts of human beings to try to change things in a cruel world. But that's just an aside.

So this paper by Christopher Lasch was, I think, wrong. I want to tell you a little bit about why I think it was wrong, but first I want to tell you the working title of tonight's talk. It actually comes out of that essay by Lasch. I want to talk about community tonight and what we mean by community, the psychology of community, the politic of community. And I want to call this talk, acknowledging my debt to Christopher Lasch, "The community as a heart in a havenless world." That's what I want to talk about because the profound mistake of Lasch's paper, in my opinion, is that there is no haven, there is no place to hide. There is no escaping the cruelty, the pain, the torture.

Many people try. People look to families, to intellectual endeavor, to relationships, to drugs, to crime; people look to politics; people look everywhere to find a haven. But there is, in my opinion, no haven. I want to talk about community not as a haven, not as a place where we can go and hide, but as an active principle, as a human, passionate, living environment which has the capacity to nourish those of us who are committed to engaging the cruelty of a havenless world. I want to talk about that kind of community.

One of the recent attacks on Dr. Fulani, the New Alliance Party, the Castillo Cultural Center, and me, was made by a grouping called Queer Nation. They put out a leaflet, which is their prerogative — we live in a democracy, or so we're told — and they did some violent things as well, but that's another issue (I don't care to critique them tonight). In their attack, one of the things they said to the Castillo Cultural Center, in the best tradition of vigilanteism, was "We don't want you in our community!" You've all heard that one, right? "We don't want you in our community!" I thought about that. "We don't want you in our community."

I was reading a batch of letters written to a judge who presided over a case that the New Alliance Party brought to guarantee our First Amendment right to demonstrate at Gracie Mansion, up at 85th Street on East End Avenue. We did several demonstrations there. Many people in that community, which is a white, upper middle class community, wrote letters to the judge. What they said in those letters was, "Don't let those poor people, those Black people, those gay people, those Latino people, those progressive people, don't let them in our community! Keep them out of our community! The property values will go down" (or something like that). "My kid will see a Black person." One letter, and this is almost a direct quote, said, "We moved over here to find an enclave where we could hide out." These letters said, "Maybe we should move Mr. Dinkins to Ellis Island so he won't be a magnet attracting these Black people around here....My kids went out to their park (this is a public park they're talking about; you'd never guess we pay taxes for it) and saw Black people....Don't come into my community....Stay out of my community."

I've been thinking about that in preparing these comments tonight. It makes me think about a lot of things — about the racism, the homophobia, the nastiness, the ugliness, the inhumanity, of what we've come to. But it made me think as well about what it is that people mean by this word "community." People throw that word around. "Community" here, "community" there, "community" this, "community" that. "My community." "Our community." "Not your community but my community." People use this word community, but what is meant by it? What do they mean by community and what is it that *we* mean by community?

Dr. Fulani [in her opening remarks — Ed.] went over some of the statistics from Tuesday, Election Day. I don't want to repeat them, though I'm tempted. Thirty-two thousand people voted for this sister for governor of New York State. What happens to those people as they're talked about in the establishment press? Well, they're not people at all to the establishment press. In the establishment press they're called "voters." And the establishment press says certain things about them as voters. It says, "They're voters and they're not enough voters to relate to as human beings. They're voters who only make up .8% of the voters who went to the polls, so let's dehumanize them. We won't even say they were there. We won't count them because they're voters and when you classify them, when you label them, when you label us, when you label the people here as voters, then you can say a whole bunch of things about us which effectively say that we don't count as people! All those folks in jail, they're not sisters and brothers in jail, they're not sisters and brothers, human beings, they're "prisoners!" They're "dangerous," they're "murderers," they're "bad people." They're "Black people," they're "Latino people," they're "statistics." They "cost us taxes." They're not human beings because they're appropriately labeled to deny they're real people. You don't think the 32,000 people who voted for Lenora B. Fulani are real people? In fact, I suspect that some of them are probably in this room right now! But the tens of thousands of those people who are not in this room tonight are not "voters." They're women and men, Black, Latino and white; they're gay and straight; they're human beings with pain and problems, with children, without children; they're living, working, eating right now, and they form a community of people, not "voters" but people, who have the courage to come together and stand up and defy being imprisoned in the categories of those people who use language like, "This is *our* community; get the hell out!"

So I want to introduce a whole new concept of community. I hope this makes sense. I want to talk about *us*. This group of people right here and all those people we relate to, our friends, our neighbors, our families, our sisters and brothers in the prisons and out of the prisons, in our communities — that 10% in the 56th Assembly District who came out and voted for Lenora B. Fulani, the million people up in Massachusetts who came out of the Black and Latino communities and passed Question 4, which eases the ballot access requirements for independent and third party candidates, which is the most democratic resolution ever passed in the history of the United States of America. I want to talk about the 227,000 people who voted for Martin Ortega to retain ballot status for the Illinois Solidarity Party in the State of Illinois. I want to talk about the 90,000 people who voted for Elizabeth Muñoz, a Chicana activist, for governor of California on the Peace and Freedom Party line. But I don't want to — and we must not let ourselves — talk about and think about these people as statistics, because they are part of our community. They are part of our community as they engage the cruelty of this heartless society.

What I mean by community — our kind of community, this kind of community, the kind of community that I just pointed to, from Massachusetts to Illinois to California — is a community which takes responsibility for defining what community is. The folks who run the show in this cruel world usually do the defining, and they do so by a lot of means. They do it with big dollars. They do it with major institutions that control the newspapers and television stations; they control the schools; they control the money. Fulani came in second to Mario Cuomo in ten Assembly Districts despite the fact that she spent $165,000 and he spent $8.3 million. This man — the governor of New York State who couldn't have lost an election if hell had frozen over — spent 8.3 million of our dollars to publicize his silly looking face all over television so that we would come out and vote for him. Think of the pornography of that, the outrage of that. I haven't even got anything against Mario Cuomo as a human being. But I have an objection to him as a pornographic star. It's pornography to spend $8.3 million when sisters and brothers are dying on the streets — that's pornography!

So they control us, Mr. Cuomo and his higher up pals, the ones who gave him that $8.3 million. The list is public information everyone should read. It's like reading the real estate listing of the wealthiest people in New York City. They control with their dollars; they control in all kinds of ways. But I'll tell you one way they control us that we have to look at. They control us by controlling the institutions which define us. They tell us who we are! They tell us how we should think about ourselves. They tell us what we should call ourselves. They say, "Oh, you should call yourself a voter." "Well, gee, I thought I was Joe; I thought I was a person." "No, check the buff card." "Did you sign?" "What Election District are you in?" "What Assembly District are you in?" "Oops, I'm sorry, we don't see your name here." "You're not a voter." "Wait a second, I'm a person." "No, you can't vote...Oh, yes, we found your card, now you can vote."

There are few activities more dehumanizing in this society than voting. Why, in a democratic society, isn't voting made easy? Why don't we have registration right at the election booth like a handful of states in this country do? Why don't young people get registered automatically when they turn 18? Why don't we do handstands to make sure that as many as possible can participate, instead of the powers-that-be doing handstands to make sure that as few people as possible participate? Thirty-four percent of the eligible electorate voted on Tuesday. I guess that means 66% of the people, the real people, said, "Give me a break Mario...Give me a break."

They define us, they define our communities. You see people defining community for you. Queer Nation says, "You people are not wanted in our community." *Your* community? Who defined that one? Who said it was your community? The community led by this sister over here [Dr. Fulani] has a very special characteristic, a radical democratic characteristic. It is a community that defines itself. That *defines itself*. That says, "We will decide who we are and how we are and how we relate, what our conditions are. We won't be defined; we won't be locked away; we won't be put in a room somewhere; we won't be put in a house, even a wonderful house like the mayor's house, or the Castillo Cultural Center or any other house. We will be a community that is in this world and we will define ourselves relative to the activity of being a place in this world, an activity in this world, a practice in this world that's going to do something about the cruelty and heartlessness. We will be an activist community of people and no one, least of all the people who control the heartless institutions, is going to tell us what our community is. *We* will decide what our community is."

Sylvere Lotringer wrote a good article called "Libido unbound: the politics of 'schizophrenia'" about 15 years ago. In it he said, "One does not cure neurosis, one changes a society that cannot do without it."

Some people ask, "How does social therapy work?" "What is this social therapy stuff?" Well, one way of curing pathology is by people taking responsibility for redefining what madness is. Dr. Fulani has a favorite quote from Dr. King. The gist of what he said is this: Maladjusted? Some people talk about the maladjusted. Who are the maladjusted? The maladjusted are those people who won't adjust to the racism and sexism and cruelty and ugliness and homophobia and vulgarity of this society. That's who's maladjusted. That's what maladjusted really means. Maladjusted? said Dr. King. Count me amongst the maladjusted. I'm proud to be maladjusted. I won't adjust to this world; I won't adjust to this society and those who really need to have their heads examined! Dr. King had a degree in theology but he was a brilliant psychologist.

How does social therapy cure? Collectively, as a community,

as a grouping of people, as human beings, we take on the responsibility for redefining what madness is. "Well," you might say, "that's crazy!...You can't define what madness is." Well, where do you think the definition came from in the first place? Do you think it was written on a stone? Is madness actually covered by the 11th Commandment? Where do you think these ideas of madness came from? Where do you think the people responsible for *DSM-III* — which is the official guide to all the varied forms of madness in our culture — got them from; who do you think they are? "Oh, they're scientists...They looked around and very carefully discovered these symptoms, etcetera, etcetera, and so on and so forth." No! People, democratically, must take responsibility for saying who we are, for saying who's crazy, how we're crazy, whether we're crazy.

To start with, we don't have enough emotions. "Oh, you mean we're not emotional enough?" No, although that's also true — but we don't have enough emotions. I mean, how many are there? "What the hell are you talking about, how many are there?" Well, just look through the psychology books. You'll find a handful of emotions there. Eight, nine, ten, eleven, a couple of combinations of them. A few more have been added. Anxiety was added in 1844, panic in 1873, but at best we've got about 15 to 20. Well, is that enough? "What the hell are you talking about?" Why don't we create more? What about all the complicated shadings of emotion between sadness and fear? What about the billions of emotional states — there are more emotions in heaven and earth than are dreamt of in their stupid psychology! We have them; we can use them; we can create them; we can define them. We can create a world in which our capacity to feel emotion is profoundly different from what it is now.

So what about us taking that on? What about us defining our community? Defining our emotionality? Defining who we are and how we relate? Not just determining it but defining it?

There are more ways of us relating as human beings than we have ever dreamt of. That's because the people who make up the categories by which we define ourselves and relate have no particular interest in our expressing our capacity to create new emotions and new ways of being. We're talking two party emotionality here! It's not just two party politics — it's two party emotionality. It's two party thinking and it's two party dreaming; it's two party living and two party loving. It's a two party system.

And if you say, "Hey, I don't fit in there," they say, "You've got an option — don't participate." And 80% of the population says, "I won't." But that's not enough, because our people are dying; because our world is cruel; because there is sadness and mortification and inhumanity. It doesn't suffice for us simply to take their third way out. Because actually they have three, not two options. It's two parties and "Stay the hell out! Don't participate...You want to participate? Two parties!" Again, not just in electoral politics. It's two party emotionality; two party life.

We want to create a community, and this sister, Dr. Fulani, is creating that community. You're a part of that community, and millions of others around the country are a part of that community; from the homeless shelters to the 56th AD, all over this country an emerging community is saying, "We will determine who we are and how we are!" That's democracy. Democracy is not plugging into their choices. It has been said again and again and again that it is no real democracy to go to a voting booth in order to select one of the choices someone has handed you. Democracy is when *we* determine the issues and when *we* determine the candidates.

Let me give you an example of what I call democracy. Why don't we suggest to some of our elected officials, the liberal ones, the ones who appear open to change, to new things — why don't we have a national referendum (very democratic, everyone gets a chance to vote) on taking the billions and billions belonging to 3%

of the people who own 53% of the national wealth and redistributing it *to us*. Hey, let's talk democracy. They say, "Oh, you can't do that!" Well, how come we can't do that? "It's not allowed; it's a private property system." But wait a second. You say it's a private property system and I hear you. I read about private property in the Constitution. But I also read about democracy in the Constitution. Maybe we got a little conflict here. Maybe if we exercise democracy the people might say, "You know, I don't mind private property all that much but there's just so much of it in the hands of so few people. If we're going to have private property, why don't we *all* have a little bit of private property? Why don't the homeless sisters and brothers have a place to live? That's the property I'm talking about." Then they say, "Why don't you go back to Russia?" I didn't come from Russia. "Well, go back there anyway."

I had a fantasy dialogue the other day. This person says, "Dr. Newman, I've heard you speak but isn't it really true that you're a communist? Aren't you really a communist?" And in this fantasy dialogue I say, "You mean like the person who won the Nobel Peace Prize this go-around, or like the person who was *Time* magazine's Man of the Decade? You mean like Mikhail Gorbachev? Is that what you mean?" And the person says to me, "Yeah, yeah, yeah, like that." And I say, "No, not like that. If that's what you mean by communist that's not what I'm about; that's not what I'm for; that's not what I'm like. I'm not for a communism which failed because it would not recognize and appreciate the significance of radical democracy or indeed of any democracy at all, any more than I am for a system which is called by other names but also doesn't believe in the democratic right of people — us, the community — to define ourselves." "Well, I guess you're not a communist," the person says. Have it any way you like; what can I tell you?

A woman I have a lot of love for, a friend, a patient, a human being, came into one of my therapy groups the other night very upset. I was very upset that she was very upset. She's very open and honest. She said she had read still another attack on our work. There was this little piece in the *Village Voice*, a nasty piece on an art auction we were doing over at the Castillo Cultural Center, a cultural center which has "a connection to the New Alliance Party." This is how people use language — "It's connected to the New Alliance Party" — as if the Museum of Natural History is not connected to the Republican Party! I've been doing this for such a long time now, I think I've become somewhat jaded — when I read the article I barely noticed that it was an attack. But I don't want to be insensitive. People were affected by it; this sister was upset by it.

What she shared with me was that she has a lot of love for me, a great deal of respect for me; I've helped her a great deal. She views me as an extraordinary and gifted therapist, but when she reads stuff they say about me, or reads my quotes, or hears me on a stage like this, she sits there and cringes and says, "Why is this dear and brilliant guy who I love and who helps me enormously, why is he being a nut case? Why can't he just be a decent middle class guy who doesn't say things like, 'The *Village Voice* is a bunch of Stalinists who are trying to stick an ice pick into the Castillo Cultural Center'? Why can't he give an appropriately balanced critique — 'Well, the *Village Voice* has its opinion; we have a right to ours...'?"

Well, *they* define a community in which we have to be balanced. Am I to be balanced when the people writing these vicious articles don't think twice about the fact that there are human beings on the other end? Am I to be balanced when these people were effectively attempting to make sure that money was not made by the Castillo Cultural Center, a significant portion of which goes to help people who are dying of AIDS and people who are homeless? Am I to be balanced when someone might be dying now because the *Village Voice* had the audacity to not be aware that there are human beings behind their stupid, vicious, sectarian, vulgar words? Am I to be balanced about that? I won't be balanced when I see people lying on the street dying because they have no home. I will not be balanced. Call me the biggest madman in town. I appreciate it. I'm a crazy son of a bitch around that issue and I hope to hell you are too. If not, just where the hell are you coming from?

Now none of this anger is directed at that sister and I love her openness and I love who she is. We have to build a community, Lenora Fulani's community, the New Alliance Party's community, which says, "Hey, we're even going to redefine anger." They've defined anger and they've treated it as a certain kind of problem. They've taught us how to direct it at the wrong people, including ourselves, and they've taught us how to be hurtful with it to other people; for men to hurt women, for straight people to bash gay people, for white people to destroy Black and Latino people. They've taught us what anger is. After all, anger is as anger does. You see, anger is not some abstraction. Anger is a practice. And they've taught us how to practice anger. They've told us who to hate and who to be angry at and what to do to those people and how to talk to those people and how to avoid those people.

We've got to redefine anger. Hey, I'm angry, but I'm going to do something else with this anger. In my community, in the community that we build, I want that anger to be a source of energy, not to destroy ourselves, not to destroy anybody, but to be used, together with all the other newly defined emotions, to build, to reorganize, to create. "Oh, you can't do that with anger. Anger is negative." No, no, no. We define anger in our community.

People in our community say, "Gee, I'm really feeling awful. I can't do anything. I can't change anything, least of all me. You talk about change and I can't change." Well, maybe we have to change what you mean by change. "What do you mean?" People have been taught to think change means "change myself." They come into therapy and they say, "I want to change me. I want me to change. I want me to be this way; I want me to be that way. I want me to look this way; I want me to look that way. I want me to be nine feet tall instead of six feet tall. I want me to be Black instead of white, or white instead of Black, or gay instead of straight. I want to have a nose that goes like that instead of like this. I want to have ears that…I want to change me. I want to change me! Give me some drugs; give me some booze; change me!"

But what if we redefine what changing means? Let's talk about how, together in our community, we can change this world of ours. What about if we're the changers rather than the objects of change? What if we are an active community of people who know how to build and change and take what we have and create new things and not simply change "me" — because it's *their* modality that says that you should change you. They have created an environment in which people are so geared toward individual upward mobility that they can get their heads high enough in the air so they don't have to notice the people sleeping in the streets of New York City. That's not *this* community.

They define things and they control us by their definitions. Those of you who follow the labor movement might be aware that a funny thing has happened in the last 20 years. There used to be strikes in America. Once upon a time workers struck — workers don't strike anymore. There are no strikes anymore — there are only lockouts in America. Redefine things.

I know what some of you must be thinking. "How can you redefine things without changing material conditions? You talk about redefining, redefining — are you some kind of weirdo idealist? You're supposed to do this in your head and then everything's better? Is redefinition going to get rid of poverty? Is it going to get houses for the homeless? Is redefining going to get more food on the table for people who are starving? Is redefining going to get 300,000 troops out of Saudi Arabia?" I know a lot of you leftists out there are saying, "Ah, I knew this Newman was some kind of Hegelian nut. Redefining, redefining; it's a mental trip; it's a guru trip. What about the material reality of it all?"

Hey, listen, we can't make a new world out of redefining things in a way which denies what's there. We can't redefine ourselves so that we can fly, because we can't fly. And there's a lot of things we can't do because of our material limitations.

But the serious issues we're addressing here are the things we *can* do materially that we're not doing because we have been controlled by their institutionalized definitions to have us be voters; to have us be locked into this community and out of that community; to have us be Black and have us not vote for white folks; to have us be gay and have us not talk to straight folks; to have us be men and be abusive to women. No! I'm talking about the ways in which we are able to do fantastically more than what we now do. I'm talking about the fact that millions of us in this country are not going out to the polls and voting in our self-interest. We are voting for people who are kicking us in the stomach. And that won't change unless we learn how to create community.

We are a part of a community that includes millions of people. I'd like us to reflect on that for a moment. Again, I want us to think about last Tuesday — Election Day — as a "Community Defining and Redefining Day." All across the State of Massachusetts, over a million human beings defined themselves as part of our community. You say, "Ah, come on, Fred. Give me a break. All they did was go out and vote for a damned Question 4." No, that's not all they did. Because if you look at the substance of what they voted for, they said, "Let's open the door to new possibilities." Television stations were saying, "Don't vote for Question 4 because if you do there will be too many new parties on the ballot and we won't be able to cover them all conveniently and people will be confused when they go to the voting booth." No one's going to the voting booth and they're worried about people being confused when they go to the voting booth!

The people who define us don't want new possibilities. How many candidates do I want on the ballot? Seventy, 80, 90, 100, a million — let's have a million candidates for attorney general! And let every one of them talk through the night on television. They'll talk and say, "I'm a this and I'm a that." But why do we have to spend all these hours listening to only Robert Abrams? Why not have national referenda on one issue after another? Why not have a national referendum right now on whether we should get out of Saudi Arabia? Why not? We have the technology to do it in two days. We have to make it happen. Radical democracy! We have to have a politic and psychology of community where we define what community is, where ultimately we define what redefine is. *That's* radical democracy.

I'm starting a new group. When I first started doing therapy about 20 years ago I was kind of locked into the traditional categories. I wasn't really so traditional but I figured I'd better do some traditional things first. So I used to see one person at a time. I used to be pretty good at it, say the right thing now and again, make solid interpretations. When folks are hurting and you help, they'll give you money. I moved out of that into group therapy, bigger and bigger groups. So this is an announcement tonight. I'm starting a new therapy group, a weekly group, and I want to have about 100-plus members in it. I want to do real serious therapy. I want to do *community* therapy. I want to have a group where people are working on their emotional problems by literally creating community and where the numbers are such that it's impossible to fake it for a year or two thinking that maybe your turn will come to do a little private therapy. There are always people in my group thinking, "I'll hang out while we're doing this building-the-group stuff but at some point, maybe a year and a half down the road, it'll be my turn." But if you're looking at 100 to 150 people, you're thinking, "My turn? I'll be dead before my turn!"

So I'm starting a new group of about 100 people, for pay. People say, "What kind of socialist/communist are you? You're always making people pay money." People say that. It's remarkable. My being a socialist or communist depends on what I *do* with my money — not whether or not you pay me. So I want people to sign up tonight for my 100-plus weekly group. To my friends I've referred to it as "mob therapy." I do small groups compared to my colleague, Dr. Fulani, over here — she's the real mass therapist. She's doing groups with millions. But I'd like you to come on board. I'd like people to see the curative element of building self-defining community.

I have another thing I want to do tonight, and this is truly crazy. I'm writing a book right now on this guy Lev Vygotsky, a brilliant guy, a Russian Jew, who died in 1934: he wrote some extraordinary stuff. I was going to talk about him tonight. I woke up in the middle of the night last night thinking about four hours' worth of stuff I could do on Lev Vygotsky — I'll spare you that. But I'd like to share something of what he said and then do something based on it. When I talk about community, self-defining community, activist community, I am not talking about cults. I am not talking about a community which goes off to Vermont or Jonestown or wherever and tries to build something which isolates itself from the community of the people of the world. I'm talking about a community of people which lives inside the broader community of people and constantly interfaces and connects and overlaps with the broader community of this city, of this state, of this country and of this world. I'm not talking about redefining community by being some inside-looking group, an inner-directed grouping. No, I'm talking about this community being an active social force which makes the demand that *all* communities — the community of human beings, women and men, gay and straight, Black, Latino and white — all of us must redefine community. I'm talking about a community which nurtures the activity of demanding and urging the redefinition of community.

The point here is that this community of ours is not just a community in this circle over here — it's a community which is constantly reshaping. It changes shape every moment. This is a Vygotskian concept. That's a hard thing to learn how to do. People are socialized to want and need stability in our culture. But the world isn't stable. Even in the best of times the world isn't stable. It moves, it grows, it changes, and we can move and change and grow and do things and we don't know it. We are socialized not to know it. We are socialized not to be aware of the fact that we can go to the right on the ballot and vote column G. We are socialized to believe that we only have *these* kinds of possibilities and not *those* kinds of possibilities.

Here's the crazy thing here, hold tight — I think we should change our shape right now. I don't want to coerce anybody so you can all do whatever you choose to do. If you want to sit, fine. But I know what I want to do and I want to ask Dr. Fulani to join me. We've gone a lot of places together so I'm hoping that she will join me. I'd like us all to get up and walk down these aisles, walk right outside the door of this high school, stand out on the street and say as loud as we can together, "NO JUSTICE, NO PEACE! NO JUSTICE, NO PEACE! *WE* DEFINE COMMUNITY! *WE* DEFINE COMMUNITY!" I'd like us to go out there for about one minute and then come on back, sit ourselves down and ask hellishly hard questions. But I'd like us to go out and tell this community that we don't have to be locked into these seats. Let's go out and define our community.

APPENDIXES

DIALOGUE ON
"CRISIS NORMALIZATION AND DEPRESSION"

The dialogue that follows is from the question and answer session directly following Dr. Newman's presentation and subsequent discussions among the East Side Institute staff and trainees.

You say that "history cures depression." Perhaps; but what are you going to do in the real world when two ambulance attendants bring in a young lady, carry her into your office, she sits in the corner, she hasn't eaten for 10 days and does not respond to anything you have to say?

Well, I'd do precisely as I described. So it must be that you're saying that that's not a proper approach for the immediacy of this crisis. All the different approaches can and need be taken. The question is not which approaches you take, it's rather what you take these approaches *to be*. This has a profound impact on the direct relationship in the real world. We are trained in such a way as to call the real world the world which exists simply at the object level of direct response to the immediate presentations. But this is the illusory, not the real, world. The real world includes the historicalness which is the process by which these objectified responses are but the immediate presentation. That's the point I'm speaking to. So yes, of course, I have met such people and I treat such patients. They come to see me and those are exactly their responses. What I am insisting upon is that whatever one's object-level approach, without the inclusion of historicalness one is effectively leaving something of enormous significance out of the treatment.

Now what does that look like? It looks like coming to terms with the historicalness of whatever immediate approach it is that you are taking. I personally believe that the approaches should be as varied as what is helpful for a human being in pain. But I don't think that, in the name of pragmatism, we should buy in on the institutional categories so as to leave the person permanently locked in that position. I've worked with many people who have gone through a process where development is rekindled by virtue of a connection to this historical process. In my opinion, if we cannot restimulate growth, then we are truly limited to aspirins. So I don't want to leave anybody with the impression that what I'm describing here is an abstraction, because it does deal with the immediacy of a situation. One must. The issue is whether you're completely organized by the immediacy of the situation. Everything that we're taught and trained to do socializes us to be thus organized. What I am urging is breaking out of that kind of training, not by way of giving up what is most valuable about it, but rather by *using* what is most valuable about it. The search for definition is an invalid search. The search for historical location is a valid search. What techniques are used along the road? All and any that are helpful. But not just treatment relative to finding some place for the person you're relating to. No, not just giving someone a drug so we can find a spot for them. Not the activity of putting a label on somebody and putting them somewhere. No, not that.

Going beyond diagnosis to treatment, wouldn't you say that the application of social therapy is to become involved actively in understanding and working on the social problems that contribute to depression and anger?

Strangely enough, I think the answer is no. In July, I gave a talk to the Congress of the Interamerican Society of Psychology in Cuba where I developed the conception of relating to the patient as a revolutionary. This means relating to someone as a human being capable of transforming her or his social environment. Whether one chooses to do so is another issue. In fact, it seems to me that it is most important to relate to someone as a revolutionary when the patient is not one. To put it candidly, I'm willing to run the risk that, if one empowers people, they will do progressive things. I have seen that when people are free from the constraints of societal definition, they do very positive, nourishing, and progressive kinds of things. Therefore, our concern is primarily to help people to become empowered and to allow their social activities to flow, as it were, from themselves. I am a very strong critic of so-called radical therapy. I think it failed, on scientific, social and cultural levels, to simply take the risk of empowerment and go from there. We have come to see that empowerment need not establish an end, because people will establish ends that are consistent with the continuation of empowerment. Empowerment feels good. Depression feels lousy. I'm ready to bank on that. People, as they are currently locked up and classified in society, are in serious trouble. They have to be helped from their state of depression into an empowered historical state. And from there, people need to be allowed to, as it were, roam free. I'll take my chance on people in history.

How do you get people into an empowered, historical state?

By finding effective means to get them out of their chains. People are powerful when they are in a position to go through a social/psychological/cultural process of coming out of the ideological, societal, political chains that keep them disempowered. I think that the natural state of the human being is powerful, not in chains. The work, then, is to help people not simply find another set of chains, or an accommodation to being in chains, or a way of painting the chains so we can pretend that they're bracelets, but rather to come to terms with the social-historical origins of those chains. This is specific to different individuals, since we all have different histories and are imprisoned in various ways to varying degrees. These histories are critical for us to take control of. Taking control of our history has, as a precondition, not simply having a cognitive awareness of it, but the restructuring or reorganizing of it. We only come to know our history by participating actively in its creation. Creating a new relationship or a new community — one that is qualitatively different, is part of creating a new history. It would be qualitatively different by being self-consciously determined, developed, built, and organized by those who participate in the process, which includes, necessarily, a constant engagement of the limiting circumstances of our current societal location. Now that's an altogether different paradigm than adapting to a societal situation. It's not adaptive to society — it's adaptive to history. I am not anti-adaptive. Let's adapt to history — not to society.

Why does this disease only select certain members of our culture?

What made the stock market go crazy on Monday [October 19, 1987]? The conditions which made the stock market go crazy on Monday were present for some time. As a philosopher of science, I have spent more hours than I care to remember attempting to distinguish between condition and cause, trying to make the subtle distinction between what are the objective conditions and what is that efficient cause that made something happen at a precise moment. I hope you don't regard this as a hedge, but frankly, my answer is that I don't think the question is answerable. Moreover, I don't even think that it is desirable to attempt to answer it. The distinction between condition and cause is ultimately not a valid distinction. Moreover, I think the search for cause is ultimately a dead-end search, one that has been more harmful than helpful.

What I would urge is that we move to search for the totalistic set of conditions.

Take a social problem like illiteracy. It is still the case that some people live right next door to each other and one person learns and the other person doesn't. One could approach the issue of illiteracy, therefore, in a way which overly focuses on that kind of issue. Or one could approach the issue of illiteracy from the vantage point of the conditions which establish the mass phenomenon of illiteracy. This is what we must do *vis à vis* the issue of depression if we take depression not to be abnormal but a normal state. What I am urging here is a mass psychological approach, which has a profound influence on every individual who participates in the transformation of the conditions which produce depression, as opposed to an approach which seeks to identify the definitional causes of a particular individual's depression.

Social therapy purports to be a theory of human life which counts on the activity *of human beings, not on the passivity of human beings. Isn't the premise that human beings are nothing more than products of our environment antithetical to the conception of the human being as active? How is this contradiction resolved?*

Let me try to answer that by talking more about depression. One of the ways we can approach depression is to try to eliminate loss. If we can do away with loss, then even by the criteria that the traditionalists have laid down, we probably can do something about depression. But most of the people who research and write about depression take both the phenomenological experience of it and the actual socio-historical phenomenon of loss as something which goes without saying. The issue then becomes figuring out what to do about how people respond to loss. *But*, what if we get rid of loss? What if we no longer have losses? Wouldn't that be a breakthrough in the treatment of depression? I actually think we have a better chance of eliminating losses than we have of eliminating depression if we hold onto losses. I think that if we hold onto losses, depression simply follows.

Scientifically speaking, then, our best shot is to go after loss and forget about depression. I don't think this has to be seen in merely grandiose terms. Loss is something we can learn to transform in the collective activity of changing the relatively mundane totalities of our daily lives. People tend to treat losses as somehow primordial: "Losses simply happen to us!" But they don't simply happen; the concept and phenomenon of loss is particularized to a specific societal organization of human life. Can we do something about that? What would it take to change the whole societal arrangement? It probably falls outside the scope of the social therapy group! But it doesn't follow that you can not make those kinds of changes within the limited environments of totalities that we relate to in our everyday lives. So it's important that you don't take what I'm saying as "we have to change the whole world and then people won't be depressed anymore." What I'm saying is that there is a methodology for the transformation of environmental and social totalities of a very mundane variety.

How can you not have loss?

Why do you have to have loss? Why do you have to lose something?

It's a natural reaction. I think it's an emotion.

When you say it's natural, are you suggesting that in all cultures — past, present, and future — people have the same reaction to, for example, the ending of a relationship? Is that what "natural" implies? *eg. - The way the Hopi Deal @ "Divorce."*

It just seems that no matter where you place a person, in any part of history, even in the future, that's going to be a reaction a person's going to have.

But it's not even true of cultures in the past. As a matter of fact, the ways in which people respond to relationships ending vary enormously from culture to culture.

Can you give me some examples?

There are a great many studies showing that people do not respond with the social behavior that we identify with the loss of relationships. There are cultures where people relate to endings of relationships as relatively natural parts of the life process. Some peoples relate to death, for example, very differently than we do. There are differences within our own culture, although to be sure, there is much overlap. But I'm trying to engage the issue of your insistence that it is a natural phenomenon rather than a societally determined one. It is not an integral part of the human being that we have to have the particular experience that you are identifying as loss. It is not natural at all. On the other hand, I'm not saying that it is unnatural, meaning that there is something wrong with it. We are, after all, products of the social conditioning of our culture, so we do, in fact, have these kinds of experience. They are deeply ingrained and profoundly reinforced, so much so that it is quite understandable that you would react to how I'm talking about loss by saying, "This is crazy! The feeling of loss is natural!" But if we pursue this a bit, we begin to see that it is not so much natural as it is, in a complex way, social. There are conditions which lead us to organize our environments in certain ways. So certainly the experience of deprivation is going to be one kind of experience in a society which is undersupplied and a different kind of experience in a society which is not undersupplied. Deprivation means very different things for different people in our culture, people of different classes, different ethnicities, etc. But again, I must add that I'm not even talking about broad socio-cultural changes to eliminate loss; I actually think that people can learn to have a different experience of loss within the relatively narrow set of environments that we engage on a day to day basis. But to do so involves learning how to transform totalities. That is the key activity; that is the activity that we are free to do as human beings.

What do you do instead of "lose it"?

Why do you have to do anything "instead of"?

You have to do something.

I used to teach Summerhill teachers who were supposedly liberated teachers. They came to a course that I gave at the Summerhill Society. I would describe radically different schools. I'd say "Let's eliminate subjects," and they'd raise their hands and say, "What will we have *instead* of subjects?" Why do we have to have anything instead of subjects? Why not just throw the whole damned category out? Changing totalities is not taking out some elements of the totality and putting in a new set of things. That is putting new elements into a formally identical totality. To transform a totality means something much more precise and complex than that activity. We don't have to have an "instead."

But to give a truly adequate answer to your question involves spelling out a whole new social therapeutic approach to depression. Since we don't have time and I don't have it totally clear, I can just begin to lay out some of the initial thinking. Why do I say that losses are bound to society more than to history? It is because I think that the social experience of life *in history* is not the experience of the alienated object which is subjective loss, but of the social process of which the object is but a description of one of its stages. Part of what it means to be in history is to experience the chair not as a commodified object, a product totally isolated from the social-productive process which led to it, but rather to experience the social-productive process. The name that we give to this relatively stable moment of its existence is *chair*. But it is possible that there are cultures, not just futuristic cultures but past cultures, where the immediacy of the productive process leads to a totally different view of the world such that what is viewed is not alienated and separated-out objects, products or commodities; *rather, the viewed experience is social process.* When the ontology of perception, i.e., what you view and experience, is social process, then the concept of loss is altogether different. In fact, it is not at all clear to me that under those circumstances loss has any meaning. Because what you actually wind up viewing is the transformation of the complex interweave of social process.

The notion of loss is very much tied to the development of commodified societies. Loss is fundamentally, in my opinion, an economic term. Does it have emotive meaning? Of course it does, because terms which are fundamentally economic come to have meaning in all areas of life. But this concept of loss is basically the elimination, destruction, obliteration of what is already the alienated product of the social process of development, production. Our world is filled with these alienated objects called commodities. Commodities behave in strange ways. For example, they can disappear. They can go out of existence in a way that social processes can't. Social processes continue. Commodities go out of existence (which is rather convenient for those who produce them). Part of what we do in the short term crisis normalization model is, as it were, to get people out of their role-determined location in society and move them (modestly, to be sure) into history so as to elongate their sense of social process so they are not overwhelmed by the wrenching of the gestalt of their life, this gigantic element, this loss. This rupture is profound when your view of the world is of a framed object — you rip that out and it is exceedingly difficult to see the world. We attempt to deal not merely with the missing object — e.g., by trying to replace it (even though it is irreplaceable) or pretending that what happened didn't happen — but with the *frame* of the picture. The primary focus is to break down that frame, because until you bust open that frame, the experience of deprivation will be so overwhelming, the sense of loss so great, that people can remain paralyzed in crisis. This positive process of opening up — rather than staying confined within — that frame, is an example of dealing with totalities rather than dealing with elements.

APPENDIX B

DIALOGUE ON "PANIC IN AMERICA"

The dialogue that follows is from the question and answer session directly following Dr. Newman's presentation.

What do you mean by adaptation to history?

An important distinction for social therapy is the distinction between society and history. A society is understandable as an historical spatio-temporal moment, an organized moment of history wherein a certain set of institutions come together in complex ways to create a certain kind of environment filled with ideological and cultural norms. But they are all, from an historical perspective, temporary, and exist intermingled with the continuity of human species development and historical development. We are all, as it were, in a schizophrenic life situation. We are all part of some society. Yet we are also part of the extended process of historical development that goes back millions, indeed billions, of years and, hopefully, if we can manage to deal with George Bush and Dan Quayle, into the future for quite a way as well.

A part of the human condition is the conflictedness between those two, because there are different values, different standards, different social actions and social policies depending upon the extent to which we relate to society and/or how we relate to history. For example, an institution like the family is societally specific;

that is, the family emerges as a certain kind of institutional phenomenon designed to, among other things, help its members adapt
to a particular society at a particular moment in the history of that
society. But this constantly raises the question of whether or not
that adaptation is likewise an adaptation to history.

Here's a concrete example, albeit an extremely hypothetical
one: Suppose a society has one week to run. It could be the case.
Some societies have at one point in their history had one week left.
We could name such societies. For example, seven days before they
dumped the Shah, the Shah was doing whatever he was doing in
Iran or elsewhere but he actually had only a week to run! He might
not have known it — the CIA apparently didn't — but as a matter
of objective fact Iranian society as constructed had only a week to
run. Question: Suppose you go to your family in that hypothetical
week and say, "Adapt me to this society. I want to be better adapted." But the society has only a week to run. Well now, that raises a
curious question: Is it helpful to adapt to that society?

This might seem like the extreme case, but it comes up again
and again, particularly in the context of a society which is rapidly
destabilizing and deteriorating. As I said before, it's not obvious
that adaptation to such a society is anything that a human being
with a certain set of values would want to do, no less could do. But
are we ready to live our lives in that "flowing river" which is the
historical process? Or are we ready to adapt to the particular
design of the beach made by the river's washing up? We all live,
after all, on that shore as well as in that river. Now, again, I don't
think that's an easy choice, but I think it becomes easier in a situation where adaptation to the society is truly an abomination, a
morally and humanly unacceptable alternative, not to mention
objectively impossible.

People come to social therapy because they're in pain. They
come because they need help. They don't come because they want

to adapt to history any more than people go to psychoanalytic therapists because they want to better understand the interrelationship between egos, ids, and superegos. Yet the treatment approach of social therapy — and people rapidly become aware of this — is adaptation directed at our historical identity, our identity not as narrowly organized and comprehended via the institutions of a given moment, but our identity as it relates to a species, a class, a people, to those historical institutions which pre-date and post-date this particular historical/societal moment.

How do we do that? Well, one of the ways is through the constant challenging of what we call the problem/solution syndrome. When people come into therapy, these decent human beings who come to us every day for help, they come to us with problems. But I've never yet seen any patient — and I've been doing therapy for two decades — who didn't come not only with a problem but with an understanding, perhaps sublimated, perhaps suppressed, of what the solution or the range of solutions to the problem was. This is despite the fact that they are willing to put money on the table for you to help them! Our problems typically come complete with some sense of what the cure is. That's societally organized. In social therapy we don't substitute our cure, which would be simply another societally organized response to people's emotional problems. Rather, we urge people to engage the *socialization* of human emotionality and human pathology. The process by which that's done is exceedingly complex.

What does that look like concretely? People come in and say, "I'm in pain; I'm suicidal; I'm having anxiety disorders. My marriage is breaking up and I'm feeling depressed." So we reply, "How do you know that's what's causing your feeling?" And they say, "Well I *know*; I always feel this way when that happens. Whenever I have a fight with my father, the next day I feel just terrible." "Well, how do you know?" "What do you mean how do I know? This is causally connected!" "Where did you learn that, *how* did you learn that, how did we *all* learn that?"

Goodwin's book suggests very strongly that certain basic emotions are constant throughout history and cultures. In my opinion, that is wrong. Now that's not to deny physiological responses — indeed one of the things proponents of this view typically point to in order to justify their claim are surprise reactions and shock reactions. They say you startle somebody and you get a similar reaction across cultures and throughout history. But the issue is not whether or not you get similar behavioral responses, or even whether you get similar verbal responses. The issue is how emotionality is organized within different cultures. There are different sociocultural ways in which emotionality is organized, e.g., the very meaning of pain, of shame, of sadness, of humiliation, along with the associated behavior, vary dramatically, as a matter of fact. Emotionality and psychopathology are as organized as anything else.

So in social therapy we raise the question of that organization, not just didactically but through a therapeutic process of urging that people work to create an environment which strives to give a reorganization to that emotional process. It's by virtue of this activity that one begins to see the extent to which our psychopathology and emotionality have been organized. It's by virtue of going through an actual process of what we call rekindling or reigniting social development that people can actually go through the process of creating new emotive and attitudinal environments — new environments not simply relative to the existing institutions — to expose themselves to the actual process of the unalienated (to the extent possible) historical production of emotionality. What happens in these groups is that people literally go through a process of resocializing emotionality. Will you "remember," some people worry, how to do emotionality "outside" the way you did it before? Sadly, yes, you won't forget so easily. It is as if someone asked, "If I learn to play the piano will I forget how to chew bubble gum?" No. You can place this new element in your repertoire and you'll still remember all the pathology — don't worry, it won't go away so easily!

Now people become frightened by this: "Will this make me maladapted to society?" "Well, wait a second, you *are* maladapted to society! What we want to do is help you be adapted to history, creating with that, anxiety." But you see, the process of creating the anxiety gives us a particular relationship to it that we did not have in the 19th century when anxiety was imposed as an adaptation to commodified reality. Because even though it's anxiety, it is the creation of our self-conscious activity in an age of panic. We create that anxiety. And I'm not saying it's good because it's ours; I'm saying it's good because we are relatively self-conscious of the process of its production. This gives us a relationship to anxiety as an adaptation to history, which is a synthesis approximating mental health in a very, very sick society. I make no huge claims for social therapy, for I don't know how well you can be in this society.

Why does anxiety have to be created to adapt to history?

The notion of relating directly, purely, unmediatedly, to history at this time is a myth. The truth is that our relationship to history has to be mediated through society until such time when out of this complex process we have the capacity to more directly relate to the historical process. I don't think any one of us is going to see this in our lifetime. To some extent this notion of relating to history is an adaptation, but not one that can be made without the inclusion of society as a mediating vehicle. We have to find some way of relating to society without the dominance of alienation carried to its pre-fascistic extreme. Still, we have to use the mechanisms that are available historically to relate to society, only as part of a triadic relationship, going beyond merely relating to society to relating to history as well.

What I'm saying, in effect, is that we have to find a way of extracting from a decadent society those institutions which are sufficiently viable for us to use in relating to history. You can't create in this society — or any other — things that aren't made up of parts that already exist in the society; you can't make something out of nothing — you'd be a bad scientist to believe in that. We have to build with the existing tools and results, and those tools and results are society's. Therefore, our relationship to those tools has to be itself an adaptive tool and that adaptive tool is anxiety relative to alienated commodified society.

So the process is actually a process of saying, "What can we effectively create within the very body of a society which has gone mad?" It's not unlike what has to happen in the process of trying to stimulate the immunological system in such a way as to fight with a system which is totally cancerous. You can't think that you can simply take the healthy parts and directly use them because they are synthesized within the holistic totality of the body. It's also true that there are elements of the system which we can use in creating whatever we can create to approximate cure.

What we actually have is this three-way relationship. I hope that our children's children's children will not have to be in the position of having to make this kind of compromise. I hope they will live in a world which is much more nourishing and supportive of people. We happen, however, not to live in such a world. And for me, the existential fact of that is the most overwhelming experience of my life.

I walk down the street, as we all do, and see homeless people. Above and beyond all the sociological and political analysis, there's the sheer fact of it. And that raises the profound issue, how could it be that we live in a society in which this is possible? It is to me such a shocking outrage and a statement not about the person on the street but about us collectively as a species. How could this be? Yet the fact is that it is so, and we can't attempt to solve the problem of homelessness by trying to go directly to the solution without mediating it through those elements of society which make it most possible to do something. Dr. Lenora Fulani, a distinguished African American developmental psychologist and activist and recently an independent candidate for President, is here with us tonight. I look at Dr. Fulani and think about her campaign for democracy. If we can make democracy live more, there might be a possibility of doing something about homelessness. We have to find a way to use those elements of an existing social system to deal with the outrage of these problems which directly confront us in history. I think that this experience, at least for me, is close to a direct historical experience. Homelessness is an historical outrage; it is an outrage to us as a collectivity of human beings that a person should be sleeping on the streets of New York. I don't even experience that as a political polemic. I think it's more than that. For me it actually feels quasi-spiritual. How could it be? But it is. We can't deny either of those things — that it is, and that we aren't in a position to confront it directly. I walk down the street and I feel a very strong pull to say, "Dammit, I'm simply going to do something about homelessness right now. I'm going to take people off the streets and put them in my home, then ring a hundred doorbells to put them in those homes, and so on. We cannot allow this! I feel that every day and every night of the week. But it can't be done. I don't say that cynically; I say that sadly.

I wasn't clear about the distinction you were making in choosing history or choosing existence. It seems that you're still choosing to exist if you choose history.

I don't think so; I'll tell you why. You see, the existential model has as its primary social picture the human being in nature. But there's no such thing, never was, never will be, as human beings in nature. Human beings have always been, from the very outset, in social history. We are fundamentally a social species. That's not to say that we're not in nature in the sense that we're in the world or the universe. But our fundamental location is an historical location, not a natural location. So in setting up this existence and essence thing, what's really being said by the existentialists is, choose to be in nature alone, forlorn, in dread, in trembling, hopeless, but still asserting your individuality. What I'm saying is that the alternative has to be between that kind of a choice and the more social, collective choice of trying to adapt and relate directly to one's historic identity.

You see, what they were throwing out in getting rid of essence was history, to the extent that they cared about history in the first place. Existentialism, survivalism, that dominant paradigm as manifest in these various curative models, is very problematic. We have to seek a location in history, not a location in nature such as Sisyphus pushing his rock. No, our identity is fundamentally social, but we have lost that in the process of what's occurred in the course of this century.

When I see Dan Quayle on TV he always looks anxious and talks like a robot. What's that about?

I don't think Dan Quayle has much anxiety left any more than the rest of us do. What Dan Quayle has is extreme panic. I think some of that was exposed during the campaign. However, what he also has are endless techniques for dealing with panic. I don't know whether it's drink or drugs — probably it's his conservatism (pre-fascistic conservatism, after all, being one cure for panic) — and I think what he is effectively able to do is hold off the panic. When you looked at him, as outrageous as he was in his most naked moments, as during the debates, what you saw, it seems to me, was the real core of the man. What you saw was a man in utter panic. This man was on the brink! Now, they kind of got it together and figured out how to give him whatever they had to give him, though it included these dreadful lines that he just kept repeating as he turned off what appeared to be at least half his mind.

But Quayle, for all his reactionary politic, isn't alone. You and I and many others are profoundly panicked by the state of this society and this world. I don't think that you can use anxiety to adapt to the threat of nuclear annihilation — it's unadaptable to. You can't possibly toss it off with, "Oh well, we might all be blown up tomorrow, but what the hell, I'll adapt to it." Or, "Oh yes, it might be that the ozone layer is being eaten away and we have a week and a half to go, but what the hell, live and let live." It doesn't make sense to speak of adapting to these things — they're not adaptable to. They are productive of enormous panic. Now, I think we all find ways to deal temporarily with that panic. But it's also possible to do something systematically, and I'm talking now about social therapeutic approaches — to get beyond panic and take up a new kind of anxiety. But I think we have to develop that anxiety.

But Dan Quayle denies he's in panic…

Oh yes, of course. He also denied that he got his father's help to keep him out of Vietnam. He denies everything. Denial of panic is one of the ways that people deal with panic. But there's a difference between not being in panic and denying panic. When I look at some of these leaders throughout the world I see an enormous amount of panic. One can perceive people in panic, not just leaders but people throughout the world. And there's reason for that panic, namely, that there's not the slightest capacity to adapt in any way to our current conditions. Again, we're not talking about the

Sierra Club in the 1950s issuing ecological alarms; the reality of what's happening nowadays throughout this world is nothing less than the possibility of species annihilation. That's not just rhetoric; that's a hard fact. I mean I'm not looking to get anyone here panicked, but we could be sitting here just days away from who knows what geophysical or sociophysical disaster. You see it in the streets. When you get three consecutive days of strange weather, people start to get weird looks on their faces as if to say "I think we might be in serious trouble." And they're right, we might be! That's a real, human, emotive experience in contemporary society; it is very profoundly a part of human psychopathology in the world in which we're living. People are constantly having to deal with the possibility of going right into overt and visible panic!

Part of what we're working with here is how to deal with that. And by the way, I'm not talking about a process which is separate from the process of dealing with people's basic pathology. Often people will hear me and say, "Oh I see, you're concerned with those kinds of problems, not the simple, basic, ordinary grocery-size problems I as a therapist deal with." But people's lives are inseparable in this way; people's basic problems are directly connected to these issues — they *are* people's everyday problems. That separation is no longer a viable or a real one. No, people don't come to see you to deal with worldly problems. They come to see you to deal with their problems. But it turns out that their problems are worldly. That's the hard fact.

In your description of passing someone living in the street, you didn't seem anxious, you seemed angry. Is there any connection between anxiety and anger?

What I'm saying is that I don't feel anxious; I feel panicked. And anger and panic are very closely connected. For one thing, anger is often a straight-out accompaniment to the panic reaction.

The behavioral-social look of people in panic is sometimes outrage which may look like anger. But I don't think my response is simply that I'm angry. It's more the case that the anger grows out of the panic which is directly related to the social frustration. And frustration invariably takes the behavioral form of anger, because the reality is that there's nothing to be done about it. One can't in any immediate sense solve this fundamentally inhuman arrangement. I believe that the experience of that is utter frustration, utter panic, utter rage. The issue is to try to find a way of creating anxiety, through this process I was describing of using whatever institutional elements are available, in order to exercise some power, modest though it may be, relative to what otherwise is simply a hopeless situation.

See, I think that if people didn't drink or take drugs or avert their eyes, or lie, or do a whole bunch of things to deal with their panic, if people simply looked at the hard reality of homelessness in America, of AIDS in America, of racism, sexism, homophobia in America, of the ecological crisis, of poverty — not only in America but throughout the world — the hard realities of an historical process, a mode of production, that had such extraordinary promise and now has demonstrably failed, we would all, if we simply let ourselves go, have a massive nervous breakdown.

The alternative can't simply be finding more and more ways of holding that off for the moment. Again, an analogy to economics: I think part of the reality of the American economy is that through a whole host of economic devices, it has been bolstered against utter collapse, but it is recognizably always on the brink of collapse. What broke through in the October [1987] stock market crash, though to be sure it was repaired, was a kind of nervous breakdown of enormous proportions. I think that we periodically see that happening at a social-psychological level, and then it's put back together through a whole host of techniques of mass psychology. This is a society that's very, very clever at developing techniques to keep panic under control. Indeed, the greatest discovery of the past 25 years in the United States of America in my opinion has been techniques for what they call riot control, techniques for panic control. And what does that entail? *How to keep outraged people from expressing their outrage!*

APPENDIX C

DIALOGUE ON "THE MYTH OF ADDICTION"

The dialogue that follows is from the question and answer session directly following Dr. Newman's presentation.

I totally agree that there is no physiological basis for addiction, being in the drug care field myself, and being around people who are on methadone and seeing how they deal with that. But what about the psychological addiction to drugs and alcohol?

Well, I don't believe there is any. Indeed, I'm very suspicious of the whole concept of psychological addiction. I'm a therapist, as you know, and I don't for a *moment* deny that people have emotional problems, that they have all kinds of issues they need to deal with. And I think it is appropriate and proper to have the best possible ways of supporting and helping people to deal with them. But I don't know what's supposed to be meant by a psychological *addiction*. The whole medical model of the 20th century grows out of the 19th century model which was the conception I said before — moral turpitude. The way you accounted for people's bad behavior was that it was in some way immoral.

I'm saying that the concept of addiction includes or is in fact the 20th century version of that same thing. I think it's a moral category; I don't think it's a psychological or physiological category. I don't think it adds anything scientifically. Without that moral platitude one can account for human behavior in terms of the circumstances and conditions that human beings have to deal with. Addiction is not only scientifically unsound, I think it's politically dangerous as hell. It leads to 33% of the American public taking homosexuality to be a disease. It's most critical that we as a people — and this is a *political* issue as well as a social, cultural and scientific issue — learn how to call things by their correct names and not employ the categories that are by and large handed to us.

Like many of you, I saw the addiction industry grow. It was startling. It became a major industry in only 20 years. And I think we do great harm by imposing this conception of addiction. It's the 20th century version of what used to be called the theory of dormative power. Back in the 17th century the official explanation for why wine made you sleepy was that it had dormative powers. And if you asked what that meant, they told you dormative power is the power of things to make you sleepy. People thought they had made a serious advance by understanding that wine had dormative power. But not only isn't that an advance, it's an *illusion* of an explanation when you don't have one and that's *profoundly dangerous* from a social point of view.

I had another question. I heard of a study where rats would repeatedly choose cocaine to the point of death, choose it over food. Is that a bogus study?

No, not at all. For example, if you invoke the pleasure principle, which is a not unreasonable one, it might lead you to say that rats — these particular rats at least — preferred cocaine from a pleasure point of view to food. Now I don't know what food they were being fed, but I don't find that the *least bit* shocking. I think probably the cocaine was a whole lot better than the food that they were giving to those rats. In discussions with young people in our communities, as well as when I worked at Queensboro, people would tell me that they use crack or heroin because it's something that they find *preferable* to any other alternative they have in their lives! We have to face that reality! I'm not *endorsing* that; I think it's terrible, but I don't think that *they're* terrible. I think it's terrible to be in a society where the use of heroin is the most preferable thing to be doing for a certain portion of our people — middle class and working class, Black and white. I think that says a great deal about our culture!

But I don't think we can get around that by saying that these people have a certain addiction, or that they have bad taste. They don't have bad taste; they have the taste that is developed by what is in fact available in a profoundly deprived culture! You can't say to people for whom there are no jobs that they're addicted. They're not working and that's enough to drive people crazy and it *does* drive people crazy! You can't say to people who are getting foul, terrible education that they're addicted to dropping out. They're not addicted to dropping out, they're having perfectly comprehensible responses to the social conditions that they face.

Now I know a lot of people are saying this is the old liberal story again — it's *not* the old liberal story again. Because it's being said in the face of *20 years* of social regression. Poverty has risen 300% in this country. We're talking about a country which, far from realizing the Great Society, promised by Lyndon Johnson, is now going down the Great Tube. It's no longer 1968 liberalism. We're talking about the need for profound and necessary changes because we are facing a *cataclysmic* social reality. And we've seen these industries growing as a function of that social system deteriorating. We didn't have an addiction myth prevalent in society when it was doing well; they had *other* myths for when society was doing well.

I have to tell you I'm confused. Now that you say that there's no such

*thing as addiction, what do you think will happen to me and so many peo-
ple who believe they are addicts?*

"What do *you* think?" is the far more important question. What
I think is what I've articulated and what I'm doing; trying to build
such psychological, political and cultural institutions where people
don't start out from the premise that they're victimized addicts.
Fundamental to social therapy is the insistence that people cannot
get help and grow and develop in psychological ways if they begin
from the premise that they are victimized addicts. This is not to say
that people don't have things wrong with them, but it's very different to have things wrong with you for lawful reasons than to have
the identity of a sick person, of a victimized person. We can't allow
ourselves to be organized around our *powerlessness* and then
attempt to do something about what's going on in our lives. I'm
not saying that one can simply do that in one's head. But if people
in their heads *see* themselves as powerless they're not going to do a
lot out of their heads; they're going to stay in their heads and be
permanently victimized. We've seen this happen in this country
where welfare is designed to organize people into a passive and
impotent position. That's not an argument against welfare; indeed
I have fought for many years for tremendous *increases* in welfare
when people don't have work because it's an obligation of our
society. But a big part of what it means to put people on welfare is
to regulate them; poor people on welfare are continually socially
coerced.

*So basically it's what do you think of yourself, not taking on the role
of a victim.*

Right. And asking the very hard question, not only *what* do
you think of yourself, but who got you to think that way? Where
did you get that from?

When that woman referenced the experiment where the rats would eat cocaine in preference to anything else, actually just about all of these animal addiction experiments are phony in the sense of their relevance. What they do is stick an animal into a very tight cage, and they stick an IV line into them. They have a tough time getting the animal to start pressing the button. The animal will usually resist quite a bit. And essentially if their choice is between food pellets and pushing the button for cocaine they will choose cocaine, under those restrictive conditions. There was a very different series of experiments done under fairly realistic conditions where the rats were given room to run around, were allowed to be with other rats, didn't have an IV line stuck to them but could just sample the material. Under those conditions they weren't addicted; as they were given fewer and fewer choices, they became so-called addicted.

I'm glad you added that. It's always important to think not only in terms of rats and other experimental animals, but that under appropriate conditions, human beings in eight weeks' time can be taught to murder women and children in foreign countries. It's important to realize that if you make the conditions coercive enough, you can get not only rats but people as well to do things that they would never think of doing under other conditions.

I'm a gay man. Before going into social therapy I was involved in a 12-step group called Sexual Compulsives Anonymous. And I got some things from that group, but anything more than zero would have been something — I didn't have much before then. This group is, curiously enough, predominantly gay men at this point. I would like to know what you think of this. I think it's pretty obvious why this group is becoming more and more successful, given that it's predominantly gay men who have AIDS.

Again, the addiction business is going terribly, terribly well; we have to face that fact. Groups are abounding. AA has the highest induction rate they ever had, something like a thousand new people a day. Why is it happening? For a host of reasons. Clearly, millions upon millions of people, all kinds of people, are searching for answers. What makes this addiction sham, this industry, so pernicious, in my opinion, is the fact that it's done in the face of the desperation of our people. Our people are *desperate* for answers, and these programs are what's given as answers. These programs work to the extent they work not because they *cure* a whole lot but because of the vacuum in this society of anything resembling developmental or positive answers. There is no country in the world — Western democracy or otherwise — that so completely lacks a social policy on health as does the United States of America. The general policy of this country is that it has no particular obligation to its people in this regard, that the Constitution does not give people the right to be healthy. Thirty to fifty million Americans have no health program available to them! Poor people are dying throughout our country because they literally have no hospitals which they can go to.

This country is so profoundly insensitive to the demands of its people that it creates the climate in which people go to quacks. You want to talk about the *real* quack industries of this country, talk about the ones that have made it! Look at some of the programs that are available for people with AIDS. Disaster programs! Now, there are truly dedicated people out there doing some humane things, but a lot of people are out there doing sham science like so-called addiction. Those kind of programs are a national disgrace, but it's America's boom industry.

Hi. I'm a drinker and a druggie. When you said I wasn't an addict, I said, boy, then I'm not powerless, maybe I should go out and smoke a joint and have a drink as soon as this meeting is over! Yet over and over again in these programs I'm told I'm powerless and I can't do that. And I think

I need to have that reinforced, because I usually get myself into a hell of a lot of trouble when I drink and do drugs. Yes, I agree that NA and AA are very individualistic in that they're not talking about society, what to do to change it to a place where people don't get addicted. However, they are places where people can come together and share a common experience and perhaps keep each other from getting into trouble.

Why is it that the options in the world are *using* or *not using?* That's the mind set of the addict. I agree with you completely — it's very positive for people to come together and share their life experiences. But how come the people you choose to share life experiences with are not a group of people who have varied life experiences? What about getting support from groups of *that* kind? My experience is that the success rate in helping people to deal with these kinds of problems is vastly greater when the group of people who support each other do not support the addict identity but support your identity as a human being, as a Black person, a Latino person, as a member of your community, your society. And I believe that the psychologists who will not allow so-called addicts into their groups are doing a criminal thing. I have worked with groups where some of the people would normally be identified as addicts. Not only do they get a great deal of help, but equally important, they *give* a great deal of help. They can support others with their social problems, their emotional problems. That kind of dynamic is fundamental for the kind of support you've talked about. I don't think it is a successful model to have addicts and addicts alone coming together.

First of all, I agree with you about addiction being big business. I look at that as exploitation of the persons who are victimized by addiction. I would like to add this point, however; no recovery program claims to cure everybody. But I would like to know wha⁺ you consider obsessive-compulsive behavior if not addiction.

I think it's part of the sham that no recovery program claims to cure everybody. Indeed, I think it's not only true of groups like Narcotics Anonymous but of psychology in general which says, "We'll charge you lots of money but don't think that we cure anybody." I think the challenge has to be met: people have every right to demand significant change, if not cure. The only reason I agree that nobody cures anybody is that I don't think anybody is *sick* in the way that they're suggesting. But I don't think it meets the challenge to say that we're not going to try to change some things, some rather important things.

Obsessive behavior? Compulsive behavior? I think those categories are equally as frivolous as addiction. Where did these psychological categories come from? We look at categories of retardation, categories which abuse and identify children, particularly from many of our poor and working class communities, as belonging on certain tracks. We look at people who identify certain behavior as requiring the use of certain drugs. But there is no hard evidence that these kinds of labelings play any significant effective role in the positive development of those people, and a lot of hard evidence to the contrary. I think you can justifiably introduce labels if they're part of a process which helps somebody. But I think if you look, for example, at the educational or mental health systems what you see is a *massive* taxonomy, endless labeling, and then the admission that really all they can do is label and perhaps employ some drugs that have been modestly effective at changing some of the behavioral characteristics identified with the pathology.

In all of the materials that I looked at, the piece that I found most valuable was a piece called "Taxonomy as politics: The harm of classification" by Stephen J. Gould, which appeared in the Winter 1990 issue of *Dissent*. Gould notes that the labeling that is done in all of these areas is not neutral; it's political through and through. They are political labels. They are designed to keep people in certain places, to track people in certain directions, and I think we have to be extremely wary of them, whether they're fancy labels with long traditions or brand new ones like "addiction." So obsessive behavior and compulsive behavior are, by and large, unscientific, not sound, and politically and socially coercive identities.

Let me press this a bit. A person has been a 15-year heroin addict, shot mainline heroin for 15 years. You tell that person in that gallery or on that corner where he's getting his next hit that he doesn't have a problem...

I didn't say he doesn't have a problem! No, he's got a *big* problem!...

But it's just emotional...?

No, he's got a *huge* problem!

Is it physical?

Yes, he has a physical problem, he has a social problem, he has a chemical problem, he could be *dying*, but all I'm saying is what do you think we've added by saying he's addicted? That's the question. What *have* we added by saying he's addicted? Except to really be saying that not only does he have all those problems, but he's a bad human being as well. *That's* what's added by saying he's addicted.

But I still don't understand what's being offered, in terms of the person who has a physical dependency on a substance that they do day in and day out, by denying that the person has an addiction or an obsession-compulsion to use this substance even against their will and to the point of destroying themselves. To say that it's something emotional or political — sure there's politics in this shit — but this person is in the grips of something more powerful than themselves...

Absolutely! They're in the grip of something more powerful

than themselves, and it's not addiction. It's the social conditions under which they are living; it's their disempowerment as human beings, and until that's transformed there's going to be no significant change in the rate of addiction in our communities. Yes, people have *terrible* problems — I'm not denying that! The addiction myth is the *cover-up* of the fact that they have those problems!

Like I said, I agree with you that the person needs to see the big picture, and that's why I'm here. At the same time, even you say that we should use whatever helps. Sure, it's big business. If people have to stand on their heads to stay clean, to stay free, that helps. So to knock anything that helps people stay clean and saves lives I think is a discredit to what people are doing.

Oh, I agree with you completely! We have to do something that helps. Should we not try to find the *best* things that help rather than accepting the position that anything that helps even a little is OK? Should we not seek out ways of helping that are in advance of these 7% success rates? I'm saying that we and others have discovered ways that are more successful — with illiteracy, with mental health, with drugs — and those programs are *not* the programs that are funded, and the reason is that they don't fit into the social control model of those other programs. We have to have helping programs that are the *best* programs for the people in our communities!

I'm sorry, but I'm really suspect of anybody who's never been an addict or an alcoholic telling addicts or alcoholics what the problem is or what the solution is.

Every dollar of every single funded program in the United States of America, every one of the billions of dollars going into the existing programs, is controlled by boards of directors, none of whom has ever had the experience that you're describing. Every single dollar! So if you're saying that you and others in this room should sit on a board, I say, "Right on!"

I still say I have gotten a tremendous amount from these programs and wouldn't be alive otherwise!

Right. And I'm sure you would agree that we have to address the 94% of the people who haven't had that experience. Because what you said right at the beginning is quite correct — you *know* that it's a big business. Well, if it's a big business we have to do something about *how come* it's a big business as opposed to a helping activity. That's what we have to do something about. You can't *say* it's a big business on the one hand and on the other hand say, "but it works." Yeah, big business works, but it doesn't work for what we as a mass of people need and that's what we have to turn around.

Dr. Newman, in the past 30 years I've seen the federal government on Indian reservations and state governments in prisons giving out lithium to children, valium and dilantin to adults. That's a big thing. Fifteen years ago the government said they were going to stop distributing valium in prisons when the stockpile went down. But when the stockpile went down people forgot about that promise — they replenished that pile. How do we fight something that big? I mean, that's real oppressive. Groups have come together to fight it, but they're not strong enough.

I think the issue is that we have not in fact come together. I think we've fooled ourselves into thinking we've come together. You know who comes together in this country to effect social change? The Democratic Party. They build massive institutions with billions of dollars — that's a coming together. Same thing with the Republican Party. What we've done is to come together to make our statement about this or that issue, but when it comes time to bring it all together to make a set of political demands regarding fundamental changes in social policy — that hasn't happened. We demand, for example, that a home is a right, and if it doesn't exist in the United States Constitution well then you better damned well put it there. We demand that health is a human right. But you can't demand that kind of social policy unless you build the kind of political organization which has the power to do it.

So we fool ourselves a lot. I go down to the marches too, and we say, "Hey, there are a million people down in Washington and that's really something." But then we need to raise the question of who does what with those million people. And there are political organizations that don't give a damned about our people, who make use of those million people and we don't get the benefit of it. If we can't build a political party that gives expression to these demands then we are just wasting our breath. Until we do that we can talk a good game but it's going to mean nothing. How many times does Governor Cuomo have to kick us in the teeth before we don't vote for him? How many meetings of Puerto Rican people will he not show up to, how many times will he insult the African American people before we say he's a bum who does nothing for us? *They don't care about protest as long as you keep putting them back into power.* They love protest — all it establishes is that we have a "free America." So there are going to have to be some changes at the level of political power.

I've been to AA and I think it can become an addiction too. I went to meetings and people would get up and say, "I've been sober for two years now, and I'm miserable, and I wish I was dead, but hey, at least I'm sober!" I think you've got to have something better than that and this stuff ain't enough; survival ain't enough!

The point I think is not to condemn these programs. Yes, all kinds of things can help people — 12-step programs, even psychiatry, occasionally help people. The serious question is whether that's what we're willing to settle for! Why are we settling for something that is failing? The psychiatrist R.D. Laing, back in the '60s, said that psychiatry is sometimes good only because it doesn't practice what it preaches. If it did what it said it was doing it would hurt people all the time, but it periodically doesn't do that so it can help a few folks. If you look at AA and these other programs, the positive thing about them is not what they preach but that they provide a context in which human beings can at least *share* some of their pain. That social process is of value. But if we accept that that is all, we are feeding into the myth of addiction. The addiction myth says that the best addicts can have is an AA meeting. You can come down here year after year and confess that you've been off booze. Well, that's not the best that our young people should have. It's the same for our educational system. They say this is the best we can have for these dumb kids who don't care about learning and are addicted to stupidity and illiteracy. That's their argument! Can we tolerate that?

I feel very empowered when you say there is no such thing as addiction. Could you say more about social therapy in terms of building environments that can help people?

Part of what's so pernicious about the myth of addiction is that the very people who do all the building are not identified in this culture as the people who did the building. I think it's very tough to live in a society where the folks who built the cars in Detroit have to go out and buy one in the store. What it means to build is simply to create the environment in which you can be self-conscious about the fact that what happens in groups, families, countries, is done by the people who build. This room that we're sitting in didn't come here by some act of grace of the Board of Trustees of Columbia University. It was built. And the problematic of a lot of these addictions programs is that they don't relate to people as people who can build and create and change what they need to.

And until we do that people will not be empowered, they will simply be addicts. They will be addicted to a society where you let yourself believe that it was done for you. It's not like we have to get special uniforms to be builders. We *are* builders! What we have to do is take off the special uniforms that tell us that we're addicts. We're wearing addicts' clothes, victims' clothes. We have to take them off; it's an undressing, not a dressing.

Dr. Newman, I want to thank you and Dr. Lenora Fulani for the work that you're doing. I started using heroin in 1965 and methadone until 1983. I came off drugs through social therapy. I learned that coming off drugs wasn't the issue, but what to do after you got off drugs, because there was only drugs to go back to. There wasn't anything else to do. So I want to thank you for your work.

I belong to a group of recovering addicts, which is an alumni association of a detox program in Philadelphia. I agree with that gentleman who asked, "After you're off drugs, then what?" We have taken on the commitment to start a program to create an environment to develop and support the practice of leadership skills. After hearing you talk about this multi-billion dollar addiction business, I'm scared. How are we going to survive? We're not federally funded; we're simply doing something we feel the need for.

The hard answer is to go directly to the community. Win that community over to support what you're doing, because what you're doing is not coming from those multi-billionaires up there, but *from* the people of the community to do something *for* the people of the community. We have to go to our people and say, "We want to show you why this must be supported by you." Communities will support these programs if we're ready to go out and do the hard work of making the demand and organizing them to do so.

I'm a single parent with two children. My one son who is 24 is not to my knowledge addicted to any drugs but he has really dropped out of society. Now, in the '60s I was an activist; I wore the turbans and I went to meetings. I was aware of how society was toward me as a Black woman. My son feels the same way, but he and about 20 kids in the neighborhood have sort of just escaped; they sit around all day and listen to rap music. He tells me that society is "beating me up and knocking me down." So how can you get these young men to come back to have the confidence in themselves and the self-esteem to want to be back in society?

What you're saying is so important. The only thing that really moves people out of that kind of totally understandable cynicism — we know what our young people are facing — is to build something successful. I almost don't care what it is, even something little the community needs. What creates so much cynicism in our culture is that there has been massive failure. We live in a country where half the people don't vote at the federal level. The reason, apparently, is that people don't think that their participating could possibly make a *difference.* I don't think it's "apathy," which like "addiction" is a nonsense term. People don't do it because they don't think it makes a difference. So we have to begin to do something that makes a difference, some kind of empowerment activity — or else people will stay exactly where your son is. When I speak with people, when Dr. Fulani speaks to students on campuses or to young people in the communities, what's being said is that *you've got to begin empowering yourself working with other people.* I don't care what form that might take.

The social workers, psychiatrists and psychologists at the East Side Institute, whom I'm proud to be associated with, go out and ring doorbells every single day of the week and ask for support because we are building a therapy center which is independent of the big bucks so we can do the kinds of things that people actually need. That activity is a component of building something which is different from those big buck-funded programs. And that has to be done at every single level; people must begin the work of building.

I'm going to school to become a drug and alcoholism counselor. What can you tell me about these programs, since there's no such thing as addiction?

I don't think that everybody working for a drug rehab program should quit, for several reasons. One, because people need the money, and two, because people can make a difference as a human being relating to another human being, not because what you are doing is carrying out the mandate of some phony-baloney program with a lot of phony-baloney language. I think I made a difference at Queensboro and I think you're going to make a difference where you're going to work — because of who we are, as human beings. So because of this these programs do make a difference, though they are set up to provide far less help than what is needed. But that doesn't mean folks shouldn't make use of them if that's all we've got for the time being. I worked with welfare recipients for 20 years; you don't say to welfare recipients, "Since they're messing with you and harassing you, don't go down to pick up your welfare check." People would look at you like you're a damned fool! You pick up the check *and* you find out what you have to do about the fact that they're messing with you! That's what has to happen!

This is wonderful! I find this whole presentation very liberating. I grew up with two-thirds of the adults I knew in my life addicted to drugs or alcohol. From a very early age I've had a response to this category called "addiction," because once people are called addicted they are no longer related to as a human being, or useful. You can hardly even relate to them in any way — you kind of have to get them out of your life. It was also a way to protect yourself because there was a lot of brutality and vio-

lence and craziness that came with drug and alcohol use. So I didn't know how to balance those concerns, because in some ways I felt safe with that category.

Oh yes, it's a very safe category. Saying that two out of three people are addicted is an easier category than coming to terms with the fact that two out of three people have no jobs, aren't in a position to get the education that they need. Those are the real, hard facts, and it's hard to face the fact that this is the reality of the lives of so many of our people. But if we settle for summing all that up as "addiction," well, it's all written off, taken care of. "Oh, I got this all explained. This isn't because people are being related to in the most racist and brutal ways; this isn't because people are being put down and oppressed and stepped on and not given the programs that they need, are being murdered by the cops and so on. No, it's because they're addicted!" And that's a safe thing to say! We've got to hear it — there's a seductiveness to that! In fact, if I would ever want to use the word "addictive," *that's* addictive. It's addictive to buy into that kind of myth. And we all internalize that, including the people in the community who are so labeled; people explain themselves and how they're living by saying, "Well, I have an addictive personality." What the hell is an addictive personality?! You think that category isn't political? You think this 12-step book put out by AA isn't political?

I was sitting up in the balcony listening to you talk and I was feeling threatened because I do follow the 12-step program. So there were a lot of conflicts going through me, because I saw a lot of things you said were true, once I really opened my mind and looked at the reality of things. Addiction is a big business, people make a lot of money at it, including our corrupted political leaders. When this brother spoke earlier and questioned what you were saying, challenged it and defended these programs, what I saw was another person going through what I was going through up there. And it scared me to see him go through it, but I understood. I had a question, but it's already been answered by you, in terms of how to build and go through the process of making people aware of what's going on. At first when you were talking I felt scared because I thought my program would have to go out the window, when in essence it's not really like that. I'm part of just a small percentage of the people who are getting help, but at the other end of that are a lot of people who are being condemned, being told, "You're an addict, you'll never get nowhere, you'll never be anything." So I understand where you're coming from.

Right. And they're using you to put those other people down.

So I understand the need for me to go out into the community and educate around these issues.

Exactly. And when that statement is made, as you so eloquently made it just now, that's going to scare the hell out of those billionaires. When you say, "We're not doing *your* programs. We're doing programs that don't *depend* on your treating me as a victim and as an addict. We're going to *deal* with this drug stuff and this alcohol stuff, but not by me becoming an addict so you can use *me* against the other 95% of my people" — when that happens, it's going to scare the hell out of those billionaires with those phony drug programs.

I agree that there is this corrupt multi-billion dollar addiction industry, built around a myth, but my only conflict is with the physiological basis for addiction, which is real....

No, it doesn't exist! People use the word "physiological" and they think thereby it must give some weight or some existence or whatever to what's being talked about. It's kind of like the way people sometimes react to mathematics, or hard science. The scientific evidence doesn't support that claim. Yes, we know that people have chemical reactions. Take some arsenic and you'll have a chemical reaction. The issue is — at the risk of repeating myself — what is added by calling it an addiction? It's that label which is so pernicious.

I work for Emmaus House, which is a treatment program in New York City, and after today I know there's going to be a big fight when I go back to work on Monday — and I'm down for the fight! I'm liberated by what you said, Fred, because I was organized by the addiction mentality and I kept wondering what the hell was wrong with me and why was I feeling so crazy in these places. And it's because I bought that bullshit and I don't buy it no more!

DIALOGUE ON "COMMUNITY AS A HEART IN A HAVENLESS WORLD"

The dialogue that follows is from the question and answer session following Dr. Newman's presentation and the brief "demonstration" on the street.

I felt like standing up on the car saying, "We define community" but I didn't think that would be right to do.

If you think they define private property you'll have those conflicts. What we're talking about is taking all the space we can grab in the process of working to redefine even their constricting definitions, which doesn't mean anything goes. It doesn't mean you can do whatever you want. What it does mean is that we've got to go a whole lot further by using what's available to us as possibilities.

This probably betrays my nationalism, but there was something I was thinking about through most of your talk. I really like this finding new ways of looking at community and redefining it, but as a gay man I also felt the conservatism of not wanting to give up what I think the gay community is, being afraid it will disappear or be swallowed up or it won't have any power.

The gay community as a separate entity *keeps* you from being gay. It doesn't give you a great capacity to be gay. What it does is effectively create a ghetto in which you are *allowed* to be gay. Don't be fooled into thinking you are more gay because they put you in a gay community. Your gayness deserves to come out everywhere.

When you said we were going to do something new, I got nervous. I thought, "Oh, what's it gonna be now?" But then when you told us what it was, it sounded so powerful and, actually, it was fun. I noticed about 10 to 15 people in the audience who stayed here inside. I was very excited to go out and shout "NO JUSTICE, NO PEACE!" but I was also aware that people were looking at me, and I was thinking, "To some people this proves we're a cult." I assumed I knew what other people were thinking and was conservatized by that at the same time that I was doing the activity and being excited about participating with all of us.

I felt really good about people staying inside. I hope we have created an environment in which people can be part of what we're doing and participate by sitting right here if that's what they choose to do. After all, there are thousands of people in this community who are not here tonight, but they're as much with us and they're doing some wild things. They might be walking out on some other street corner doing who knows what! I think it's very important, and I'm not just saying this in the spirit of "everyone's allowed to do their own thing," but because I believe in a democracy which runs even deeper than that.

I think everyone has a right to participate and help to build and change things as they are able and see fit. So I think the people who were sitting here are in some profound sense as active as the people who chose to go outside. And that's fine because what we're building is just that kind of community where people can participate in all kinds of ways, including "not participating."

People should have that right. And we have an obligation to create an environment where people can live and be with us and be a part of us and relate to us doing that.

It felt good going out there. But the way things are defined in this country, that was civil disobedience. So who defines?

The activity of civil disobedience, as practiced by its greatest practitioners — Dr. King, Reverend Sharpton, and many others — is designed to raise that very question. To oppose the definitions of what is civilly obedient in the name of some higher or more profound statement. We seek to move, not in accordance with the powers that constrain us, but in accordance with a commitment to humanity which gives us not only the right but the possibility to challenge them.

I think that's a large part of what civil disobedience is about. We have to be disobedient in all kinds of ways. Disobedience has to be our watchword. Again, I don't mean people should go out and do things that are going to get them hurt or be dangerous or hurtful to our cause, but rather that we will collectively do things which challenge the right of those in power to define what we are allowed to do. In that sense, I think we have to be politically disobedient from morning to night!

When we did the demonstrations over at Gracie Mansion and we brought that court case, one of the things they were saying to us was, "You're not supposed to do demonstrations at Gracie Mansion. The proper place for these demonstrations is at City Hall." We said, "Wait a second, we want to demonstrate at Gracie Mansion because we want to be disobedient. We have a Constitutional right to do it and we want to make a particular statement, which is that we're not going to go to the arena you want to put us in because we want to stand up and say we're being disobedient and violating your norms." Now the worst of things happened for them. When we went there, no one had demonstrated at Gracie Mansion for decades. After us, ACT UP and other groups started going up there to demonstrate. Just the other morning the hospital workers demonstrated there at 7 am. I think the people of the city have to be aware that this new community will go into every part of the city and say NO JUSTICE, NO PEACE! — not just into Harlem, not just into Bensonhurst, not just into the Village, but right on Park Avenue. We're going to protest Park Avenue because it needs to be protested, because there are homeless people and we can't tolerate Park Avenue while people are living in the streets. Such acts of disobedience need to be undertaken.

How do we work with a primarily transitional homeless community that's been together for about a year [Emmaus House in East Harlem]? We're working folks. We work hard every day; we study and do other things. Taking about 60 people, men and women, young and old, how do we create an environment, a community, a heart in a havenless world? We're all homeless; give us a clue.

Emmaus House is an extraordinary place. I have enormous love and respect for what you've done, for what Mamie Moore's done with you. We can't allow ourselves to be defined by a house or a description of our people which fits into the appropriate categories for certain purposes. We have to openly define ourselves as an ever changing and growing community of people so that we do the activities of that active community. It must be the case that the people at Emmaus have as their fundamental identity being part of a human community of people who are defining themselves in the spirit of changing a world which makes it necessary to have an Emmaus House. The people in Emmaus House, in my opinion, must be constantly working to "do in" Emmaus House, because if that's not being done then all you are doing is reinforcing the social conditions which make it necessary to have Emmaus House — an extraordinary place which we're lucky to have, given those conditions. That's got to be the active, working, day-to-day, hour-to-hour principle — how do we "do in" Emmaus House?

Now there's a million ways of doing that. I have a handful of answers; Dr. Fulani has many more; you have some; Mamie has some; everyone in this room has some. I think we have to come to see that this redefinition of who we are is fundamental, so that we don't become bounded by the walls of the New Alliance Party or Emmaus House or Castillo or anything else, so that we not fall victim to that kind of narrow sense of community. That's what we must work on together and I'm there to do it to the extent I'm needed to and wanted to and so are other people here. I think everyone in this room tonight has to see Emmaus House as a place you go to because it's a part of your community. Everyone has to go up to Emmaus House and say, "I might not be homeless but I'm here because this is part of my community and the people here are part of my community." And we have to form and shape this community with absolute respect for the integrity of who people are, who you are. That respect is part and parcel of our creating a broader self-defining community.

"Homeless?" "Homeless" people are people *they* define. Homeless people are human beings. They are our sisters and brothers who, given what's going on in this world, don't have a place to live. They're not hopeless: they're brilliant, they're dedicated, and because of the conditions in which we currently live they don't have a place to live. They live in the street — that's the tragedy of this culture, of this environment, but let's not fall into the category of "homeless" in a way that denies what active living human beings can build.

What do you mean by taking all of what we have available as options and building community as it applies to youth?

A hard but honest answer to "What do we have to build with?" is that what we have is a lot of pain, a lot of conflictedness, a lot of rage. In many cases what we have is people's creativity, which we can still grab hold of. We don't have a lot of material stuff. What we have are not only positive things but painful, negative things. And we've got to take all that stuff and build.

The Barbara Taylor School, in my opinion, does that better than any school in the United States of America. The Barbara Taylor School takes children's conflictedness, their pain, it takes who they are, and exposes that, brings that out and says, "This is what we have to build with and learn from." As working people and middle class people who aren't that 3% who have billions of dollars, we can't afford to turn our backs on *anything*. We have to build with what we have.

Social therapy means the creation of an environment, an educational environment, an emotional environment, a political environment, a work environment, an artistic environment, in which people take the actual things we have in this world, painful and cruel as it is, and use them to build something. And it's beautiful to see that. It's beautiful to see that school because I know the materials — the creativity, the openness, the compassion of yourself and other adults and the children — and I know that you use what is very painful to expose and you build something which is very real and very much ours. That is extraordinary! That you are doing that is extraordinary. That's what can help our children; in my opinion that's all that can help our children.

I'd like to know how to get beyond this divide-and-conquer type thing among humans and learn how to address people.

We have to learn how to build community by recognizing the extent to which and precisely how we are divided. Dr. Fulani and I have spent years working on building what I think is a wonderful political-personal relationship. I love her as dearly as I love anyone in the world. She is an extraordinary human being. We have never for a moment denied that there are very real differences in terms of where we come from. In fact, we take those differences, and the antagonisms that have been socialized into us, and say, "*We* will control these rather than these controlling us. *We* will take control of who we are, including how we have been made to hate each other." That's hard work. The easier thing by far is to be cynical, to be skeptical and say, "Listen, this guy talks a good game, but it's the same old nonsense; it's not real."

When people ask me who I am, when people ask Dr. Fulani who she is, we both believe we owe them more than an explanation. What you've got to put on the line if you're going to take yourself seriously and ask others to take you seriously is an ongoing, 24 hours a day, seven days a week *practice.* You have to build something and say, "There it is. You want to know what I'm about? Go look at Castillo. You want to know what Fulani's about? Go look at the New Alliance Party. Go look at social therapy. Look at what we're building. Look at this room. Look at what we're opening up and building for people." Forget explanations. Anyone can make up a good explanation. All you need to know is how to bullshit. The issue is what do you do; what is your practice; what's there, what's open? I think you have a right to demand that and be ruthlessly honest about our differences in the spirit of building commonality. That's fundamental.

I'd like you to talk about what a cult is. I know that a lot of people use that word as a sledgehammer in reference to us. What I do at NAP or Castillo are things that I've done in many different places in many different ways: in the civil rights movement, in high school, in church. So it becomes very confusing when enemies turn around and say, "That is the behavior of someone who's in a cult and doesn't know any better." What is a cult?

The other thing I'd like you to address is this notion of community. I have very strong experiences of being in a certain kind of community. I spent about 13 years getting sober in AA. Two things that were said over and over were "Let the people in AA love you until you can love yourself," and "crossing a bridge back to life." There was this sense that being in this community involved being separate from the world, being wrapped in some kind of cocoon. And after I had been in for a while, I heard a lot of people in that community say that one of the things we have to do to be sober and stay sober is to take action in the world. I took that seriously and that's how I ended up in the New Alliance Party and the Castillo Center. For me, that was crossing the bridge back to life and taking action in the world.

When you talk about community as you talked about it tonight, it seems to me that there is no time when one goes someplace out of the world in order to be in the world, that the process of growing doesn't involve being away from the world; it involves coming in and going out, coming in and going out. It sounds like a constant, and I'd like you to talk about what the dynamic of that is, how it feels, what it looks like, what some of the difficulties are, because it's difficult for me to grasp and deal with. I'd like you to talk about that dynamic because I think it's very different from what I've heard about or experienced before. In other places, church, school and so on, there is this sense that you are in here and not out in the world, and being in here gives you some kind of strength to go out there. It seems, though, that you're suggesting that the biggest change has to be destroying that kind of wall in our heads because it doesn't exist in reality. It's just something someone thought up.

What cults are is a difficult question to answer because everyone has their own definition (so I can only give my answer). As with everything else, there are the acceptable cults and unacceptable cults. So, for example, when you talk about official programs that get dollars, places like Synanon [the drug rehab program], they are cult structures. And they are perfectly reasonable. I'm not pro-cult and I'm not part of a cult but I don't want to get into a heavy attack on cults. Cults make sense in this world. It is an ugly world for many people. It is a horrible world. It is a painful world and people are looking for havens in a heartless world. When families don't provide that, and they don't for many, people go elsewhere. They look for cults; they look for programs; they look for wildernesses; they look for all kinds of experiences through drugs and alcohol.

What I understand to be fundamental to a cult is that it is a temporary or permanent withdrawal from life into an inner directed experience, largely out of the feeling that you can't cope, don't want to cope, want to say to hell with it, and want to create an environment in which you have control and which would be separate from the world in which you feel fundamentally powerless. What I'm saying is that the problem with the cult is not just that it's a naughty word, that it conjures up images of Jonestown or whatever; the problem is that cults give the illusion that one can, in fact, find a haven, that there is a real wall that one can hide behind.

But look what happens with these programs. I'm deeply moved that you're here, an active and creative performer and poet and so on, but what is the actual rate of success of those programs, of AA? By their own account their success rate is around 8%, and I think they're probably lying.

This notion that we can hide somewhere and prepare ourselves for life is itself one of the illusions and definitions put out by those people who essentially want to keep things as they are and have lots of people who aren't participating get the hell out and go someplace else. It's the people who advocate methadone, which is a stronger drug in many cases than the drug people were using before they got hooked on it. *They* talk cult, cult, cult. The truth of the matter is that the powers-that-be have been supporting cults of the acceptable kind for a very long time.

What we are, ironically, is the absolute opposite of a cult. I think they wish we were a cult! If we were a cult we would simply find a place and go hide out. But here we are, not pulling back from our world and our people. We are insisting that we go out into the world, that we engage in social change, whether it's thera- peutic, political, cultural — whatever social form it takes. So this is all about what's necessary for human growth, which is the process of saying, "I don't have to go hide anywhere. That's *my* street out there." What the hell do the people on 85th Street mean when they say, "You can't come over here because you're invading the priva- cy of my enclave"? What are you talking about? This is *my* world. This belongs to *my* people and *my* community, not in any narrow sense but in the sense that we will define who we are and how we are and not have that imposed on us. So I believe deeply in radical democracy, in self-defining community and not in cult.

Who defines cults? Usually some ideology or some hierarchy. We're not looking for a cult because cults don't make basic changes in the world. What makes *that* is people who get together to create new possibilities and build, saying, "This belongs to us." That's what human growth is all about. I don't think growth comes from looking inward in an inner-directed group. I think it grows from a community defining itself and saying, "Hey world, we are here! Check out the New Alliance Party. Check out social therapy. Here we are. We're standing outside, here on Irving Place. Look at us, Irving Place." Because we are people. Look around this room, see who we are.

That's what I think it's all about; in that is enormous growth potential, the growth of possibilities beyond our wildest dreams. Our dreams, after all, are limited by *their* categories. *We* should decide what our dreams are going to be. I don't want my dreams decided by Lever Brothers or ITT. I'd like for us to decide what our dreams are, the good ones, the bad ones, the sexy ones, the not so sexy ones. I'd like us, the people, our extended community, to decide that — not their television.

First of all, I'm scared to death just to be standing up here talking. But I've learned that I'm a powerful Black gay man — and expressing who I am allows me to continue to be powerful. I also identify myself as a person who doesn't use substances anymore. I was into a life that I thought I could never get out of and I have some dear people in my life who have introduced me through social therapy to what life is about and that has helped me stop. I also am involved in a cult, as you say. But one thing I've learned about cults is that if I don't make a difference while I'm in this cult there is no need for me to be in this cult.

A person I love dearly told me I was crazy to go on a job interview and say that I was gay. But I got the job. I'm seeing that it just showed me that I can continue to use my growth and my development to be who I am. My question is how or what could you give me right now to help me continue to be who I am, because right now I need your support to help me be powerful like you are.

I'll give you something. I think you've got to start to push other people's development just as hard as you've pushed your own. You have a right and an obligation to help us, me and other people, to help us grow with the same energy that you've pushed yourself. That's how we make that energy social, so we're doing that for each other. I want you to give that same energy to everybody. I think you've got something very important to give and you can't just give it to yourself because that's selfish — you have to give it to the whole community.

I was very excited when you talked about redefining emotions. As you know, Fred, I try to be right all the time, and I was thinking about how redefining emotions is so much more human than doing emotions "right" and having emotions in categories. I was wondering how we do that work of defining emotions on the bigger level of our community, not just one group here, another there. How do we do that in the community of people across the country?

That question sets up a division between this group of 15 people over here and the rest of the world. But there isn't any such division. Some people say to me in social therapy, "Isn't it great! This worked out great here, but how can I take this other places?" My answer is, "You can't help but take it other places." It goes with you. The issue is whether you're going to allow yourself to not take it other places. When we make changes, we might be in a room called a "therapy room" but, as I point out again and again, the therapy room is on 72nd Street; it is in Manhattan; it is in New York; it is in the Northeast and it is in the world. Part of the problem of traditional therapy is that it is based on attempting to make that separation between therapy and the world. We have to work to see that there is no such separation, except insofar as those who would have us remain separate have defined that separation into existence. We have to work to redefine it out of existence.

Let's be serious for a minute. Let's suppose one night in group we come up with 16 of the most incredible and fantastic emotions ever heard of. We could come up with some emotions we don't have names for yet — fantastic emotions, unbelievable stuff. You think you're gonna keep that a secret? You think no one will hear about it? Now I don't want to be flip, but when people create things in complex social ways, those things make their way out to our environment because of how socialized our human environment is at this point in human history. We live in the most socialized environment that this species of ours has ever created. The issue is not our *capacity* to socialize; the issue is our readiness to use the socialization that's already there on our behalf rather than to divide us in such a way as to keep us from being able to share the benefits of our humanity and our creativity.

Look at the arbitrary divisions in this world. There's a boundary here, a boundary there. When I was teaching philosophy years ago, I used to talk about this. I'd put up a map, and I'd point to the boundary lines, and I'd realize, as I was exploring this, that people actually thought, at some level, that there were these lines out there. They believed that these were pictures of lines that went around this country, Zaire, or went around another country. But there are no lines out there! Are there different peoples? Yes. Do these peoples have separate histories which are rich and meaningful? Yes. But they're not histories in isolation. They're social histories, they're interrelated histories.

I'm here seeking help and support from you. I'm a member of a community in Philadelphia, a very strong community that's building a context for people to make changes in their lives. We've talked about anger before, and when you said that we "practice" anger, I realized my practice of anger oftentimes turns into abuse of others and myself. You spoke of using anger as a source of energy to reorganize and create; you talked about change and what you mean by change. It's a challenge. Seems like when there's a challenge in my life I feel more comfortable. When there's no challenge and I let others define who I am and what my place is, I tend to get confused and react to the conditions that they have fostered on us. I'd like further elaboration.

One of the things they sell (they being these who do the defining for us) is some degree of comfortableness. They say, "Listen, be more comfortable — let us define." But then that raises the question about anger, doesn't it? Because I don't think there's any way you can understand that anger unless you look at it relative to how comfortable you are with someone else doing the defining. If you want to do something about that anger you've got to do something about taking responsibility for defining who you and that community and me and we and all of us are. That energy's got to be used to do that. Until you do this work, I think that you might have a little comfortableness but you're going to have all the pain and torment of that anger, and all the hurtfulness of what you yourself recognize you do with it when you've got it. So, yes, there are some tradeoffs in this life.

I remember a person in therapy with me for years who used to say, "I hear what you're saying; I like what you're saying; I appreciate it, respect it, but when I think about making these changes they seem to me to be very inconvenient." They are! They're *inconvenient.* I think a lot of us are going to have to be inconvenienced *vis à vis* some of the privileges that we have — be it as men, be it as straight people, as white people, be it whatever the modest privileges you get in a hierarchical structure. So this one's got a little more than that one, but meanwhile none of us have what is there to have if we were, collectively, to build self-defining community. So I never deny it when people say to me, "Won't I have to give some things up; won't this be inconvenient; won't I be uncomfortable?" Answer — yes, that's right. Now if what you're saying — and I know you're not saying this because you wouldn't be here if you were — is "I don't want to give up any comfort," I say, "Well, what can I tell you?" When men say, "I want to hang on to my male privilege, but when I hear you speaking I hear you saying I should give up some of it," I say, "Yeah, that's true." But you've got to have a hard look at all that follows from being given that privilege.

I was thinking about the issue of community, having been around lots of communities, from the family to the Black community, to the alternative community, to the arts community, to the vegetarian community.

In some ways I had been looking for a haven and never found it. I've also been having a reaction to these communities that have already been defined in ways that don't liberate or empower me as a human being.

Working on Dr. Fulani's [1990 gubernatorial] campaign for the past three months I've seen that word "community" used in its most debased forms — the gay community, the Black community. I was thinking about being told over and over again to get out of "our community," and then standing up and saying, "Who made it your community?" What are the lines that separate yours from mine and ours and the millions of people in the world? I was thinking about having that experience in '88 [Fulani's Presidential campaign], when we traveled around the country building a community of people who would fight for democracy. You responded to a question earlier by saying that there isn't this separation, that making the assumption that you have to get together is wrong, and is a barrier to the thousands of people who are part of a broader community called humanity. What do you think of that?

You've got to break out of this notion of community or not-community defined by consciousness. You've got to break out of "this person's here, that person's there, what is the consciousness, do you feel a part of this, do you feel a part of that?" The operative principle for community is *building*, creating something. If there is one person out in Wichita right now who is a New Alliance Party and Fulani supporter, our job is to find a way of building with her or him, not creating some consciousness but *building* something together. We take what we have and we find a way of building something no matter what it is, no matter where the people might be. When we build, we create community, and when we don't build, no matter how much consciousness there is (now permit me to use one Marxist term) we have "false consciousness," alienated consciousness, illusory consciousness.

I think that's a whole lot of what cults are about. There's an illusion of togetherness, and that's real to people. People feel they need that in a pained world, but it isn't real because it's not something people have built. The issue is to build and find new ways of building constantly. We talk about that at Castillo all the time — new ways of producing things, not just producing new things but new ways of producing things.

When you say building, does that mean like building a campaign, building a play…

It's building whatever — building a house, a play, a relationship, it's building a life, a farm, a telephone hookup once a week, a newspaper. Building is human beings exercising our social skill to create something. Then we have built something which has a relationship to the world and to us, because we've built something together. We are a building species. Unfortunately our skills as builders have been exploited. That's what happens. Our skills, talents, capacity to build, get ripped off again and again. We have to reclaim that, not just through a mentalistic act, but through the collective activity of building community which builds. Not only do we build community, but we build communities that build — building communities. We take that out and people often get upset. "I don't want you to build. This is not the proper way of building."

No one is talking about violating laws. It turns out that the powers-that-be want to constrain us even from functioning within the laws. You know what it looks like to work at the voting booths in the Bronx or Brooklyn or wherever, if you're an independent party? They say, "Who the hell do you think you are, coming up here and asking for a fair, democratic election? How dare you!" You say, "I'm sorry, but doesn't it say that in the Constitution?" "Constitution! This is *my* community; to hell with the Constitution!" "But, we got on the ballot, Fulani's on the ballot, we deserve to have things done properly, here are the books, here are the laws." And they say, "Take those books and get the hell outta here." You say, "Wait a second. If that's what we're going to accept, then we can't be creating our community." It's a fight.

They say, "You're crazy, you're a cult, you're illegal, you're communists, you're gay, you're straight, you're Black, you're white." The New Alliance Party has been accused of every contradictory thing in the book. You can't tell if we're bad because we're gay or we're bad because we're straight; whether we're bad because we're communists or we're bad because we're not communists; whether we're bad because we're Black or we're bad because we're not Black. But what they're really saying is, "You're bad. You're no good. We don't want you. Get out of here. You don't belong here!" What *we're* saying is, "Says who?"

I was thinking about growing up and being defined into all these categories: a wimp, a teenage alcoholic, this, that — being bad and being really wrapped up in that, really believing those categories. I'm learning that to the extent that I buy into those categories it deforms me; I'm having to take a painful look at the fact that my being in a wheelchair must have a lot to do with my emotionality. Then I think I must be crazy, about what Dr. King said about being maladjusted, and I think maybe it really isn't so bad to be crazy.

I really don't want to be heard as in any way glorifying craziness. Craziness, as you well know, is very painful. The issue, however, is what we do with our pain and our craziness. It's whether we use that experience in a way that does something for our community, for our people, for ourselves.

I think it's very important not to slide into the glorification of pain. Pain is not glorious. Oppression is in no way glorious. The issue we're talking about is how we relate to that — how we are socialized by the powers-that-be as victims who can do nothing else with it save to experience it and suffer from it, as opposed to our taking those very things, that very pain and madness, and using them in ways that are progressive and developmental and humane.

That's the issue. Let us not glorify the pain; the pain hurts. It's no good and those who make it happen should be identified. But we don't have to do with it what they've told us to do — *we* can define what we do with that pain, not them.

So many people have been burned by the white left movement so many times, including those who are Black, those who are gay. That's why, when I go to the piers, organizing for NAP, I feel like a white leftist, trying to get people's phone numbers and trying to get them to a meeting. I'm sure if I feel this way that's what I'm projecting. Do you have thoughts on this?

Who made you a white leftist? Where did you get that from? Who did that to you?

Some radical friends in college.

Well, why don't you just remember the good things that happened with those people, and get rid of the other part? I think a lot of leftists, white, Black, Latino, but maybe particularly white leftists, have some kind of need to have that identity in order to justify their concern for other human beings. That's bullshit. You have a right to be concerned about your sisters and brothers, Black, Latino, white, without having to have a label to justify your feeling that way. So you need to be here, live your life, be who you are and not get caught up in those labels. Moreover, a lot of white leftists, once they have that definition, never go near the Black community that they had to take on a definition to justify caring about. That's something to move beyond, and you need to contribute that experience to this community as part of the building process because you're not alone in that.

Fred, I have a complicated question. First, I want you to talk more about the two party system and the defining aspects of that, along with addressing this fight we've been having at Horizon House about there being no such activity as "not getting high." We can so easily get organized to help people around what they're not going to do. So I was wondering if you could tie these two together — the two party system and this activity of getting high or not getting high.

The ideological essence of two partyism, if you think about the social-psychological core of it, is winner-take-all. Think about that. That's why these people who defend it, quite specifically defend *two-party* democracy — not three-party democracy, not four-party democracy, but two-party democracy. They defend a position which has as its ideological centerpiece that if you haven't won, you've lost.

There is no respect for historical social process, the ongoing life activity which is actually what we all participate in. For example, people who voted for Fulani are related to as nonexistent because she didn't *win*. The winner is real and the loser is real but degraded and dead or out. So two partyism is a competitive winner-take-all mentality; it's part of the social fabric of our entire culture. That's critical in terms of this other issue you're raising because I think we have to learn something about the fact that life and experience and development and growth are all about social process, not just about the commodified end product. We have to talk about what we're doing in terms of the social process and not as a negation of this or that — don't be a this, do be a that, don't be one of those, do be one of these. Definition which imposes these different labels that say you're a this and a that is a denial of the fundamentality of social and historical development. When we talk about self defining community — the brother before was talking about coming out and saying who he is — we are talking about finding out who you are, what you're giving expression to. It's the activity of saying it; it's the activity of socializing it. We are social people. We have been privatized by a whole lot of labeling, but we are a social species. Everything we do is social.

I remember being really, really angry at you, Fred. I remember that, because I had just discovered my new identity as an addict. It was the first time I had an identity and I felt very comfortable and safe with it. But you know what the trouble is? Sometimes you get bored with an identity after a while. After three, four months, you say, "Gee, this is boring."

I read your article on "The Myth of Addiction," and some lights popped up in my head. I had just gotten out of a rehab at the time of that discussion and I loved it. I spent four weeks there. I had an insurance card so I got to go to a really nice place; people made my bed and I got fed really well. I had a great time. I don't think I could have done it much longer — people telling me what to do — it was like being a kid again. I needed that; I needed to be a kid for a month.

One thing I got bored with was that everything was in terms of me being a drug addict. I'd say, "I'm angry." They'd say, "That's a drug urge." I'd say, "No, I'm angry 'cause I hate my job, because I'm worried about money, 'cause every time I read the newspaper or see someone really suffering it cuts through me. I'm angry and it's real and it's not a drug urge." They'd say, "Ah, denial!" AA helped me. It made a lot of sense and I still go, but I got really bored with constantly defining my life as an addict. It made me obsess more about doing drugs.

I didn't want to come tonight. I think you're really crazy and I didn't want to be involved with you, but I came because I knew that even if I didn't agree with you at least you made me think. So I thought if I came tonight you would get me thinking again and you did do that.

I was really moved by what you've been talking about all evening, and in ways you've been answering my question. I worked on Jim

Mangia's campaign in San Francisco [1990 campaign for Board of Supervisors] *and I've been thinking about when we were working in the Black community. I felt so welcome, but I didn't feel I was welcoming them into my community, even though I was putting out that Jim was endorsed by the Reverend Al Sharpton and Dr. Lenora Fulani. How do you change that? I still think of it as their community, instead of welcoming people into our community.*

Well, aren't they in our community?

I guess I still only think of people who are out working on the campaign as our community.

No, I think the reason you have a hard time bringing them into your community is because they *are* in your community. The difficulty you're having is being in that total community, because I think you still think in terms of "Well, they have their community; I have my community." The people who participated in many different ways in that campaign are all part of community. I don't mean that's just true by definition but by virtue of the particular activity in which folks are engaging by building the New Alliance Party.

It's not the same thing as the Democratic Party, where all they do is talk about voters. There, it is true that they have no relationship except for the voting relationship to their constituencies. But in terms of what we're building that can't be, because of the very nature of what it is that we're building — because this is a challenge and it is a self-defining community. If we lived by their definitions it wouldn't exist. You read the papers after Election Day. Independent parties aren't even listed. That's the degree to which they go out of their way to make us nonexistent. "You don't exist." We've had to fight for ten years to get the results of our candidates listed in the paper. Their position is "You're not a Democrat, you're not a Republican — you aren't real."

A few months ago I came over to Castillo and I also started therapy at the East Side Center. It really blew my mind. It still blows my mind every time I go there. It's changed a lot in my life. I was in ACT UP, and I'm no longer a member though I sometimes still align myself with them, and I was a second lieutenant in the army and I'm not in the army anymore either. I want to thank my therapists Nancy Green and Bette Braun for getting me to that point and my friends for getting me here tonight. What I've learned from this community is how much can be given, and I want to learn how to go out to communities that I'm still part of and give with the same intensity.

There's lots of different ways of interpreting what people say, what they mean by it, so you always run lots of risks when you use words that are in the marketplace, but to me one of the things we've been most deprived of in this culture and society is the experience of giving. Giving is an extraordinarily growthful experience; it's a humanizing, socializing experience. But I think we've been culturally deformed into a mentality of "don't give, get." I've written a lot about sexism and how men are socialized — essentially how we're *all* socialized — to be rapists. The fundamental rule informing men's socialization in our culture is to relate to women in such a way as to get as much as you can while giving as little as you can. That's the dominant socialization in our culture. Obviously that's profoundly oppressive to women, but it's also oppressive to men because its self-destructive to think that the totality of what it means to be human is to get. That is a dehumanizing credo. We are less human when we don't work at learning the activity of giving. So you need to continue doing what you need to do to learn how to give, and you are doing that.

Fred, you talk about how there shouldn't be any labels, white, Black, all that stuff. I'm thinking if people take pride in themselves that doesn't make the person less, any more than it does the rest of the community. So when you talk about community you should strike that label out too.

I agree. What I'm saying is that I think we can give the greatest expression to our Blackness or our Jewishness or our gayness in the context of a community of people where we don't have to worry about being separated and isolated from other people in order to be Black, or Jewish, or gay. I agree completely. I support the pride we have in who we are and where we come from. In fact, it's that pride we have to give expression to in a broader social community.

BIBLIOGRAPHY

Adorno, T.W. (1951). Freudian theory and the pattern of fascist propaganda. In G. Roheim (Ed.), *Psychoanalysis and culture*. New York: International University Press.

Akbar, N. (1985). *Chains and images of psychological slavery*. Jersey City, NJ: New Mind Productions.

Akbar, N. (1991). *Visions for black men*. Nashville, TN: Winston-Derek Publications.

American Psychiatric Association. (1980). *Diagnostic and statistical manual of mental disorders* (3rd ed.). Washington, DC: Author.

Bacon, F. (1960). *New organon*. New York: The Liberal Arts Press.

Brown, P. (1973). *Radical psychology*. New York: Harper Colophon Books.

Bruner, J. (1987). Prologue to the English edition. In L.S. Vygotsky, *The collected works of L.S. Vygotsky, Volume I*. New York: Plenum.

Buck-Morss, S. (1975). Socio-economic bias in Piaget's theory and its implications for cross culture studies. *Human Development, 18*, 35-49.

Bulhan, H.A. (1985). *Frantz Fanon and the psychology of oppression*. New York: Plenum Press.

Butterfield, H. (1962). *Origins of modern science*. New York: Collier Books.

Castillo, O.R. (1971). *Let's go* (M. Randall, Trans.). Willimantic, CT: Curbstone Press.

Cole, M., Hood. L., & McDermott, R.P. (1978). *Ecological niche-picking: Ecological validity as an axiom of experimental cognitive psychology* (Monograph). New York: Rockefeller University, Laboratory of Comparative Human Cognition. [Reprinted in *Practice, 4*(1), 117-129]

Coleman, J.W. (1976). The myth of addiction. *Journal of Drug Issues, 2*, 135-141.

Collett, L. (1988, July-August). Step by step: A sceptic's encounter with the twelve step program. *Mother Jones.* [Reprinted in *Utne Reader*, 1988, Nov./Dec., 69-76]

Conason, J. (1982). Psychopolitics. What kind of party is this anyway? *Village Voice, 27(22).*

Coyne, J.C. (Ed.). (1986). *Essential papers on depression.* New York: New York University Press.

Deleuze, G. & Guattari, F. (1977). *Anti-Oedipus: Capitalism and schizophrenia.* New York: Viking Press.

Fanon, F. (1963). *The wretched of the earth.* New York: Grove Press.

Fanon, F. (1967). *Black skins, white masks.* New York: Grove Press.

Feyerabend, P. (1978). *Against method. Outline of an anarchistic theory of knowledge.* London: Verso.

Fingarette, H. (1988). *Heavy drinking: The myth of alcoholism as a disease.* Berkeley: University of California Press.

Foucault, M. (1975). *Madness and civilization: A history of insanity in the age of reason.* New York: Vintage.

Freud, S. (1984). *Civilization and its discontents.* New York: W.W. Norton & Company, Inc.

Freud, S. (1977). *New introductory lectures on psychoanalysis.* New York: W.W. Norton & Company, Inc.

Fromm, E. (1973). *The crisis of psychoanalysis.* Middlesex: Penguin.

Fukuyama, F. (1989, Summer). The end of history? *The National Interest, 16,* 3-18.

Galileo, G. (1914). *Dialogues concerning two new sciences.* New York: Dover.

Goodwin, D.W. (1986). *Anxiety.* New York, Oxford: Oxford University Press.

Gould, S.J. (1990, Winter). Taxonomy as politics: The harm of false classification. *Dissent,* 73-78.

Habermas, J. (1971). *Knowledge and human interests.* Boston: Beacon Press.

Herman, E. (1988, Summer). The twelve-step program: Cure or cover? *Out/Look: National Lesbian and Gay Quarterly.* [Reprinted in *Utne Reader,* 1988, Nov./Dec., 69-76]

Holzman, L. & Newman, F. (1979). *The practice of method: An introduction to the foundations of social therapy.* New York: Practice Press.

Holzman, L. & Newman, F. (1987). Language and thought about history. In M. Hickmann (Ed.), *Social and functional approaches to language and thought.* London: Academic Press. [Reprinted in L. Holzman & H. Polk (Eds.), *History is the cure: A social therapy reader.* New York: Practice Press]

Holzman, L. & Polk H. (Eds.). (1989). *History is the cure: A social therapy reader.* New York: Practice Press.

Hood, L., McDermott, R.P., & Cole, M. (1980), "Let's try to make it a nice day" — Some not so simple ways. *Discourse Processes, 3,* 155-168. [Reprinted in *Practice, 4*(1), 103-116]

Hood, L., Fiess, K., & Aron, J. (1982). Growing up explained: Vygotskians look at the language of causality. In C. Brainerd & M. Pressley (Eds.), *Verbal processes in children.* New York: Springer-Verlag. [Reprinted in *Practice, 1*(2-3), 231-252]

Jacoby, R. (1976). *Social amnesia: A critique of conformist psychology from Adler to Lang.* Boston: Beacon Press.

Kant, I. (1929). *Critique of pure reason.* New York: St. Martin's Press.

Kuhn, T. (1970). *The structure of scientific revolutions.* Chicago: University of Chicago Press.

Laing, R.D. (1983). *The politics of experience.* New York: Pantheon.

Lasch, C. (1976). The family as a haven in a heartless world. *Salmagundi, 35.*

Levine, H.G. (1985). The discovery of addiction: Changing conceptions of habitual drunkenness in America. *Journal of Substance Abuse Treatment, 2,* 41-57.

Levitan, K. (1982). *One is not born a personality: Profiles of Soviet education psychologists.* Moscow: Progress Publishers.

Lichtman, R. (1977). Marx and Freud, part three: Marx's theory of human nature. *Socialist Revolution, 7*(6), 37-78.

Lotringer, S. (1977). Libido unbound. The politics of "schizofrenia." *semiotexte, 2*(3).

Luria, A.R. (1978). Psychoanalysis as a system of monistic psychology. In M. Cole (Ed.), *The selected writings of A.R. Luria*. White Plains, NY: M.E. Sharpe.

Marx, K. (1964). *Economic and philosophic manuscripts of 1844*. (M. Milligon, Trans.). New York: International Publishers.

Marx, K. (1967). *Capital* (Vol. I). New York: International Publishers.

Marx, K. (1971). *Grundrisse: Foundations of the critique of political economy*. New York: Harper & Row.

Marx, K. (1973). Thesis on Feuerbach. In K. Marx & F. Engels, *The German Ideology*. New York: International Publishers.

Marx, K. & Engels, F. (1968). *The communist manifesto*. New York: Monthly Review Press.

Marx, K. & Engels F. (1973). *The German ideology*. New York: International Publishers.

Newman, F. (1987). Crisis normalization and depression: An approach to a growing epidemic. *Practice, 5*(3). [Reprinted in L. Holzman & H. Polk (Eds.), *History is the cure: A social therapy reader*. New York: Practice Press]

Newman, F. (1989). Seven thesis on revolutionary art. *Stono, 1*(1), 7.

Newman, F. & Holzman, L. (in press). *Lev Vygotsky: Revolutionary scientist*. London: Routledge.

Oates, S. (1982). *Let the trumpet sound: The life of Martin Luther King, Jr*. New York: Mentor.

Peele, S. (1975). *Love and addiction*. New York: Signet.

Peele, S. (1977). Redefining addiction. *International Journal of Health Sciences, 7*, 103-124.

Peele, S. (1988). *Visions of addiction: Major contemporary perspectives on addiction and alcoholism*. Lexington, Mass.: Lexington Books.

Peele, S. (1989). *The diseasing of America: How the addiction industry captured our soul*. Lexington, Mass.: Lexington Books.

Piaget, J. (1923/1955). *The language and thought of the child*. London: Kegan Paul.

Piaget, J. (1924/1968). *Judgment and reasoning in the child*. Totowa, NJ: Littlefield, Adams.

Plog, S.C. & Edgerton, R. (1969). *Changing perspectives in mental illness*. New York: Holt Rinehart Winston.

Quine, W.V.O. (1964). *From a logical point of view*. Cambridge, MA: Harvard University Press.

Reich, W. (1970). *The mass psychology of fascism*. New York: Farrar, Straus & Giroux.

Rothman, D.J. (1971). *The discovery of the asylum: Social order and disorder in the new republic*. Boston: Little Brown.

Russell, B. (1912). *The problems of philosophy*. London, New York: Oxford University Press.

Schaef, A.W. (1987). *When society becomes an addict*. New York: Harper & Row.

Shaffer, H. (1987). The epistemology of addictive disease: The Lincoln-Douglas debate. *Journal of Substance Abuse Treatment, 4*, 103-113.

Szasz, T.S. (1961). *The myth of mental illness: Foundations of a theory of personal conduct*. New York: Harper & Row.

Volosinov, V.N. (1987). *Freudianism: A critical sketch* (I.R. Titunik, Trans.). Bloomington: Indiana University Press.

Vygotsky, L.S. (1962). *Thought and language*. Cambridge, MA: MIT Press. (Newly revised, 1986, by A. Kozulin.)

Vygotsky, L.S. (1978). *Mind in society*. Cambridge, MA: Harvard University Press.

Vygotsky, L.S. (1987). *The collected works of L.S. Vygotsky, Volume I*. New York: Plenum.

Welsing, F. C. (1991). *The Isis Papers*. Chicago: Third World Press.

Wertsch, J. (1985). *Vygotsky and the social formation of mind*. Cambridge, MA: Harvard University Press.

Wilson, A.N. (1978). *The developmental psychology of the black child*. New York: Africana Research Publications.

Wittgenstein, L. (1953). *Philosophical investigations*. Oxford: Blackwell.

Zinberg, N.E. (1984). *Drug, set, and setting*. New Haven: Yale University Press.

ABOUT THE AUTHOR

Fred Newman received his Ph.D. in the philosophy of science at Stanford University in 1963. He is the co-author with Dr. Lois Holzman of *Lev Vygotsky: Revolutionary Scientist,* to be published by Routledge in 1992. Dr. Newman is the founder of social therapy and of the East Side Institute for Short Term Psychotherapy, the post-graduate program in social therapy. He has been a practicing clinician, supervisor and consultant to community organizations for over 20 years. Dr. Newman has lectured extensively throughout the United States, in Cuba and in England on the relationship between psychology and politics. He lives in New York City.

Other books available from Castillo International

Independent Black Leadership in America: Minister Louis Farrakhan, Dr. Lenora Fulani, Reverend Al Sharpton

The Man Behind the Sound Bite: The Real Story of the Rev. Al Sharpton